Faithing It

BRINGING PURPOSE BACK TO YOUR LIFE!

Cora Jakes
COLEMAN

DEDICATION

I dedicate this to every faither, to my family, to my
friends, to my followers, to my leaders. I dedicate this to
Nehemiah. I dedicate this to God, for without Him
I do not know what faithing it truly means!

Peace, Love, and Faithing It

Your Sister, Your Friend, Your Family, Your Leader

Cora Jakes Coleman

All photos used by permission

DESTINY IMAGE® PUBLISHERS, INC.
P.O. Box 310, Shippensburg, PA 17257-0310
"Promoting Inspired Lives."

This book and all other Destiny Image and Destiny Image Fiction books are available at Christian bookstores and distributors worldwide.

Interior design by: Koechel Peterson & Associates
Cover design by: Brandon Coleman
Cover photographs by Rance Elgin Photography

For more information on foreign distributors, call 717-532-3040.

Previously published in Hard Cover in 2015 under ISBN: 978-0-7684-0789-1

Reach us on the Internet: www.destinyimage.com.

ISBN 13 TP: 978-0-7684-0910-9
ISBN 13 eBook: 978-0-7684-0790-7

For Worldwide Distribution, Printed in the U.S.A.
1 2 3 4 5 6 7 8 / 19 18 17

TABLE OF CONTENTS

Faithing It

FOREWORD
T.D. JAKES SR.

My daughter directs our children's ministry. She is in charge of helping us reach the young minds and hearts that attend our church. The irony of it all is that it was only yesterday she was the student and not the director, the child and not the parent. Whatever she did in between it was always done in church. Right or wrong, weak or strong, church is all she has ever known. She is the progenitor of my anointing, the epitome of my expectation. Cora is on a path with destiny that cannot be aborted.

The body of Christ welcomes a handmaiden whose journey though many tumultuous times and heart-breaking disappointments, has been crafted and designed to minister from a place of both experience and example in shaping a narrative for the souls of men. To say she is a jewel is an understatement. In fact not even an ultrasound would show you how vast and infinite her heart opens to those who need and hurt. I've watched her grow and explore, evolve and increase in wisdom and stature all in anticipation of this moment of impact to her generation and my own.

As witty as a comedian, as prayerful as a church mother, she wields a precocious ability and sobriety beyond her years. To be sure, Cora is an intricate mixture of contemporary ministry and old-school prayer. Her refreshing humor and unexpected wisdom will take you to a new place that will bless your life. As her father, both her mother and I, walked her through the perils of adolescence, a journey filled with nearly escaped mayhem and adventure. As arduous and daunting a task as it was, no commendation or human accolade awards us as parents like the validation of watching her evolve. She is a consummate mother, a devoted wife, and a daughter of the King.

Her flames of faith were ignited in part through the disappointments of being denied the birth of children. All she wanted in her whole life was children. Every time the headlines showed a baby discarded in a dumpster by an uncaring mother, we wept for her. She rode through the endless tests, medicines, and process of infertility clinic after clinic, desperately seeking her children. Little did we know that her excruciatingly painful journey of disappointment only helped to reveal that she would birth not through her womb, but through her words, a generation of Kingdom kids far beyond her wildest dreams. I've seen her adopt children both spiritually and naturally and bring vagrants inside out of the cold. I've watched her when she fed others at her own expense (and many times at mine) from near and far away.

She was the child who would bring anybody from anywhere into our home and into our lives, leaving us scrambling to prepare for the unexpected beneficiaries of her loving heart! Anything we gave her, she would likely give to one of her friends who needed something. Raising her increased my prayer life and decreased my finances as she thought we could feed the neighborhood and fix almost anyone she met that day from the grocery store to the gas station and almost nearly anywhere!

I want to share a story that occurred when she was still in diapers. I took her to see the doctor who, after careful examination, advised me I would need to admit her into the hospital due to a severe case of meningitis. I could hardly see the road as I drove first to my mother's house (for moral support) and then to tell my wife, her mother, that our first daughter was infirmed enough to be admitted. My mother and I faced her mother with the disturbing news, trying to explain that our daughter was going to need to go immediately to the hospital that day. As young parents we were both mortified. Minutes seemed like hours and hours seemed like days as we went through procedure after procedure. Her arm ended up bruised and swollen through misplaced IVs, and her brain ended up swollen from an improperly executed procedure. It seemed like everything that could go wrong, did. Finally, with much prayer and deep travail, we overcame and brought our baby home to lay on my chest as she did at that age, listening to my heartbeat for a rhythm that eventually and usually lulled her into a relaxed state of being and sleep that we all desired! It would be years before I realized that like the decree on the life of Moses, satan's fury against our child was in all actuality fear of what she has now become.

Today out of the ashes of despair she now rises to teach lessons on faith that have been sprinkled throughout her entire life! If you have ever faced a challenge for which your circumstances made you wonder if you could survive, this book is for you. If you have a faith that needs to be managed, massaged, or has been maligned by disappointing news and bleak conditions that defied human rectification, here's an answer coming through the pages ahead. It is no surprise that a child that was on the enemy's "hit list" from the beginning would find her inaugural literary work to be so rightly called *Faithing It*.

When she was born we were barely getting by, struggling to survive, we were literally on the verge of homelessness. Yet in that environment that was riddled with repossessed cars and often less than nutritious meals, she was born and raised. She watched her mother and I pull our family from the brink of annihilation to the basking light of promises attained. In short she has nursed on the breast milk of struggle, been fed on the tears of pilfering parents who were on the brink of bankruptcy, and finally wrapped in the rewards of a committed life to Jesus Christ, we reported complete and total victory! Health? Restored. Finances? Reclaimed. Family intact! We made it here by faith!

Now I see what the fight was about. It wasn't a battle against me. It wasn't a battle against her. It was the reckless fear coming from the defeated foe whose tactics were derelict in their intent to stop her from reaching you. Her message is a faith-building, courageous commitment to help you bridge the gulf between the circumstances you face and the future you are destined to attain. With all the pride of an effusive father, who marches his daughter down the aisle to her beloved, I hand this book to you. As her father, I am just a voice crying in the wilderness. I've come to say to you to prepare your heart and mind. She has processed to this point to turn misery to ministry. This is the moment where I pass her power and pain off into your hands with the intent that when you have finished reading her thoughts, you will attain a deeper sense of purpose.

Ladies and Gentlemen, brothers and sisters, I introduce to some and present to others, my daughter, and God's servant, Cora Brionne Jakes-Coleman. Receive her and the mustard seed faith she brings to your garden of thought. The next words you read will come from Cora. Receive her words as she plants the thoughts that will enable you to go beyond making it to Faithing IT!

PREFACE

People often ask me what it's like to live with someone who's famous. I tell them, "It's like this. By the time I turned eight years old, my name was officially 'Bishop Jakes' daughter.'" Not that being T. D. Jakes' daughter is a bad thing, but suddenly my personal identity as Cora Jakes was a thing of the past, and I had a front-row seat in the "fish bowl" life of a high-profile preacher.

No pressure, right? Wrong! There was admittedly an undeniable pressure to become something more than a little girl who dreamed of being a mother, playing with baby dolls, and wearing Mickey Mouse afro puffs in West Virginia. In the midst of trying to establish and maintain my identity, we relocated to Texas—which felt like being thrown into a museum!

Now, I can't tell you my whole life's story in this little preface, but I will share more as we unpack this concept of "faithing it" together throughout this book.

I *can* tell you that I figured out pretty quickly that trying to be "normal" in the family fish bowl was not going to be an easy task, but that did not stop me from trying. And it didn't stop my partners in crime either—my siblings.

We learned from our parents that families stick together. Jamar, Jermaine, Dexter, Sarah, and I grew up being watched by the world. The fact that we were under constant scrutiny only drew us closer. As the children of a famous preacher/celebrity (take your pick) we were overwhelmed. There was so much pressure to get everything right and certainly never make a mistake. We learned how to hold our heads up high even when our feet were trembling from the world falling apart beneath us. We figured out how to be strong at our weakest moments and, sadly, we learned that not everyone is your friend and means you well. Some people are simply around as vultures, just waiting to scrutinize you…just like patrons in a museum.

As I grew older, I did eventually make trustworthy friends and I developed a deep compassion for people. I still dreamed of being a mom, and the desire to take care of children only grew inside my heart. But as innocent as my life was on the surface, I was secretly going through an emotional hurt.

At the age of ten years old, I was molested by a young boy in a bathroom stall at my elementary school. It was heartbreaking for me. I knew this boy, and I trusted him. After being violated by someone I trusted, I understood for the first time that life was not always going to be easy and I wasn't exempt from hard times. For a long time I rehearsed all the things I did wrong. It was not until several years later that I accepted that I was a victim of circumstance, and there was nothing I could do about it.

I am typically a very strong person, but some things can shake you to the core. I can honestly say that it was through my relationship with Christ that I overcame this trauma. Even as a little girl, I knew I was called to be something bigger than what I could see at the time. Mind you, I have always known that with great privilege in life you will have great obstacles, but as a young girl I didn't realize how great some of those obstacles would be. I'm grateful that my parents taught me that with faith in God you can get through anything.

My life, purpose, and the promise of God came with great obstacles and heartbreak along the way—a series of circumstances that I will share later in this book. But I can tell you that those heartbreaks and storms forced me to develop a true faith in God. With maturity comes wisdom. As I grew older, I learned that I had to partner my faith with my fight, and it was at this point in my life that I developed a term I use called "faithing it."

"Faithing it" means that we must learn how to develop our faith and go after those obstacles with faith. You are a conqueror because you are faithing it. You are a fighter because you choose to be. You cannot get to great purpose, promise, and legacy without great tribulation, but you can trust that everything works together for good in God's timing.

You cannot get to great purpose, promise, and legacy without great tribulation.

Speaking of timing, you chose this day and this hour to read this page. I believe God's timing is at work right now, and it is my hope that when you turn the last page of this book you will go back into your life with a better understanding of who you are, why you are, and what your storms mean for your ultimate destiny and purpose in life. So are you ready to stand up and fight with me? "Get ready!"

Faithing It

INTRODUCTION

F "aithing it." What does that mean? It means that in order to get through our problems and bypass our circumstances, we must fight with faith—and without a faith fight there cannot be a win. Faith is obtained by God! If we choose to speak faith and fight obstacles with our faith, we cannot lose.

Are you in a struggle right now? I want you to know that you are not alone. God has you in His hand! You *will* make it, and I'm here to tell you that there is not just one way to win, but there are several ways to win.

I wrote this book because I love you, and I do not want you to feel alone or be alone. I want to be clear. Just because my earthly father is known as "the world's bishop," that doesn't mean that I am above you. I am coming to you as a friend and sister to encourage you to leap into your dream, purpose, and promise. My hope is that you walk away with a better understanding of who you are and what your struggles mean in connection to your ultimate destiny.

Before we begin this journey together, I want to tell you a story that I tell to audiences everywhere I speak. This story is really what led me to faithing it. This story is why I'm telling you to fight with faith for your purpose.

The "Accident"

Without a faith fight there cannot be a win.

I was twenty-two years old, engaged to the most wonderful man in the world, and thoroughly enjoying my work as a nanny and babysitter. One evening before going off to work, I told my mother that my hips and back hurt badly, but I wasn't sure why.

That night on the way home from the babysitting job, I was driving and talking to my fiancé on the speakerphone when my green arrow light came up to turn left. So I began to turn, and suddenly I looked up to headlights coming directly at me. I immediately prayed, "God, get me out of this." The truck rammed into me going 40 mph. My air bag burst in my face and glass shattered everywhere. My car caved in on me.

I was scared. This was the worst car accident I had ever been in. I remembered one thing. I prayed God would get me out of this. I believed God would get me out of this when the collision ended. I opened my eyes. My coat was burned from the airbag, and all I could hear was, "She's dead! She has to be dead!" The fireman came running to my car, and I opened my car and stood up—without a visible bruise or scratch—nothing. I was just sore.

I didn't go to the emergency room that night. I went home that night asking God, why me? Why would You cause me to go through that? What was the purpose of this? I woke up very sore the next day. My mother took me to the doctor.

During the CAT scan at the doctor's office, they found a 7 cm cyst on one ovary and a 9 cm cyst on my other ovary. The doctor told me that I was days away from my fallopian tubes twisting and shutting down my reproductive system.

Why Me, God?

I was stunned. All I ever wanted to be was a mother. Everything that I dreamed about, everything I hoped for would have been impossible had it not been for a car hitting me at 40 mph. If the devil had his way I would have been dead, and everything that would allow me to produce would have been dead.

You may not know the why, but sometimes the hard things happen to us because we are being saved from the enemy destroying our ability to produce. Whether spiritual or natural, the enemy is after your seed. You may have just been hit hard and you may be in pain, but all of this is leading to your salvation.

God saved me in a unique way because God is a unique God and He has to orchestrate things accordingly. Had I not gone through the hurt, the soreness, and later the surgery, I would have been in a lot of trouble. Later, the surgeon discovered that one of the cysts was much larger than they originally thought, and because of that I would have to lose one of my fallopian tubes and one of my ovaries.

One hit by a car led to me to discovering two cysts, the loss of an ovary, the loss of a fallopian tube, and a news flash from the doctor that it wasn't probable for me to get pregnant without going through in vitro fertilization. Needless to say, I was devastated by the news. I saw the pain of the process, and I was hurt by the facts in front of me. I wanted to live in the "Why me, God?" but had I not gone through all that, I wouldn't have gotten to the great rewards of my life.

What's Your Story?

So what's your story? Do you have unanswered questions about the circumstances in your life? Are you wondering when your rewards are coming?

I want to invite you right now to join me in faithing it—fighting with your faith to produce purpose. If you decide to faith it, the enemy will not control your story, your win, or your life. This is *your* time to move forward with zeal, tenacity, and determination. This book is going to inspire you to believe God, and push you to stretch and develop the fighter in you.

Are you ready to stand up and faith it with me? I want you to know that I believe God's best is just ahead for both of us. Let's talk.

Faithing It

MY STORY

Faithing It

ONE

You Are God's Book— Respect the Process

You saw me before I was born. Every day of my life
was recorded in Your book. Every moment was
laid out before a single day had passed.

(PSALM 139:16 NLT)

God is the author of your story! Every good story has a multi-dimensional character who experiences inner struggles, outer conflicts, and a satisfying "aha moment" where everything finally comes together for that character. You can't go to a bookstore, pick up a book, tear out the happy parts that you like, and then move on. If you pick up that book and you want those eight pages that you like, then you will have to buy all the other pages. And to live a successful life in all the other chapters of your book, you're going to need to faith it to the last page! God is crafting a marvelous book about each one of us, and in order to get to complete wholeness we must first understand our life is a series of processes all built to create us into the person God wants us to be. Don't worry! Your "aha moment" is on the way!

I started dating my (now) husband, Brandon, six years ago and boy we were head over heels in love! When you are that in love, you have the tendency to want to move really quickly. Whenever we would feel the "urge" to move quickly, Brandon would look at me and say, "We have to respect the process." At the time, though, it was so difficult. Although I knew what he meant, I had to patiently realize that there was a process that had to be implemented in order for us to get to our ultimate goal. We loved each other and we were grown, but it was not a time for "urgencies" and we had to respect the process. I had to grow more, and he did too.

Don't worry! Your "aha moment" is on the way!

All great things come with a process. Was it hard for Brandon and me? Indeed! At first it was very hard, and then it became easy as God grew and matured us. We faced trials for sure and gained major perseverance, but at the end of the day it was our respect for our process that got us to our goal. Really, in all honesty, trusting God *is* the process. Allowing Him to lead you is the ultimate maturity.

You Can't Skip the Process

You have to understand that "the process" is a normal way of life. When you think about the basic things of life, there's a process. When you are getting ready to cook for your family, you pick something out, then you build a grocery list, and then you have to go get the groceries, and preheat the oven, and prepare your meal. The meal cannot come forth without a process, and if you do not go through the process your family will be hungry. Even when you are tired, working, and things are going crazy, you have to cook and you have to go to the grocery store. You cannot skip the process. No matter how easy the meal is, you cannot skip the process to get there.

When you are crying out to God for Him to do something and it does not come through, you wonder, *Lord, why are You blessing everyone else connected to me, but not blessing me?* It is in that very moment in the middle of your WHY that God is telling you to respect the process—"trust Me." It is in your maturity and completeness where you realize God is for you, and what He said He would fulfill, He will, but you must trust Him.

Our lives are living testaments of several processes both big and small. In our relationships of life there is a process. The point is, you can't run away from the process. You have to face it. If you want to be a wife, a husband, or even someone's significant other, you have to go through a process.

Being in a relationship you will have obstacles, ups and downs, but it's all a process in order to get you to your promise. God is asking you to face your process, face your trials, and when you can believe God in the midst of your trial, then, and only then, you will not lack anything. Your promise is in your problems. Those problems are there so you do not lack anything. God wants you to mature and become complete. Now when we look at "complete" I know that can be confusing, but it means that He wants you to be whole—He wants you to be full. The book of James tells us about the process that brings us to maturity:

Consider it pure joy, my brothers and sisters, whenever you face trials of many kinds, because you know that the testing of your faith produces perseverance. Let perseverance finish its work so that you may be mature and complete, not lacking anything (James 1:2-4 NIV).

It's all a process in order to get you to your promise.

Perseverance as defined on Google is "steadfastness in doing something despite difficulty or delay in achieving success." James 1 tells us that the testing of our faith will bring perseverance. So God was simply saying, yes, we will face trials, and yes, it is going to be hard. But the good news is that our current hardship is going to develop steadfastness in whatever we do, despite difficulty or delay in our leap of faith.

Are you looking for purpose? Chances are your purpose and your plan are right there in your face. Let me explain how this happened to me.

The Chapter in My Book that I Didn't Like

As I entered adulthood, I felt pretty steady and secure. I had realized one dream of working with children, and God loved me enough to allow me to meet the love of my life—an amazing man and artist, Brandon Coleman a.k.a. Skii (Sky) Ventura, and my life as far as I knew it was going great. Then I hit another obstacle. I mentioned in the introduction to this book the accident that I was in when Brandon and I were engaged to be married. Since that time, I've been in the fight of my life. I am currently dealing with the diagnosis that I will not get pregnant without fertility treatments due to PCOS (Polycystic Ovarian Syndrome). This very diagnosis is one of the reasons why I wrote this book.

After hearing such horrible news, right when we were ready to marry and start a family, I was heartbroken. I didn't like this chapter in my book at all! Yet again, here I was going through "everything that a young woman goes through." For years, I dreamed of becoming a mother, not to mention the fact that I had "mothered" countless children in my day care work and as the Children's Ministry Director of the Potter's House of Dallas. Now to hear I would not have children—I was disappointed beyond belief. But I did not let that stop me from trying, preparing, and getting ready to become a mother.

Often we let what the world says detour us from our desire and from what God said would happen. Then instead of even trying, we stop fighting altogether. Not me! I shook myself off and I looked for ways to make my dream come true. I became a mom to my beautiful daughter through adoption. I experienced the miracle of choosing my beautiful daughter. You don't have to birth a child in order to be a mom. With that being said, never make a backup plan for what God promised you. Keep the faith in the promise! When I was a little girl, I had a dream one night of being a mom to a son. I am holding on to the promise of my son from God, and I won't and can't stop faithing it until it comes to fruition.

You have to make up your mind to fight for your promise! The power is in your fight, so FIGHT FOR IT! You can do it.

Faithing It with Perseverance

God is developing your purpose through your trial, and it's likely that you are currently in the process—meaning a series of actions or steps taken in order to achieve a particular end. The process of life cannot come without perseverance. Beware! You can lose your promise when you do not match the two together. It is important that whatever you go through in life, you go through it with perseverance while faithing it for your promise.

Whenever I think of perseverance, I think of my favorite story in the Bible—Job (pronounced Jobe). Maybe you've heard someone say, "It's been a Job day." That means, "I am having an incredibly difficult day and everything that *could* go wrong, *did* go wrong!" Job was a man of God, and an entire book of the Bible is named after Job and is dedicated to his story. Let me tell you a little bit about Job!

You see, the Bible says Job was an upright man, and because of the greatness that he sought, he was chosen to go through great trials. How crazy is it that? We get chosen to go through great trials when we are Christians? What sense does that make to go through problems when you are a child of the King? What if I told you that you were chosen to go through trials because you are a child of the King seeking righteousness, and the enemy wants to destroy your promise and your ability to prosper?

Here's how it went down. Satan went to God in heaven to accuse the people on earth. (Satan still accuses God's people, even today.) When satan accused the people living on the earth during Job's day, God said to satan, "Have you considered My servant Job?"

Satan replied, "No wonder Job's so righteous. Look at that hedge of protection You've put around him! Take down that hedge and I'll get him to curse You" (see Job 1:8–11).

God allowed satan a limited access to Job, and Job lost everything but his life. He got sick, he was shaken, he was broken, yet he never once cursed God—although he did curse himself. There will be times in life when you wonder where God is, and He is standing right there, but He is taking you through the process in order to bless you. You must understand that the enemy is not hitting you without God's permission. You need to know that the importance of Job's story is that the enemy had to go before God before even touching Job. Your circumstance does not come without granted approval from the throne. It is also important to note that the enemy is not a creator—he is an imitator. If he attacked Job, then he will attack us, too. Whatever the enemy presents to you is just a reconstructed situation that he has used before.

Job's friends thought he was crazy. His wife turned against him and even tempted him to sin! She said, "Why don't you just curse God and die?" What a test! But Job still trusted God while he was in his process, and he never stopped believing in God.

Whatever the enemy presents to you is just a reconstructed situation that he has used before.

You are designed by God to persevere. You are designed to face trials because you need them in order to get to the promise. Before you can get to what God has for you, you will have to face adversity.

Processes are not easy. Think about all of the conflict and struggles a main character goes through in a novel or even a movie. Those intense struggles make the "aha moment" even better! So keep faithing it, no matter where you are in your process.

From the Process to the Promise

Sometimes we have to process our mind, friends, and family before we can get to our promise. The overall point is this: Are you willing to go through the process in order to get to the thing God wants for you? Even if it means losing everything in order to gain more in the end?

Philippians 3:8 says, "Yet indeed I also count all things loss for the excellence of the knowledge of Christ Jesus my Lord, for whom I have suffered the loss of all things, and count them as rubbish, that I may gain Christ."

You see, there is much to gain! Not only will you obtain God's promises for your life, but you walk out of your process *knowing* Jesus!

Let's consider Jesus. Jesus was a carpenter. He created things, and He was a builder. Jesus was God in the flesh, and it's only natural that we will go through processes in life simply because Jesus was a builder. He was a carpenter, and carpenters know more than most that there is a process in everything that you want to create. They understand that you cannot make something without a process.

Step out of who you think you are and who people think you are, and begin to walk in what God spoke over you. And just in case you did not know who God said you are, then you need to just walk in the simple fact that you are a child of the King of kings. You are a child of a carpenter, and He is building you into something beautiful. Molded and created in His perfect image, you can walk in the fact that you are called to be great.

I believe that fighting and faith go hand in hand. That's what gets us through these obstacles—our ability to stand before the mountain with faith and a fight and command the mountain to move. It *will* move!

Every superhero has a villain, and every hero has a backstory.

God is molding you to be great. He is molding you to overcome. He is molding you into completion and maturity. You are not forgotten. You are worthy of your dreams and hopes. You are not being punished; you are being processed. You deserve to gain all God has for you. Do not limit yourself because the storms are raging, but look at the storm and say, "I will trust you, Lord." If you were not meant to be anything, you would not have trials to face. If you were not meant to be strong and great, then you would need no molding.

I wrote this book because I believe in you. As your sister in Christ, I am here to faith it with you so we can rise up together against the enemy and break his chains!

You are God's book, and right now, today, you are living out a page in that book. Is today's page overwhelming you? Do you feel alone in this chapter of your life? As your sister and friend, I want to tell you that it is through your hurt that you become a hero. Every superhero has a villain, and every hero has a backstory. Will you let me pray for you right now?

I pray that God give you the grace to endure the pain of the process. I pray that God open your eyes to see the people who are for you and the people who are not. I pray that God allow you to embrace this in a new way where you understand that your storms have been meant to make you grow stronger. I pray that God ignite the purpose and gifting inside of you, that you might be able to go after your purpose with everything that you have. I pray that faith be your encourager, that faith be your pusher, that faith be your strength, and that you begin to become a faither. I pray that you take on this challenge to become better than who you are, that you do not look behind you, and that you do not let the enemy keep you bound in the past, but that you challenge yourself to be even better than who you think you are supposed to be. I pray that you give God the ability to do great things in you. I pray you get something out of this journey, and that you understand that I am here for you, I am faithing with you, and, trust me, we are going to win and I pray you know that.

Scan this code for Cora's Chapter 1
PRAYER FOR YOU!

Or Visit

WWW.CORAJAKESCOLEMAN.COM

Faith Affirmations

This chapter is designed to affirm and show you that it is in your ability to understand that just because you are being processed in pain, it doesn't mean you aren't going to get to the promise. So often we don't take advantage of the lessons that could be learned if we would permit ourselves to walk through the process of life and let God lead us. Many times we will allow ourselves to be so consumed by our suffering in the process that we do not seek or hear the answers to our problems in the Word of God. Is it easy to get through the process? No! As I said, it is extremely hard to get through it, but when you are getting through it with God, it is much easier than trying to accomplish it on your own. What do you require of yourself in this process? How do you allow God to be shown in your storms? Why is it so easy for you to give up on God? Why is it so easy for you to give up on yourself? These questions are a part of examining yourself in this process. If you are unwilling to learn the foundations of your surroundings, you will never be able to explain why you crumbled. If you won't face the enemy of yourself, you can never see what God is trying to do for your life in the pitfalls. You were born to be greater than what you are going through, but as long as you let the villains in your life destroy you then you will never get there.

Faith Points

God is the author of your best-selling story! He is daily crafting each chapter to make you the person He wants you to be—the best possible you!

All great things are the result of a significant process. Writing a life story is an ongoing journey that God wants you to enjoy. Having respect for the process allows God to lead you to ultimate maturity.

Your life is a living testament of ongoing processes, which need to be faced head-on. When you believe God is in the midst of every challenge, you will overcome each one.

Your purpose and your life plan is before you. God allows you to experience ups and downs throughout life to build you into the most incredible person you can be.

Don't accept or allow what the world says to deter you from reaching your God-given desires. God has promised His children ever more than you can imagine. Keep faith in the promise.

God develops your purpose through trials and challenges—which are all part of the process. Persevering and pushing through each tough time assures you Jesus' promise of an abundant life.

You are a child of the King, which makes you a target of the enemy who wants to destroy your promise. But...God is greater than the enemy in every way. Whatever comes your way, God knows you can handle it—because He is with you all the way.

Sometimes you have to process your mind, friends, and family in order to get to whatever God wants for you.

There is much to gain—promises, joy, and a more intimate relationship with Jesus.

Every superhero has a villain, and every hero has a backstory. Fighting and faith go hand in hand. Your ability to become a superhero means defeating the villain by standing firm for righteousness, facing obstacles, and winning each battle.

Faith Activations

The next time you face a problem, confrontation, or battle of the mind, stop what you are doing for five to ten minutes and pray that God will give you the grace to endure the pain of the process. Pray to embrace the storms in your life because you know God is holding your umbrella.

Determine to be a faither by writing ten ways you can keep the enemy from gaining any ground in your spiritual life, your home life, and your work life. Then put those ways into action!

Take time to reflect on situations when the enemy tried to overwhelm you. Do they seem to be reconstructions of the same issues? If yes, take steps immediately to deal with and eradicate any area in your life where the enemy seems to have a foothold.

Faithing It

TWO

"Faithing It" Through the Chapter I'm in Now

For if you live according to the flesh you will die;
but if by the Spirit you put to death the deeds
of the body, you will live.

(ROMANS 8:13)

Who or what is the villain in your life's story? I'd be interested to know what came to your mind just now when I asked that question!

I think it can be extremely helpful to locate yourself where you are right now in the process to your promise. Sometimes our own emotional reactions to the storms of life can rise up to be the worst villain in our lives. I know from experience that our inner struggles can squeeze the life out of us if we allow them to hang on. Other times the obstacle in front of us looks impossible to move because it's so big.

Remember, every superhero has a villain, and every hero has a backstory. So let's locate ourselves and what process we are in right now in our backstory.

First, in every good book there is a beginning and an end. The pages in between represent the process we've been talking about. The best way to think about processes is stages. I believe that stages of grief are very similar to a cycle that we go through in the daily process of walking out God's promises.

Let me be clear about one thing. I believe that our flesh has to die by the end of this process. Let me talk about this for just a moment before we define the stages of grief.

You may wonder what I'm talking about—our flesh has to die. Well, it's important to understand that in order to gain purpose you have to be willing to sacrifice your own fleshly desires for God's will for your life. We must be willing to spiritually sacrifice within ourselves and kill those things that are not like God in order to reach our purpose. You are only as strong and as blessed as what you are willing to sacrifice to get it.

> *For if you live according to the flesh you will die; but if by the Spirit you put to death the deeds of the body, you will live* (Romans 8:13).

You have to be willing to sacrifice your own fleshly desires for God's will for your life.

Stages of Grief

Grief comes into play when we have to completely sacrifice ourselves so that God can use us in the end for His overall purpose and glory to be fulfilled. I believe that, like the stages of grief, our process may come in different orders and times in our lives, but at the end we've met each process.

The stages of grief are:

- Denial

- Isolation

- Anger

- Bargaining

- Depression

- Acceptance

Let's talk about it, and how my mind breaks each one down.

Denial

People go through levels of denial. First, we don't believe in ourselves. We may hear God speak to us about what is up ahead, but we can see our own weaknesses and think, I will never get there. I'm not good enough or smart enough or strong enough.

If we are in denial, then we will begin to isolate ourselves from everything and everyone.

Isolation

We isolate ourselves because we are afraid. First, we can be in denial and don't believe in ourselves. Second, if we were to surround ourselves with God's people, then God would use those people to speak inadvertently into our lives. Simply put, we are not ready for other people to believe in what God has for us, so we go through isolation.

The beauty of this stage is that it is in the various levels of our isolation when God speaks to us the most. You may find that the times you spend alone are the times when God begins to give you the most direction.

But there is a difference between healthy isolation and unhealthy isolation. Devotional time and isolation are not the same thing. Isolation that does not produce a stronger relationship with God is unhealthy isolation. But if your time away from the doubts, fear, and outside voices brings you closer to God and closer to believing His promises for your life, that is healthy isolation. The bottom line is that some form of isolation is experienced during your process, and that isolation will either lead you to success or oppression.

Anger

I explained earlier that our flesh has to die in order for us to truly live. That dying to flesh often doesn't feel good. Sometimes it angers us when we don't get results immediately or we assume that the sacrifice of our flesh doesn't matter to God. If we do not see God acknowledge our sacrifice in the time frame that we think that it should happen, then we have the audacity to get upset! It's at this point that we can be tempted to stop faithing it and either run away or go back into the world.

It's okay to be angry, but it's not okay to stop fighting.

We must lay hold of patience to be able to stand and wait for God to acknowledge us. Don't forget, my friend, that the reason we sacrificed our flesh to begin with was so that we could gain purpose, power, and our promise. You cannot get any of that without God! So we sacrifice our flesh to get something out of God's hand, and when He doesn't move as quickly as we want Him to, we get angry.

To this stage I say, "Get over yourself. You win because God fought before you got there." Think about this—God had to be patient with *you* to get you to sacrifice in the first place! So let me encourage you to be patient and wait for God's timing instead of getting angry in your own timing. Our anger comes because we want to make God do our will instead of trying to operate in God's will. When you can release yourself from your own expectations, then you release God to be able to work for you. Anger is a natural emotion, but it is not a healthy emotion if it is not producing a benefit to you.

It's okay to be angry, but it's not okay to stop fighting.

Bargaining

The next step in our process or grief stages is bargaining. I relate to bargaining so well—mostly during my wanting a husband (LOL). I found myself wanting to stop going through so much pain from bad experiences with past boyfriends, but I was in a process and God wanted to bring that pain to the forefront so He could heal me.

I can remember after accepting my call into ministry, I sacrificed my flesh for the better will of God to come forward. Right away I asked God, "Please, Lord, if You send me my husband right now, I promise I will appreciate him, and I will praise You in advance and even more when he comes. I know that You are able to do this for me!"

Now, when I accept God's call and His will, I cannot bargain with Him for my will and my desire. My hope is that as you read this right now, you will pray:

God let my will line up to Your will. And if my desires don't match Your desires for me, Lord, then help me to desire even more what matches Your will for my life.

We must understand that God has the best deal for us so we don't need to bargain with Him. Yes, sometimes He will place us in situations in life that will make us sad, and that we may not value, but His ways are higher than ours. If we choose to walk with Him and not bargain with Him, then we are already on a level of success in our walk that we may not have ever been able to reach before!

Depression

How you deal with this next stage is up to you. Truthfully, we all go through some point of depression in our process to success and purpose. Usually, we encounter depression at that moment of God's test when He asks, "Will you trust Me?" For Job, it was the moment when he cursed his own life.

There are different forms of depression that are associated with the stages of grief. One type is a response to the reality of the overall loss. Sadness and regret are the primary two things that drive that particular type of depression. You may question the cost of your sacrifice of flesh:

- What it will mean to go after my purpose?

- How will it impact the people around me, especially my family?

- Am I good enough to obtain this type of dream and purpose?

This is the time when you need to evaluate the people around you because, in that moment, when everything looks hopeless, you need someone to believe with you. You need friends and family members who will recognize your hope to become something bigger than your obstacle so that they can help to push you through.

Now the other type of depression isn't as obvious, and in some cases it is handled during the time of isolation. At this point, you find you have to let go of people or responsibilities that are holding you back from your purpose. It's the time when you have to truly accept that you have evaluated your friends and your surroundings, and God has told you who is for you and who isn't, and you have to accept that separation is necessary and you have to say good-bye. Let me tell you, it's not easy. But on the positive side, make sure that you find the people that you know are for you whether you are wrong, right, fail, or succeed. Just spend time with them and get affirmation and support from them.

Acceptance

Acceptance is my favorite stage. This stage is often overlooked and, ironically enough, it is the one that takes the longest to get to. Let's just look at the definition. *Acceptance* as defined in *Webster's* is "The act of accepting; the fact of being accepted." The reason I picked that definition is because we often have a hard time accepting that God has accepted, called, and chosen us.

Acceptance takes the longest time to get to because we then have to understand that we didn't sacrifice ourselves for nothing, and that God is going to use us even though we've made mistakes, even though we've handled some things in the wrong way. The act of accepting comes when you are able to accept the fact that it's okay to make mistakes, and God can still use you for something bigger than yourself.

The acceptance comes in when you realize the pain, depression, and anger are to benefit you, not break you—when you are able to understand that, the Bible says the enemy will come in like a flood and the weapons will form, but God will build a standard against it, and they won't prosper. It is your choice to either concentrate on the flood and the weapons or to focus on the standard God builds. When God builds the standard, the flood and weapons set against you will not prosper. Most of us are drowning in an invisible flood. It's easy to say that the storm will rage and there is power in your pain. The reality is the power is in your perspective.

I've walked through these stages of grief, and let me say that it has not been easy. After twenty-six years of living through heartbreak, struggles, problems, and tribulation, I can tell you that because of my life's journey, I know where God is taking me. I can only imagine where He is taking you. What has God spoken to you in times past? Whatever God has spoken to you, the fact that you decided to take this journey indicates it must be a pretty big deal indeed.

The power is in your perspective.

Don't Call It Quits!

You will go through the storm in order to develop your fight. You will go through the trials in order to develop your fight, and when you develop your fight then you must let that strength and that fight grow and finish in you. You must let your storm finish in order for you to mature and gain everything you are praying for. The beautiful thing about the Word of God is that when you truly spend time in the Scriptures it breaks down and you receive revelations about your placement in life that will truly wow you.

Are you about to call it quits? Don't do it! I believe in you. I believe God has greatness in store for you. I believe that God is molding you because you are great. The beautiful thing about diamonds is that they come from deep within the earth, from the bottom. Diamonds can also be found in water. I am calling out the diamond in you. Diamonds are created through massive amounts of pressure and heat. If the pressure is too low, the diamond cannot form. If the heat is not hot enough, the diamond can't form. Before it becomes a beautiful ring, that diamond goes through a series of cutting processes. Dare I say God is allowing you to be cut to shape your story into something beautiful?

God is bringing about clarity to your life right now as you read this. And this is step one to the beginning of your greatness. Please know that God is breaking you into something beautiful, and your purpose came with a process. There is beauty in your breaking, and I am here to tell you that if you respect the process, you can get to the promise.

One of the most difficult things about the process is that we usually don't know when the struggles and storms are going to stop. Most of us know when the beginning of our storm started. It is in that moment when your back is against the wall and everything is falling apart and you do not know what to do. The thing is, you can never know when it is going to end.

Can you imagine being in your Job stage? You are covered in boils, children died, friends turned away from you, your spouse tells you to curse God and die, and you do not have a clue when it is going to be over? The hardest part about the process is that you have to believe God and you have to hold God's hand even if you do not know where He is leading you or how long it's going to take to get there.

A few years ago I did a project in which I was blind for a day. I went out into the world without the ability to see, with only my friends to lead me, and that was the hardest part of the project. That was the day when I learned how God wants us to depend on Him. He wants us to be able to be led by Him even if we do not know where He is taking us. I had to learn that first. Step one of the process was to believe and be led by God. If you choose to take God's hand and walk with Him, He will get you through the other steps.

Your trials have come to make you complete. Job went through the trials and the problems and the hurt, but when he matured and became "complete," when he handed it all over to God, he got back more than he started with. Could it be that God is placing you in your Job process so that He can get you to your big promise? Are you being persecuted or hated like Job? Are you enduring loss or sickness like Job? This has powerful meaning because some people would look at that meaning and say, "Dang, that's awful!" But that definition is what *people* saw him as, and not what God saw him as.

God said, "Have you considered Job, that there is none like him on the earth, a blameless and upright man, one who fears God and shuns evil?" (Job 1:8). Job walked in what *God* said, not in what people said. The problem that we have is that we are walking in what people said and not in what God said. If you flipped that definition, you could go on to say that is what the devil felt about him.

The devil wanted to persecute Job and he hated him. You see, you have people in your life who are speaking things about you and defining who you are by where you are.

People's Opinion or God's Opinion?

Your trials have come to make you complete.

We need to get something straight. We are God's book, and He's not writing our book to impress the people around us! Furthermore, it is God who will get the glory on the last page of your book, not the devil! And God isn't trying to place us on the top-ten best seller list so we can outrank and outdo the people around us. We need to decide right here and now whose opinion matters to us the most—God's opinion or people's opinion?

You are God's book and He is writing His story about you right now. I am here to tell you that you are designed for such a time as this, and that God is for you. I know that at times it can seem like He does not hear you, and you are lost in the middle of this world. I want to remind you that God is fighting for you and, as long as you trust Him, then nothing can hurt you or be against you.

The Bible says in Romans 8:31, "What shall we say about such wonderful things as these? If God is for us, who can ever be against us?" The world cannot be against you, your friends cannot be against you, your family cannot be against you, even you cannot be against you! Nothing, I mean absolutely nothing, can be against you. You have to believe God that your circumstance is not your outcome, it is simply your process. Putting God ahead of your storm allows Him the opportunity to lead you out of it.

You need to stop allowing the people behind you to tell you who you are and look ahead of you where God is. Some of us need to place God ahead of us instead of trying to figure it out on our own. Your circumstances, both past and present, cannot define where you are called to go. Do not let where you are today hinder where God is trying to take you tomorrow.

Job tossed and turned. He battled and cursed his birth until he finally gave it to God—and that is when his process ended, and he lacked nothing. The timing of your process is not the same as everyone else's. God is seeking a different process for you. You must understand that if you start desiring where someone else is, then you will have to take on their process. You are not allowed to pick and choose what you want to have from someone else's blessings.

Your circumstance is not your outcome, it is simply your process.

You see, we get in a habit of fake rejoicing. You know what I mean. Someone gets something you have been praying for, and you clap, jump up and down, and you thank Jesus for them, but on the inside you are envious. On the inside you are breaking apart because you wish you had what they had. You say that and you stand there in your hurt and you do not realize that you can't pick and choose.

We All Face Trials

Let me make this simple. Jessica gets a job Ashley has been waiting for. Ashley graduated from college, has a great family, and loves the Lord. Ashley says to Jessica, "Oh, that is wonderful." She is happy for Jessica, but on the inside she is jealous of Jessica's blessing.

Ashley does not realize Jessica was beaten all her life by her parents, has tried to kill herself several times, is struggling with a crack addiction, got the job by the skin of her teeth, and if she did not get the job she would be evicted from her apartment. Ashley just saw Jessica's job offer and immediately wanted to be in Jessica's position, but if she took the job she must also take Jessica's process and her struggle. Ashley does not get to pick and choose.

Be careful whose life you envy, and be careful what you ask for and where your heart of jealousy lies, because, at the end of the day, you too are going through a process. Are you so busy wanting another person's blessings that you can't see that God called you to be a diamond so you do not need to be reaching for copper?

I know it's hard to look at other people's dreams come true and try to rejoice for them when you are in your process, but the thing is you do not know their story. You do not know what it took for them to get to their promise. *We all face trials*, we all face storms, and just because the people around you are getting blessed does not mean that God forgot you. It means they finished their part of their process for that particular promise, and now that process is done, they will go through another process. They trusted God and let it go. They believed God for the impossible, and they allowed God before them. It is important in life that you do not blame God for your circumstance, but that you humble yourself under the hand of the Almighty God and allow His control over your life.

Be careful whose life you envy.

Trust me, I get what it is like to look at other people and want what they have and want to be where they are. When Brandon and I were dating, my sister got married and the people around me were getting engaged, and I wanted that. I wanted Brandon to just hurry up and propose already—even though I knew it was not the right time, and we were still growing. I had to walk through my storm, not my sister's, not my friends', but my storm. Brandon and I, whenever we felt weak, broken, or felt an urgency to jump ahead of the process, we would remind each other we were respecting the process, and, oh boy, did I say it was hard? (LOL.)

We wanted to just run headfirst into what we believed was right for us, but God wanted to mature us and complete us before we could get married. We had to respect the process. If we had jumped in our timing instead of God's timing, then we would have missed out on the process, and if we missed the process then we would not have gained perseverance, and without perseverance we would not have been able to make it to completion. We had to trust God's hand over us and not allow anything around us to detour us from God's path for our lives.

So now I ask you: What would happen if you stopped right now and said, "I am over the process and I am done with this"? Could you be ruining your wholeness in Christ because of your lack of respect to walk with Him through the process?

Listen, I don't want you to give up. What am I saying? You *cannot* give up. I will not allow you to! Do not lose hope, and do not become envious of the people around you getting blessed. You have to understand that your story is unique and God is creating a best seller for Himself out of your trials and circumstances.

God has not forgotten about you, and He will do what He said.

I am speaking to the broken, scared, hurting, and lost *you*. God has not forgotten about you, and He will do what He said. I know you are rejoicing for the people around you and still wondering when your turn will be. I want to tell you that it is through fire, shattering, and processing that God molds a beautiful diamond. And a diamond is well worth the wait.

Let me pause here to say that I am honored that you are allowing me to be a help to you. Will you let me pray for you now?

I pray that you have faith that is bigger than a mustard seed. I pray that you desire faith that is bigger than that. I pray that your faith is to speak for, to fight for, and to push for. I pray that you understand that the power of your faith can produce your purpose. I pray that you understand that this is the beginning of something bigger than you can even fathom. I pray that you become a supernatural thinker because God can do exceedingly and abundantly above anything you could ask or think, so I pray that you begin to think supernaturally so that He can do above that. I pray that you think big, believe big, and that you know big and supersede big. I pray that you understand that this faithing it thing is not just a thing but it is an ethical term that you will begin to live by that you will faith fight to your purpose. I pray that you understand that the enemy is after your faith because he understands the power behind it. I pray that you take a hold of your faith and use it to benefit you, not shake you. I pray that you become a faither. Amen.

Scan this code for Cora's Chapter 2
PRAYER FOR YOU!

Or Visit

WWW.CORAJAKESCOLEMAN.COM

Faith Affirmations

We all go through stages in life, and it is never really the stages that bother us, but the in-between time. What do I do while waiting on God to bring me to acceptance? I wish I could say there were some steps for that, but there really aren't. What I can tell you is that you must be just as willing to accept your lows as you are your highs. The only way to be truly successful in anything is to always consider where you went wrong and what lesson can be learned from it. More often than not, God has a solution for your situation; you just haven't opened your mind to the idea of what He has for you because it's not comfortable. As long as you are looking for the easy way to get to your promise you will always be negotiating and never navigating your way through. We all have highs and lows in life. We have ups and downs, journeys we would rather leave uncharted, but it is in the uncharted territories of life where we receive our greatest lessons. Just like with a diamond, you can't find it unless you are willing to go through some uncharted territories and some dark places. You have been called out of the shadow, but that doesn't mean you will never experience the valley of the shadow of death. Sometimes God will take you to a dead place to show you the power you have to speak life!

Faith Points

Emotional reactions to life storms can be the worst villain. Don't allow inner struggles to squeeze the life out of you.

To fulfill your God-given purpose in life you must be willing to sacrifice your fleshly desires for God's will.

You are only as strong and as blessed as what you are willing to sacrifice.

When dying to self (Romans 8:13), believers encounter similar experiences to the six stages of grief after a loved one dies. Face each stage with confidence, knowing that the Holy Spirit is with you all the way.

Quitting is not an option during the process of faithing it. When you spend time in the Word of God, you will receive revelations about where you are in life and what wonderful blessings are in store for you.

Don't blame God for a temporary situation that isn't to your liking. He can and will turn your mourning into dancing (Psalm 30:11).

Do not lose hope or be envious of others. God is creating a best seller for Himself out of your trials and circumstances. He knows you will triumph over every problem—He's writing the book from beginning to end!

The enemy looks for ways to cause you to doubt God and your faith in Him. Stand strong and don't give up or give in.

Faith Activations

Write the stages of grief; and after each word, write an instance that relates to a time in your life. Did that experience make you stronger, bitter, sad? Could you have handled the situation better?

Schedule a time, perhaps set a timer for 45-60 minutes, when you can blindfold yourself and then go about your daily chores at home. (Ensure someone is also at home who can keep you from harming yourself unintentionally.) Experiencing temporary "blindness" will give you a sense of how dependent you are on God to lead you through the darkness of every storm.

Write Philippians 4:8 on a slip of paper or 3x5 card. The next time someone tells you the situation is hopeless, your family member won't be healed, your financial circumstance won't improve, or any negative statement, immediately push those statements out of your mind and spirit. Reject all negativity by reading and memorizing Philippians 4:8.

Faithing It

THREE

Fighting Faith

*Because of your unbelief; for assuredly, I say to you,
if you have faith as a mustard seed, you will say to
this mountain, "Move from here to there" and it will
move; and nothing will be impossible for you.*

(MATTHEW 17:20)

"Process" has a sister, and her name is "Faith." When I am in a stage of process and I am fighting with my faith, I call that "faithing it." And here's the good news—as long as you fight with your faith there is nothing you can't do!

It is through faith that your promise is possible.

It is through faith that your purpose is fulfilled.

And it is through faith that your process finally comes to a victorious end!

Faith defines your level of outcome. If your faith is big, your blessing is big. We can see this by going back to Job. Job had big faith and so, after his process and his struggle, he had a big blessing.

As long as you fight with your faith, there is nothing you can't do!

Some of us do not have enough faith so we are not moving toward a big outcome. That's why Jesus stressed, "Because of your unbelief; for assuredly I say to you, if you have faith as a mustard seed, you will say to this mountain, 'Move from here to there' and it will move; and nothing will be impossible for you" (Matthew 17:20).

What Are You Believing In?

I wonder—what level of faith do you have? What level of faith do I have? Does our faith match up with the blessing for which we are asking of God? Does our faith match up with the promise God told us we'd receive? The problem is that we are asking for big blessings, and we have so little faith that we aren't seeing results.

Without faith in our process we are not going to make it. To begin with, we know that the biblical definition of faith is this:

> *Faith is the substance of things hoped for, the evidence of things not seen* (Hebrews 11:1).

The breakdown of that statement? You must believe in your promise and know it is coming even if you do not see it.

Can you believe without fight? Can you have faith without fight? I say no.

Merriam-Webster's defines *faith* as a strong "belief in something or someone." Some of us choose to have more faith in things we *can* see instead of what we cannot see. Faith is a strong belief in something.

Now, let's think about you and your process. What are you believing in? What are you trusting God for in your life? Is the enemy defining your faith or are you defining your faith? Sometimes we can become so interested in the blessings that we *can* see, that we have no faith in God's ability to do the things we cannot see.

The other half of *Webster's* definition of faith is a strong belief in someone—"a person." Some of us have trusted people to give us something instead of trusting the God who is preparing a place for us. It is time for us to start putting our strength in God instead of our logic, our thoughts, and our opinions.

Can you believe without fight?

Jesus' statement about faith in Matthew 17:20 came because the disciples did not have faith in their ability.

Here's the story from Matthew 17. A man with a demon-possessed son came to Jesus for help. What is so amazing about the story is that the father says, "I went to the disciples and they could not heal him." Now, Jesus spoke to the demon and it was removed. The disciples were shocked, and they wanted to know why it did not work for them. That's when Jesus responded, "Because of your unbelief; for assuredly, I say to you, if you have faith as a mustard seed, you can say to this mountain, 'Move from here to there' and it will move; and nothing will be impossible for you" (Matthew 17:20).

Don't Wait to See Before You Believe

They did not have faith in themselves. They did not have that fight within themselves to cast the demon out. Without belief in your power through Jesus, you have no power. Jesus is calling for a believing generation, a faith-fighting generation!

We can get so caught up in what we can *see* that God cannot use us.

We can get so consumed by doubt in our own ability that God cannot use us.

We can get so lazy in our belief in God that He cannot use us.

We need to get our power back!

Too often we wait to see it before we can believe it, and we don't match our day-to-day lives with our faith in God. Do you have faith enough to believe what God said and move on it, even if He does not give you a sign? In the days before creation, God was just God. He did not have to give any signs, numbers, or a divine message through a prophet. He was just God. We (myself included) have gotten caught up in the "God, show me a sign" prayer. Really, all that means is, "God, I do not really believe that I heard You, and I need You to confirm Your voice because I have strayed so far away from You that I do not know for sure if that is You." Have you strayed so far away from God that you are not confident that you can hear His voice? I understand. I was there.

It's possible that you are still in the same process stage and going through the same test over and over again because you have disconnected from God's voice, and He is simply testing your faith. We repeat prayers over and over again as if God did not hear us the first time. Yet Jesus told us if we have just a little faith we can move a mountain. He did not say we would have to repeat over and over again to the mountain before it moved. Speak one time with just a little faith. Jesus did not repeat to the boy over and over again to be healed. He spoke one time, and it was so.

So my question to you is, have you gotten so broken that you cannot believe? Have you gotten so cut that you do not believe in your ability or your relationship with God? Are you choosing to allow your circumstance to detour you from the plan God has set before you? Have you forgotten God's voice? Are you praying for signs and wonders because you have lost your faith? Are you so lost in your process that you forgot you are a child of God?

Faith for the "Now Generation"

There was a time when I wondered, why did Jesus say we can move a mountain and not a rock or a pebble? And why did He not say, "If you have faith like a mountain you can move a mountain?"

Then I began to evaluate myself and us as a people. I came to the conclusion that those words from Jesus are prophetic for the "now generation." One time Jesus even said, "You are an unbelieving and perverse generation." Even people who were alive in Jesus' day were losing faith and belief in themselves. If you lose faith and belief in yourself, then you lose faith and belief in God. He knew that we were going to start losing our faith, and He knew we would have mountains, and in a plea for us to believe that He can do it *all*, He said, "If you can just have faith the size of a mustard seed, you can move your mountain." He asked for something small. He stressed that if you had that small thing you could move that big thing. A mustard seed is about 3 mm in size. Jesus was pleading with us, "If you just believe this small, I can do something so big!"

The sad part is that we use this Scripture as our "go-to prayer" when we are at our breaking point. Then we say, "Lord, You said if I have faith the size of a mustard seed, I can move mountains. Please, Lord, move this mountain!" At that point we're thinking, *Surely I have more faith than the size of a mustard seed!* Unfortunately, we do not, and that is why we end up staying tossed around in our storm.

You cannot ask God to decrease your struggle until you ask Him to increase your faith. When we pray for our dreams and they do not happen right away, we can allow our circumstances to chip away at our faith in God. Or we can choose to allow the cutting to shape us and yield to the skillful hands of the Master Carpenter, Jesus Christ.

You cannot ask God to decrease your struggle until you ask Him to increase your faith.

So this chapter is a match that I am placing in you. I want you to know I understand that in the middle of a broken place it is hard to believe God.

With God you can achieve the unthinkable, and with God you can conceive the impossible. The biggest part of this struggle is faith.

We can tell our thoughts to "faith it"! To faith your logic (meaning your thoughts, your opinions, and your perspective of life) is to announce to your logic, "God is seeing me through this because I can't see for myself."

I recently made a decision to faith my logic to trust God in all that I do and that whatever happened was all in God's hands. I prepared myself for this choice by writing to God the things that I wanted specifically. I prayed to God once for what I needed and I stood back and praised Him for it in advance.

Why don't you do that too? You can write down what you are seeking, and begin to believe God like never before—even if you are writing for God to help you believe. You cannot remove yourself from a stagnant place without first realizing that you have placed yourself there by not believing in God, and not believing in yourself, and not fighting your storm with faith. You have to want to be better in order to get to better. You have to want to leap in order to get to the top. If you can start faithing it (fighting with faith) then you have the ability to conquer this.

Jesus Ministered from the Cross

Consider Jesus. Jesus was broken, bruised, and beaten, and we believed in Him. And it was in His breaking that He became a King. He was a carpenter in the process of greatness, and it was after His beating, after His bruises, after they nailed His bleeding body on the cross, and He rose again, that He became a King.

My friend, God is breaking you into your crown. I want you to understand that without believing what He said and fighting, you cannot get to the other side. God used His crucifixion to *be* a ministry. And here you are, waiting to be healed and come out whole before you minister from your own cross. When Jesus ministered to the people and hung from the cross, He went through His process in the face of His people.

Post Up!

It's time to get your faith back! It's time for you to face yourself and ask God to reignite in you the passion for Him so that you can fight the enemy. It's time for you to realize that you were built in the image of a man who was broken for us. Theologians will be quick to interject that Jesus did not endure physically broken bones, but Jesus said at Passover, "Take eat. This is my body which was broken for you!" (see Matthew 26:26). So I am saying His body and His emotions and His spirit were cut, broken, and shaped into perfection when He obeyed God and went to the cross.

Where is *your* fight? Where is *your* faith?

You are standing in the middle of your storm, saying, "I trust You, God," but do you?

Do not allow the beating of your process to take away your faith. You need to fight back. The enemy cannot take what you do not put in his face. My daughter watches *Dora the Explorer* animated TV series, and one of my favorite things is when Swiper (the enemy) shows up and he wants to take something from Dora, and they have to say, "Swiper, no swiping," and sometimes he goes away, but sometimes he takes something, and they say, "Aw, man!" But they immediately start searching for what he took, and try to put it back in its rightful place. We can learn something from Dora here. Do you just say, "Aw, man!" and walk away? Or do you fight back and begin to search in your spirit.

Allow God to stir up the fight in you. It's time for you to begin faithing it. Things are going to happen to you, and you are going to get hurt, but we have already learned that is your process, and now we know that we have to match our faith with our process. Stop praying for mustard seed faith. Ask God to give you faith the size of a mountain. What would happen if you faced your trial with mountain-sized faith? A mountain-sized fight!

My daughter is in kindergarten, and a little boy was bullying her. Almost every day she would come home with an incident report that he scratched her, hit her, or did something just crazy. My husband sat her down, and began to show her how to protect herself and post up.

We told her, "There will be all types of enemies in your life, and when they approach you and they try to hurt you, then you have to protect yourself. You have to fight back."

Next time she went to school and he tried to scratch her, all she did was post up, and he backed down.

What would happen if you were in the middle of a whirlwind, and you just posted up with faith? Is your faith strong enough to stop your storm? Is your faith strong enough to stand up for itself?

You may be believing God for a relationship, a healing, a house, job, car, or anything. Whatever it is you believe God for you must understand that it is through your faithing that you get it. And if mustard seed faith can move one mountain, imagine what mountain-sized faith could move. It's time for faithing. It's time for real faith! God is calling His children. You must hear His voice and know it's Him and move by His perfect will. It is in your sincere trust and belief in God that you can be saved from the dangers that the enemy brings. Sometimes that danger is real.

My Struggle, My Story

Did you read the story about my accident in the introduction?

I was in the worst accident of my life. Although I came out of it without a scratch or a bruise, I found out the next day during a CAT scan that I had a 7 cm cyst on one ovary and a 9 cm cyst on my other ovary. In short, that one car accident led to me discovering two cysts, the loss of an ovary, the loss of a fallopian tube, and a news flash from the doctor that it wasn't probable for me to get pregnant without going through in vitro fertilization (IVF).

God gave me a wonderful husband that had enough faith to fight for the both of us. We went through the IVF cycle, and it didn't work out. That was another pain, and I asked, "God, why me?" But that led us to adopt our beautiful daughter, Amauri. We rested and went through another IVF cycle. I went through the acupuncture, the pineapples, and the legs up, and all the tricks, and we found out it didn't work this time either.

A few months after going through the pain of the failed fertilizations, my godsister Michelle called me. She wanted me to go with her into the birthing room, and I did. I witnessed the birth of my godson, and I was honored to cut the umbilical cord. Since that day, I have been gifted to raise him. He is an amazing gift, one I wouldn't have even accepted if I was pregnant.

Why am I telling you all of this? I am telling you this because I want you to know that no matter what you're going through, you can overcome and be victorious. I could have spent my time crying over the loss of my ovary and fallopian tube, or I could thank God because I am still able to overcome and win and be victorious.

Not Bound by Brokenness

Don't spend any more time asking God, "Why me?" You have been considered for the struggle because there is something great to be produced through you. You have been considered for the struggle because God is about to make you a survivor and a successor of your storm. Don't focus on the broken, focus on the blessing. You don't need to worry about the pains of process and the *why me?* Really, you must ask yourself, "Why not me?" For every broken piece God is planting a blessing. You are not being broken for no reason, you are being broken on purpose. You are going through the pains because God is about to birth something beautiful through you.

You are not bound by your brokenness, you are lifted from it. I could still be looking at the car accident, but I stepped into the purpose of the pain. Stop searching for the why me, and start searching for the blessing. If you don't, you will miss out on what God has and where you are meant to go because you have stopped yourself from soaring. It's time to soar, sweetheart, soar. God chose you because you are called to be of great power.

Don't focus on the broken, focus on the blessing.

Your struggle is because you have a purpose.

Your struggle is because you are powerful.

Your struggle is because you have a message.

When you can understand that you aren't the average person, then you will know that your purpose is powerful. Your pain is powerful. You are a Kingdom kid, so you will have to go through some things, but catch what I am saying: You will go *through* them, and by faithing it, you will get to the other side!

You are covered by the blood of the Lamb. If God is living in you, then you have a hedge of protection camped around you, and whatever storm the enemy brings you must rear up like Job and know that your God is greater, bigger, and stronger than anything you could be facing. Your time to believe God is now.

You are whole when your fight matches with your belief. The woman with the issue of blood bled for twelve years. She was hurting, but as soon as she heard Jesus was near she got out of her bed, and she took her fight and her faith to Jesus. She crawled and climbed through the crowd and moved while bleeding to get her healing. She did not care about the people or the crowd! Her faith and her fight was to press in far enough—she just wanted a piece of Jesus' clothing to touch. She believed after bleeding for twelve years, "If I can just get to His hem I can be healed."

How many of you can believe God like that after twelve years of being broken and hurt? You can put your shoes on and drape yourself and climb through a crowd to get to your promise. And if you remember, when she climbed through the crowd and she touched His hem, Jesus immediately knew He had been touched. When He turned around and saw her, He pulled her up and He said, "Go, for your faith has made you *whole*" (see Mark 5:34). That goes back to our first chapter: God is pulling you up through a process so that you can be whole.

I want to speak to the tired you. You have been hurt time and time again. Things have been taken from you after you pled with God to hold on to them, and now you do not believe God cares for you. You do not believe God hears you. I want to tell you that He hears you, and He is there with you, and He's holding you, but it is your faith that He is after. If you will trust God, you can get to His hem.

You cannot pray to a God you do not believe in.

You cannot pray to a God you have lost faith in.

You cannot pray to a God you do not even have mustard seed faith for.

Get Real with God

My faith has been shaken at times, but my heart for God wasn't. I understand that as a child of the King, I must go through things that will shake me. I understand that just as any relationship sometimes I will get upset with Him, I will get sad with Him, I will get hurt with Him, but I will also get happy with Him, overcome with Him, reach milestones with Him, fall more in love with Him. The point is, I will be with Him! I am in a relationship with Christ so that although He slay me, shake me, and crush me, I will trust that at the end of it all I will receive a crown.

You have to be real with God. He knows your every thought. He knows you are mad when it does not work out the way you wanted it to. He knows that you are breaking apart on the inside. He knows you are confused, He knows you really wanted it, but I want you to start trusting Him for the expected end of your trials.

I know. You are probably saying, "Cora, how?" You are being cut to be beautiful, and God is not saying no because He does not love you. He is saying no because it is not time, and that if you draw unto Him then He will draw into you. It's easy to get a no and find your faith shaken, but that's why I am calling it a challenge. Because no matter how hard you get cut, no matter how bad it is, you have to look and say, "Though You slay me, no matter how hurt and heartbroken I am, I will trust You."

That is how you do it. Trust Him in your brokenness. Trust Him in your heartbreak. You trust Him in your anger, and you tell Him. You share with God your truth. When I had to go through heartbreak, I had to go before the Lord with my truth, saying, "God, I really wanted that! I am sad, angry, hurt, and heartbroken that you did not give me what my heart desired. I feel like You don't care about my desire, my hope, or my vision."

Part of having faith in God is believing in Him when things don't make sense—believing God when things don't work out.

The enemy's motive is to destroy your faith in God, because if the enemy can take your faith then he can take your fight. You are empowered by God when you choose Him above the pain you are going through. You need to believe God can and will be greater than your storm. A storm walked through alone is a storm that cannot end and will not have peace, but when you walk through your storm with God then you have peace and power. You will have the access to get through it because of who you have decided to work with.

A Choice to Make

As we end this chapter together, I want to challenge you today to make a choice. I challenge you to stand in the face of negativity and say, "I rebuke you, devil, for making me not believe God for what He said. And today I am faithing my logic, my thoughts, and my perceptions."

Obstacles will come—face them with faith. More importantly, face them with God.

Give God all of you. Stop hiding from God and begin to reveal yourself. Remember, He knows all and sees all. Be willing to be submissive and open to giving Him the embarrassing things. Open your heart to God—the broken pieces, the hard and hollow pieces, and open it up to God. You can be great, just strengthen your faith.

You are empowered by God when you choose Him above the pain you are going through.

When you fight with faith you are fighting for purpose.

I'm talking to you—yes, you! Don't let your storms shake your faith so much so that you have been shaken out of the ring. It's time for you to get your faith back—claim your power back. You deserve the ability to win. In fact, you have earned the right to win. You are stronger than you think, and this shaking was supposed to stop you but no more.

You won't be hindered by the storm. You will use the storm to catapult you into your destiny. God needs you to overtake the Kingdom.

You are reading this page in this book because God wants you and me to talk about this right now. I want you to know that God isn't against you—He wants you to win! The bad stuff happened, and you were hurt but you aren't dead. You still have life. You still have fight! So it's time! We are not to sit down in our hurt, sadness, anger, and brokenness anymore. We are fighting with faith. Today, starting right now, this moment, we are faithing it!

I have such an earnest desire to see you cross over into your promise! Please, let me pray with you!

I pray that God strengthens your faith in this season and that you open up to Him. I pray you are vulnerable to God. I pray that God refreshes your relationship with Him and shows you that He is for you. I pray that God lifts you up before great men, and that He walks you through the steps that are needed in order for you to pursue your purpose. I pray that you begin to resist the devil and confront the enemy that is within. I pray that your strongholds be broken and that the yoke that has you bound and that has made you stop trusting and stop having faith in God, I pray that it be loosed right now in the name of Jesus. I pray that this moment right now you are ignited in purpose and that you begin to develop a real relationship with Christ. You are great! I pray you begin to walk in that. In the name of Jesus, it is so. And so it is. Amen.

Scan this code for Cora's Chapter 3
PRAYER FOR YOU!

Or Visit

WWW.CORAJAKESCOLEMAN.COM

Faith Affirmations

In the real scheme of things, we are all prewired to be willing to fight for what matters the most to us. We will go for it, and we will conquer many things in life because of the will to fight for what we believe in and hope for from God. We will fight for family, friends, and even for ourselves, but when it comes to faith, it is almost as if we have allowed our faith to become not close enough to us to fight for. We have allowed ourselves to be consumed by the attack as opposed to being reminded of our power. We must have even more zeal and tenacity in our fight for our belief system in God than we have in our fight for man. To be a ride or die for Christ is something that we don't really hear very often. You are strong enough to combat this giant. Understand that the enemy is not the type of enemy to give up so you need to not give up either. Stay the course, fight the good fight of faith, and press on anyhow. You can accomplish this, and you will win. But if you give up now, you'll never get the promise that is waiting for you at the end of this fight. So I challenge you: Don't become weaker in spirit simply because the enemy is screaming loudly at you. Stay strong and fight for your faith. Believe in your faith, trust in your faith, and don't give up.

Faith Points

You will receive your promise through faith. Your purpose will be fulfilled through faith. And through faith your process will come to a victorious end!

If your faith in God is big, your blessing is big. When you fight with faith, you will win everything!

Believe in your promise and know it is coming—even if you don't see it right away.

Who is defining your faith? God? The enemy? You? Only God knows the end from the beginning. Trust in Him fully—not in your own flawed logic, thoughts, and others' opinions.

Belief that through Jesus you have the power to trust and obey will ignite your faith for greatness in your spiritual walk, family relationships, career advancement... all aspects of your life.

Don't allow yourself to become so broken that you can't hear God. Have faith, listen for His voice. He is continually calling you to Himself.

You can't ask God to decrease your struggle until you ask Him to increase your faith. Allow God to shape you by yielding yourself to the skillful hands of the Master Carpenter, Jesus Christ.

Don't focus on the broken, focus on the blessings. Don't ask, "Why me, Lord?" Ask yourself, "Why *not* me?"

You are empowered by God when you choose Him above the momentary pain you are experiencing.

Faith Activations

Write down in a notebook or tablet what you need to move ahead in life. Be specific. Then pray to God for what you need and praise Him for it in advance.

Of the list you wrote, what are you willing to believe for? Pray for? Fight for? Rewrite your list if necessary to reveal the most important needs in your life. Then faith them!

If you are standing in the middle of a storm, write down several ways you think the storm can be calmed. Pray for God to show you what direction to take to sail through to the other side of the raging winds and waters.

Faithing It

FOUR

The YES in the Burning Bush

The Lord your God, who goes before you,
He will fight for you, according to all He
did for you in Egypt before your eyes.

(DEUTERONOMY 1:30, AND ALL OF CHAPTER ONE!)

One of our needs as human beings is to know who is with us. Who believes in me? Who's got my back if things go wrong? It's possible to become so caught up in ourselves that we cannot see that God is our back support. Let me share a story from the Bible that I hope will encourage your heart, because I want you to know that you are not alone.

I want to bring you to a moment in the life of Moses. Moses was tending to the flock as normal when in the distance he saw a bush. The bush was on fire, but it was not burning down to the ground. He decided to go toward this bush to see this strange sight. When he got there, the Bible says that God called for him from within the bush, and Moses answered, "Here I am" (see Exodus 3). Now you must understand, that is the step that so many of us are missing. God calls for us to invite us into His purpose, but because we are so astray from His voice we do not answer. When God announced Himself, Moses hid his face because he did not want to look at God.

God is our back support.

Moses was told to go and save the Israelites because God had heard their cries. So many of us are crying out to God, and we do not even realize that He has come or that He is sending someone on our behalf to save us. The beautiful part of this is that Moses in his humility questioned God: "Who am I to go to them and demand this?" And the response from the Lord is what brings me to back support. God said to him, "Go, and I will be with you." I want you to realize that it is not about you—it is about who is with you. God was Moses' back support as he traveled back to Egypt to get the Israelites to the promise. God told Moses, "I have your back. I am with you."

This is the big YES in the burning bush! God says, "YES, it is time for Me to send you into your destiny, the purpose for which I made you." Moses has questions, but ultimately he says, "YES, I will do all that You say." There was a yes to purpose and a yes to going. And when God says yes, He gives a promise to go behind Moses and be his back support. If God says yes to you and others don't, it doesn't matter, as long as you say yes in response to God!

So when the Israelites started acting funny and trying to rebel, Moses was like, "Wait a minute, did you not see that God went before us and fought for us, and got us out of our storm? Did you not see that God was with us?" Moses was angry then, and we need to watch that we don't become the same people he was angry with!

The Trap of Vulnerability

After the people complained in his ear, Moses was discouraged and he was vulnerable. So Moses and Aaron left the presence of the people and went together to the door of the tabernacle. The glory of God Almighty appeared to them there! God told Moses and Aaron to take the rod with them and go to a large rock in the wilderness. But instead of striking the rock with the long staff, God told Moses to speak to the rock. Now, speaking to a rock is strange but, remember, I told you that you can't be afraid of strange things if you're going to get to your destiny with God.

Moses and Aaron got all the people to gather around the big rock, but by that time Moses was so frustrated with the people he said, "Hear now, you rebels!" (See Numbers 20.)

Moses was told to speak to the rock, but the sin of the people made him so angry that he struck the rock instead. In short, this emotional outburst caused Moses to disobey God. Because of his vulnerability, he was easily manipulated into emotional outbursts and unchecked anger, and he missed out on leading the people into the Promised Land. You will miss out on your promise when you remain vulnerable to the wrong thing. When you become vulnerable to anger, then it consumes you. You can be sure that the enemy works very well with anger. When you become vulnerable to bitterness, it consumes you and the enemy works well with bitterness.

Whatever you are vulnerable to will consume you. I want you to become vulnerable to God so that He can consume you. You are stronger than you know! When we don't understand how God could allow certain things to happen to us, we can start to push away from God. Don't do it! The more you push away from God, the longer you leave the door open for negative spirits to enter. Stop giving the enemy access to doors he should've never had the key to. Don't make yourself vulnerable!

Worship while you wait for victory.

When we read the full text in the first chapter of Deuteronomy, we find that the people were in rebellion. They were so close to the Promised Land, the land flowing with milk and honey. God had blessed them and wanted to bless them again. Moses told them to go in, but even though they trusted Moses before, they did not trust him this time.

Become vulnerable to God so that He can consume you.

They said, "Well, send someone up there before us to see if it's okay." Instead of saying, "God said go, and it is well," Moses said that the people had a good idea, so he does it. The people were manipulating Moses' faith.

The people were untrusting. They sent people up to look over the Promised Land to see if the land was good, and even after hearing it was good they still rebelled against God. They allowed their surroundings to put fear in them. The people were taller and the walls were bigger, and they allowed that to keep them from moving forward. Because of their lack of trust and unbelief, they even went as far as to say the Lord hated them!

That's when Moses stepped in and told the people, "The Lord your God, who is going before you, will fight for you, as He did for you in Egypt, before your very eyes" (Deuteronomy 1:30 NIV). He reminds them how God showed up for them in Egypt, how He carried them from their struggle to safety, and even in the midst of all of that they still did not trust God, and they continued to rebel against God.

Moses is really just letting them have it! They did not allow God to be their back support and show them the way. Because of their inability to trust God, even after they had trusted God all this time, they were forbidden access to the Promised Land. How many of us are allowing our fear of what we see keep us from believing God?

Moses walked into Egypt and with God's power delivered them from their struggle, their process, and led them over the sea. Moses got them to safety and showed God's miraculous works, and they still rebelled against the Lord. Moses had believed in God all this time, but after so many years he allowed himself to be wavered and manipulated. So because he allowed the people to shake him, he was forbidden from the Promised Land as well. He tells them basically that Caleb and Joshua are the only ones who followed the Lord, and they are the only ones, along with the children under twenty-one years of age, who will be able to inherit the Promised Land. When we choose not to trust God, we choose to lose our inheritance.

A big part of allowing God to be your support is allowing God to lead you. That means God is both behind you and before you. The people Moses allowed to challenge his faith and his ability to hear from God kept him from the Promised Land. The leadership to the Promised Land was given to Joshua. Sometimes we allow the people around us to change our thoughts and waver our faith, and we miss out on our blessing because we slipped on our faith.

After Moses read the people their rights, then they wanted to fight, but by then it was too late. God said, "Do not go up and fight, because I will not be with you. You will be defeated by your enemies" (Deuteronomy 1:42 NIV). You cannot wait until your promise is taken to believe God. You have to believe God in the ups and the downs, no matter what it looks like. The minute you lose God's support, the minute He isn't with you, then your enemies will defeat you.

They did not know that God was their back support, and Moses was being used to guide them through as God instructed him. He was trying to get the people to understand the God of hope, support, and fight he encountered at the bush. He reminded them, "God went before us and fought for our people." He tried to get the people to see the God he had trusted all this time. They would not believe.

What Kicks Us Away from Our Promise

What kicks us away from our promise? Could it be that we can talk about the storms God took us through, but we cannot trust God in the storm we are standing in?

What kicks us away from healing the broken? Could it be that we believe that we have to be perfect in order to be used?

God chose Moses from a burning place. Even though Moses stuttered and had low self-esteem, God chose him and God believed in him.

The beautiful part is that God chose him from birth, for just as he was drawn out of the water he would draw His people out! And it was because of Moses' heart toward God that he was able to be used. He was not a prince anymore, he was just Moses and he was used by God to move all of the Israelites to freedom.

In the end, when God talked to Moses from the burning bush, He was telling Moses, "Yes, I believe in you." Ultimately, Moses said yes to God. Equally important, Moses took that one "I believe in you" from God to leap into his destiny. I want you to understand that your destiny is tied to the yes in the burning bush. It is not about where you are standing, it is about where your heart is and what you are walking toward. God knew your purpose from the beginning of time, and He knew that you would have an encounter with a burning bush of your own, and that you would have to choose to either walk with God or wait for the people around you to make your choice for you. You cannot allow the people around you to define where God chooses for you to go.

Your destiny is tied to the yes in the burning bush.

What would have happened if Moses had said, "I can't," and walked away?

What would have happened if Moses had waited for his friends to say, "Yes, Moses! You can do it!"?

What would have happened if Moses had waited for the world's yes instead of walking on God's yes?

We can wait for the world to gratify us, and in that waiting we have missed that God already said yes. This is a good place to check ourselves. Have we been so consumed by getting our friends to support our dream that we have missed our encounter with God's yes? We can lose what was meant for us while waiting around for the world to support us.

Walking toward the Strange Thing

Moses was tending the flock when he saw a strange thing. How many of us are missing God because of our inability to walk toward the strange things? How many of us are waiting for someone to say, "Oh, yes, you are called to be great," instead of believing what God already said? Is it possible that we are trying to find our place in the world when God has already given us an assignment? What do you do when you have missed God's approval waiting on the world's yes? I need you to realize that the only support you need is the support of God's belief in you, and God's yes. Move in what God said, not what the world said.

I am reminded of Sarah when the angel told her she would conceive and she laughed (see Genesis 18:1–15). Some of us are hearing strange assignments from God, and we are laughing. How long will you laugh at God's promise because you think you are too old or it isn't naturally possible? Sometimes God is bringing forth amazing miracles because of your amazing storm, and if you would understand that God is with you in the midst of the storm then you will be more open to the miracle. We must know, believe, and walk in what God said for us to do and stop waiting for natural responses to a spiritual revelation.

God Is Your Back Support

I want to talk to you about allowing God to be your back support. You cannot wait on the people around you to push you, and truth be told if you are waiting for your friends to give you a yes then you are not dreaming big enough. You need to have a vision and purpose so big for your life that the only person who can make it happen or see it through is God.

Who are you allowing to be your back support?

Who are you allowing to speak into your life?

Who are you allowing to motivate and push you?

When Moses was standing at the burning bush, he was nervous and did not know what to do. God was already preparing a place for him. He was already getting the people prepared for Moses. We need to know that if God gives us an assignment, He is already working on the people ahead of time. I know what you are saying—if God prepared the elders and ministers to listen to Moses, why not Pharaoh? It's because of the need for the process. Moses had to have a challenge in order to get the people to the promise. Even when God knows you are going to win in the end, that does not mean you will not have great challenges.

If you can acknowledge God as your back support, and you can know God is preparing the people for you ahead of time, then you can move forward. So we understand first that God is our back support, but the other wonderful thing about the story is that Moses also had his brother, wife, and sister. Part of what made Moses so powerful is that he had support backing him. He had God, his family, his wife, and his people. You cannot move forward until you have people behind you to push you to your next level. It is in God's power that Moses was able to move miraculously. Moses believed God, and he did everything God told him to do to get the people to the promise.

If you do not have your family to support you, then you move on that one "I believe in you" that you hear from the Lord. You move on that one "you can do this," and you move on the one encounter that you have with your figurative burning bush. Moses had an encounter with God for every new step he had to take. After his first encounter, he became sensitive and vulnerable to the Spirit of God, so much so that he was consumed and visited by the Spirit of God. Why am I saying this? Because Moses took that one go from God, and he matched it with faith. That's how he fulfilled his purpose.

Let God Move You

What would happen if you took that one yes from God? How many people could you get to their promise if you used your one yes from God to move you?

Moses took that one yes and plagues were initiated and lives changed.

Moses took that one yes and the people followed him.

Moses took that one yes and his enemies were behind him.

Moses took that one yes and moved all of God's people into the promise.

All that action started with that one simple yes. When you can go when God says go, you can move through the water and obtain your purpose. My hope is that you do not stand at the burning bush waiting for other people to believe in the yes God gave you, but that you move and carry people to the promise. Walk out your yes to God and He will surely keep His yes promises to you.

You must allow yourself to have the encounter with God so the Spirit can consume you. When people see God's power in you, then they will get behind the God in you. Stop trying to lead yourself to your purpose and promise, and allow God to lead you.

I daresay that you can challenge God to use you in a major capacity according to your storm. I refuse to allow the Lord to let the enemy take me through great tribulation, and me not come out stronger, bigger, better, and more powerful than when I started. My storms must match my impact of ministry. I refuse to allow the enemy to believe that God will not get the glory out of every storm, mountain, and adversity that I face. I am more than a conqueror, and I know that God is with me. Once you understand that you have the ultimate support, then you can do ultimate moves.

My storms must match my impact of ministry.

When I was seven years old, my father sat us all down and said God told him to move to Texas. At the time it was crazy. We had a good life, we were in a nice home, and we knew no one in Texas. All of our friends and family were in West Virginia. None of that mattered. My dad had a burning bush encounter, and God said go, and he moved on it. We were nervous but we understood that if God said yes to Daddy, we were going to go. We supported my dad's burning bush moment, and we moved. When we moved, my dad moved over ten families with him. Just as Moses did, my dad went on God's yes and he pulled families into the promise. My father allowed God to be his back support and, because of that, he was able to pull other people out.

When we moved, doors began to fly open, and it's been the most amazing experience of our lives. When you can trust God, He can move you to your destiny. When you can trust God, He can show you things you know not of. It was then at an early age that I understood if God speaks to you, even in fear, nervousness, and uncertainty, you move no matter what. If you have crazy belief, then God can do crazy things. We had an expectancy of greatness, and God gave us just that.

What are you expecting from God? The win is in your ability to believe that God is supporting you, even in the worst of times.

All great things come through because of support. When you are about to start a diet, you look for an accountability partner. You lose more weight when you have an accountability partner than when you don't, and that is because greatness comes with support. Greatness happens when you have someone cheering on what you think is impossible. Greatness comes when you understand that you cannot do this without help. If God gave you a yes or a go, that means He has your back. That means that He is with you, and He is your back support.

We all fall short of the glory of God, but the power is in your ability to get back up.

The power is in your ability to chase after God.

Our power is in our search for Christ and our understanding that there is beauty in our broken things. Then we can say, "I am strong, and God gave me a yes and I will run with that."

Hear God and Say, "Yes"

Say yes to the process, yes to the test and trials. Later on, we can look at our trials as treasures and then we can win in the end. You will go through ups and downs, but stand on the yes that God gave you. Some of us have moved because we thought it was God speaking, and we are now realizing it wasn't Him. You know who you are in Christ, and once you do that you can redevelop your relationship with Christ, and once you do that then you can hear from Christ.

Some of us have to admit we have strayed, and our prayer life needs to be: "Lord, help me to redevelop my commitment with You. Help me to run back to You. Help me to hear You, and do not allow me to walk toward my will, but only Yours."

If you text friends, Facebook friends, or tweet friends more than you talk to God, then you cannot hear Him. You have to be so close to God that there is no doubt in His instructions to you. You have to be so close to God that the people around you see God in you. That does not mean you should go around quoting Scriptures every hour and become overwhelmingly spiritual. That means that you show your pure heart toward Christ. You are not always going to get it right, and there are going to be times that you fall, but when God is your back support you can do anything.

Some of us have placed people where we need to place God.

Some of us have placed people's opinions of us where God's thoughts of us need to be. Some of us must step away from our own will and step into God's true desire and hope.

The people rebelled against God and began to worship calves, commit adultery, murder, and just jump into the world. After all God did for them, they left His presence. They left behind His instruction and they rebelled. We cannot become the people of the world—we must become the changers of the world. We cannot begin to break the rules God placed and pray for the blessings of God. We must be renewed from the inside out, and allow God to be with us. What made Moses powerful was not the bush or the staff or the plagues. What made Moses powerful is that God said, "Go, and I will be with you." Some of us have gone without God being with us, and then we wonder why miracles are not happening. We have to understand that it was the God with Moses who made him powerful.

We cannot become the people of the world—we must become the changers of the world.

With God, I Can Do This

Your power is in God, not in people. Your power is in your walk in Christ, not in your actions in the world. When Moses said yes to God, God did not once bring up where Moses came from. In fact, He used new things to show His support of Moses. Do not limit God's ability by staying in what you went through during your process. It is your walk toward Christ that makes you great, not the steps you took without Him.

The Bible says, "With God *all things are possible*" (Matthew 19:26 NIV). It's a simple Scripture, and we hear it often, but we must live by this Scripture.

I cannot be great without God—it's not possible.

My marriage cannot succeed without God—it's not possible.

My job cannot succeed without God—it's not possible.

I will not get that raise without God—it's not possible.

My child won't survive cancer without God—it's not possible.

My parenting won't be a success without God—it's not possible.

You must be consumed by God, supported by God, and standing with God because with God *all* things are possible! With God I can do this!

Let God fight your battle. Let Him in. Let Him bring forth your success through your submission to Him. God is a better fighter, better provider, better leader, and just better all around than we are. You will win when you remove your hands off of God's plans for your life and let Him orchestrate it.

Moses looked at the people, and he pleaded with them, "Wait! God fought for us. We got here because of God."

Wait! You cannot become great without back support. Your hope, your legacy, and your promise are in the God who supports you.

I am eager to pray over you right now!

I pray that God will be your first choice of support. I pray that you begin to see yourself through the eyes of God. I pray that you would begin to walk in your destiny without pain and hurt weighing you down. I pray that you would remove your hands and begin to fight with your faith. I pray that God grant you the desire and discipline to be able to obtain what He has for you. I pray that you are able to stand before your mountains and command them to move, and they be moved. I pray that you stand up for your purpose and you gain your power. I pray that you begin to live life and make every decision count. You will come out of this by the power of the Holy Ghost, and I thank God that you are free to be with God, and, being with Him, you are free and it is so and so it is by the power of the Holy Ghost. Amen.

Let's continue this journey of faithing it together...

Scan this code for Cora's Chapter 4
PRAYER FOR YOU!

Or Visit

WWW.CORAJAKESCOLEMAN.COM

Faith Affirmationns

Your "yes" is valuable because you need it to be given from a place free of complaint and full of truth. I used to fast and pray, but I would complain throughout and then get upset when I didn't receive the promise. Your "yes" in your situation with God must be given from a place of great strength and foundation. Where there is complaining there can't be a promise. You must give yourself the focus of being disciplined in what you said "yes" to and believing God anyhow. Your "yes" isn't valid if it comes from a heart of anger, resentment, guilt, or regret. It just simply can't build from there. I challenge you to give your "yes" from a place of great humility and discipline so that you can obtain the promises of God.

Faith Points

You can't be afraid of "strange things" if you're going to reach your God-given destiny. Walking toward strange things (as Moses did) may be where God will meet you with His greatest gift. Know, believe, and walk in what God tells you; stop waiting for natural responses to a spiritual revelation.

The enemy will use anger and bitterness to break you down and prevent you from receiving God's promise. Pushing God away opens doors for negative spirits to enter. Don't allow fear to keep you from believing in and turning to God.

God believes in you—no matter what flaws you have, no matter where you came from. He knows your heart and loves you dearly.

While waiting for the world or friends or your job to support you, you may miss your life-sustaining encounter with God.

God's vision and purpose for your life is so big that He is the only One who can make it happen. Trust Him.

If you text, Facebook, or tweet friends more than you talk to God, you won't be able to hear Him. Placing God closest to you brings joy and peace.

Faith Activations

After meditating on the following questions, write a few sentences as answer to each:

- Who are you allowing to be your back support?
- Who are you allowing to speak into your life?
- Who are you allowing to motivate and push you?
- Have you allowed the Spirit to consume you?
- Are you trying to lead yourself to your purpose and promise?
- Are you allowing God to lead you?
- What do you expect from God?

FIVE

Delights, Desires, and Dysfunctions

Delight yourself also in the Lord, and
He shall give you the desires of your heart.

(PSALM 37:4)

If I could invite you into my home right now at the beginning of this chapter and sit down with you over coffee, I would ask you this question: What truly delights your soul? I mean, what thought can make you smile even when nobody is in the room?

For me, I'd have to say that nothing delights my soul in this life as much as welcoming a new baby into the family. It doesn't matter if that baby is my child or my niece or nephew, there is a delight that stirs the waters in the Jakes and Coleman families whenever a new life is given to us to nurture. That new little one is ours, but a stranger, really. We don't know yet if this baby will play football or play the piano. We don't yet know this little one's favorite color, and we certainly don't know everything this baby's future will hold! We all realize that in the days and years ahead, this precious child will consume much of our time, talents, and treasures. We will spend our time and treasure in what delights us. Jesus said, "Where your treasure is, there your heart will be also" (Matthew 6:21). So where we spend our extra money—that is, the money outside the cost of living—is a pretty good indication of what delights our heart.

But money is no object when it comes to caring for a new son or daughter. We know that it will take time and patience to get to really know this baby. We realize that there will be midnight feedings and rocking chair prayers in the weeks and months to come. Sacrifices will be made to ensure that our baby receives every natural and spiritual blessing that we can give. Yes, it will take a lot of work and sacrifice, but that is nothing compared to the sheer joy of getting to know this new little person and developing a special relationship together.

We will spend our time and treasure in what delights us.

Do you know God feels the same way? When we are born again, He longs to spend His time, talents, and treasure on this newborn child of God. His love for us just increases day by day.

Of course, a newborn doesn't stay tiny forever. That baby will walk, talk, clap, and eventually eat solid food. For a few years, the mother and father are the central joy of that child's life. We all know what happens in adolescence—separation. It's at that point that a child rightly desires separation from his or her parents in order to establish personal identity. I can't say I look forward to the separation part, but it's all a normal stage of growth.

The Spirit of Adoption

It is at this stage of adolescent growth that a child decides whether or not to adopt the parent! Seriously! We know God is good and we may even call Him "Father," but have we allowed that spirit of adoption to flood our souls until nothing and no one delights us like Father God? Maybe we don't need Him in the same way we did when we were first born again, but we still need Him! And He needs us! He wants us! God says to us, "Delight yourself in Me, and I'll give you the desires of your heart."

No one knows us like Father God. No one.

Sometimes we abandon our destiny because we wander off looking for other amusements and delights. God's purpose and dream may fade into the background as we pursue other interests. If that's you, ask God right now to restore you back to His dream and His purpose for your life.

If you do not identify your promise, purpose, or dream, then you don't know what you are fighting for. Do you delight in the Lord? Is your time with God the highlight of your day?

There is so much power and purpose generated when we set aside time alone to delight in God. Of course, we have to stop communicating horizontally via Twitter, Messenger, Snapchat, Facebook, texts, and e-mails, but if we will lay all that aside and listen, God wants to say something to us!

We often get stuck in the part of the Scripture that says God will grant us the desires of our hearts, not understanding that it first said that we must delight ourselves in Him in order for those desires to be granted. So the question then is, how do you know what you want to do? He grants you the desires of your heart according to how much of your heart you have given to Him.

How do you know what your purpose is? This is not a question that comes with an easy answer. But I have found that what the enemy tries to block you from the most is the thing that you are supposed to be going after. In reality, the enemy isn't fighting you for your purpose; he is fighting you for your power. He will try to distract you with any number of things to keep you from pressing and delighting yourself in God because he knows that's where you get your power. The enemy knows that if you head toward delighting yourself in God, then God will open the doors to grant you all your desires. And it stands to reason that when you have the desires of your heart and you are able to see the power of God, then you become more compatible with God, which makes you a force to be reckoned with!

God wants to say something to us!

If you've spent time with God, then He's already put some of those desires within you. You have that passion deep inside somewhere, but the enemy keeps presenting you with distractions to keep you from the very thing that you should go after. The enemy tried to block my fertility, and that is because I delighted myself in God to fight for my promise. With God on my side, I began faithing for my power. Satan is trying to stop me from being a mother. He is trying to stop your progress and your pressing in to delight in God. What is your desire? Delight yourself in God, and you will be able to produce your desire. This is all part of faithing it.

One of our God-given purposes on this earth is to be fruitful and multiply. It's easy to say that this purpose pertains just to women and men being able to have children, but I challenge you to think bigger! God wants you to be fruitful in all things and to multiply in all that you produce. It's important that you know that the very reason you have a desire to do what you want to do is because God placed that desire in you. If God was good enough to place the desire in you, then He should be good enough for you to walk toward and to link up with. If God is for you, then nothing can be against you.

In my personal life, adoption became a focal point of my communication with God. I was diagnosed with infertility even after telling God my entire life that all I wanted was to be a mommy. I could've given up, but instead I decided to get under God's umbrella. When I delighted my life, my marriage, my home, and everything in God, He granted me the desires of my heart by giving me a beautiful daughter. What a joy it is to my heart when she calls me "Mom."

What you must realize is that just because you delight yourself in God doesn't mean that you won't face opposition. You may endure ridicule, backlash, haters, and unwanted and unmerited opinion. If God gives you a yes, just keep pushing and don't give up! I don't care what your desire or what your dream is, when you delight in God and your relationship with Him, then nothing can stop you! In fact, blessings will overtake you, the light will shine on you, and all will work out according to God's perfect will.

Dysfunction, Distraction, and Detours

Now let's talk about the real issue here, and that is dysfunction, distraction, and detours that prevent you from getting to God. If you don't delight yourself in God, how can He can grant you your desires?

How can dysfunction prevent us from getting to God? Dysfunction means that we depart from the norms of social behavior in a way regarded as bad. Oftentimes, our surrounding relationships and self-view can be dysfunctional. When we have lived so long in a dysfunctional point of view, it's hard to recognize, hard to face, and even harder to get out of. Are you staying in relationships you know aren't producing the good fruits of peace, love, joy, righteousness, and self-control? Do you see yourself as valuable? Do you see yourself the way your Father in heaven sees you? You can identify your desires all day long, but if you aren't willing to face your true dysfunctions then you will never get to your desire.

Do you see yourself as valuable?

If you relax in a dysfunction, you introduce distractions and invite detours into your life. You will find you are never carving out that one-on-one time with God and it becomes less and less of a priority to delight yourself in Him. If you don't delight yourself in God, your heart's desire will not be given.

Evaluate My Three Ds

So here's a challenge! I want you to evaluate your dysfunctions, distractions, and detours. Identify the relationships or other things that you have allowed to detour you from your expected purpose, power, and promise. Handle your three Ds so that you can get your three Ps.

Please do not blame other people for the actions you took to relax in your dysfunction. Face yourself. Take personal responsibility for where you are right now so that you are able to forgive yourself and go toward your purpose. You could spend the rest of your life being comfortable in this dysfunction or you could take this challenge so that you can get to your purpose. We talked about this earlier when we discussed who's got your back, but sometimes we can allow the people around us to weigh us down. We can stay within a dysfunction so long that we can't even support ourselves or a God move. So it's time for you to loose yourself from your dysfunction, stop entertaining distractions, and turn around from your detours.

Perhaps you're asking, how do I do that, Cora? What do I do? This is what I did: I created my circle, and I asked myself several questions about my circle, and here it is—a little bit of homework.

1. Are they giving or taking away from me?

2. Do I grow from the things they speak to me?

3. What do they bring to the table?

4. How do I function having them in my life?

5. Are my friends pulling me toward the world or toward God?

"Birds of a feather flock together." How true! When you are able to evaluate your surroundings, then you are able to evaluate you. Hopefully, as you consider these questions, you will be better able to understand the principles behind your morals and core compass. In other words, what makes me tick?

A lot of who we are can be seen by what things and which people we allow in our company. That is why Scripture says to delight yourself in the Lord first. God has this beautiful way of introducing people into our lives, people He wants us to get to know—and not just for our personal benefit. He wants us to bless others too. But if we engage in lengthy times of fellowship with people who aren't seeking God, we will find ourselves drained, distracted, and detoured away from God's central purpose for our lives. Eventually, we will lose the power of God in our lives because we don't really know Him.

When you are able to evaluate your surroundings, then you are able to evaluate you.

It's important that you are walking with God, because when you allow the world to consume you, then you are giving someone else who is willing to walk with Him the access to your gift. Therefore, when you look up and see your idea that you dreamed about being pursued by someone else, you cannot be upset. You would still be with your purpose if you didn't allow toxic environments and toxic people surround you and hold back your power. You must be spiritually strong first so that you can obtain, manage, and walk out your purpose.

Having a vision for purpose, power, and promise doesn't matter if you have no faith to walk it out. Such vision won't matter if you have no God to walk it out with. So make sure you know what you want because you can be so involved in your distractions, detours, and dysfunctions that you birth a stillborn of purpose. You can sit there and hope that you are able to give life, but toxic people in toxic surroundings cannot produce life. However, if you've chosen to step out of those toxic surroundings and walk toward God's purpose for your life, God will meet you.

Today can be a new day. You have picked up this book and you are taking this challenge! You have just been introduced to faithing it in your spirit and you can choose to delight yourself in the Lord from this point forward. You know now that when you delight yourself in the Lord, then and only then can God grant you the desires of your heart. Think about it. To obtain your gift and birth your purpose, you must be willing to be consumed by God more than your dysfunctions.

Delight of My Soul

We talked about dysfunctions, distractions, and detours, so now let's talk about delight. *Delight* means "to please, to give a feeling of happiness." Your life is a testament of what you have done for God. So now we have to ask ourselves, have we fully delighted in the Lord?

Is my life pleasing to God?

What am I delighting in?

Am I pleasing the flesh?

If we please the flesh before Christ, then we can't complain that we don't have our true heart's desires. We must be willing to face the wrong parts and fix them according to God's will.

I told the Lord what I wanted and I lined myself up with Him, using those questions I gave you a few pages back. I gave God my true repentance and got delivered. I want to share more on this a little later, but when I started lining up and voiced my desires, God started placing my steps in a direction where I could walk. He pointed me right toward my promise and my purpose!

Face yourself, forgive yourself, and align yourself.

You can't have everything your heart desires until God is pleased. And in order to please God, you must be willing to face yourself, forgive yourself, and align yourself. Get ready to please God first in all things and crucify your fleshly desires.

Can you truly say that God is pleased right now with your life? This is not just about identifying your desires, but it's about the destination to your desires.

Consume Me, Jesus

So now we get into how to be consumed by Jesus Christ. If we are unable to pray, we are unable to be consumed by Christ. We must be willing to give everything that we are to God. We must be willing to recognize that it is not religion but relationship that God is after. We want to communicate and trust Him with every part of our lives.

Pray that you will love yourself enough to want everything that He has to offer. God wants to consume you, become one with you, become compatible with you! And when you have given Him all of you and you have allowed Him to consume you, then He has become the desire of your heart.

When Jesus Christ consumes you, He consumes your thoughts. Your thoughts are His thoughts! If Jesus consumes you, then you begin to birth your promise. Your surroundings are no longer toxic and you are no longer toxic—what you birth is healthy! Now it's time for you to produce and walk out in purpose so that it can grow, mature, and take over.

When you cleanse your surroundings and your thoughts, you are no longer toxic; rather, you are consumed by God and one with Him. It's so beautiful! You have become one with God and He has changed your name. Think about it. If God can do exceedingly and abundantly above anything you could ever ask or think, then your thoughts are His thoughts. Then you will tap into the fact that your desires have become whatever God thinks of you. His thoughts are higher than your thoughts so your desires for yourself match God's will at this point. Get ready! When you make this step, your blessing will begin to overtake you and God begins to open doors for you. He pours out a blessing in every aspect that you do not have room enough to receive it all. That's why when people first get saved, great things begin to happen and doors begin to open. They are consumed with Christ! If we are consumed with Christ, then we are ready for the world and the attacks. Our belief system is not shaken, and we understand our call. Everything is new and happy because we have been reborn into Christ, into a nontoxic surrounding.

It's possible that later, as a maturing saint, you may have fallen into allowing your toxic surroundings to consume you. And now you are watching other people grow while you have fallen in love with a toxic environment.

"NO MORE!"

NO MORE! I speak to your toxic surrounding and I command it by the power of the Holy Ghost to be gone. I pray right now that you, my friend, be loosed from the captivity of toxic relationships, and that God shift those old friends into position and alignment with His perfect will. I speak to you to be consumed by God Almighty! Let your desires be toward God and of God so that you can break loose from generational curses. I pray right now for you, that you would be free from the yokes of bondage that you became accustomed to and have fallen in love with. I speak liberation in every element of your life! I speak liberation from every spirit that is surrounding you and consuming you that is not of God, both knowingly and unknowingly. You will walk in freedom. You will walk in liberation from this day forward. You will birth purpose, you will birth power, and you will press forward. Today you are reaching, and you will gain power according to God's great power and anointing resting inside of you. It is so and so it is.

Scan this code for Cora's Chapter 5
PRAYER FOR YOU!

Or Visit

Faith Affirmations

In order for you to grasp ahold of the true desires of your heart you must continue to examine your life. Are you doing things that please God, or are you more focused on pleasing your agenda? Oftentimes we don't get our desires because we put ourselves in a position to take control of our desire and vision. As a result, when God wants to take us somewhere, we choose resistance over submission. You can't please God if you don't believe in His ability. You can't please God when you're always trying to work things out for yourself. If you can't trust Him to give you what you want or need, how can you trust Him to do anything else? Some of us are so controlling that we are deliberately not listening to the instructions of God because they don't match our desire. Stop trying to micromanage God, and instead walk in the things of God.

Faith Points

No one knows you like your Father God. No one.

If you don't identify your promise, purpose, or dream, you won't know what you're fighting for—or what you're living for.

You must first delight yourself in God the Father for Him to grant your heart's desires.

When you delight yourself in God, blessings will overtake you, and His light will shine on you—all will work out according to His perfect will.

Dysfunction dims your light and prevents blessings for yourself and others who depend on your light to see them through the darkness.

If you relax and accept dysfunction in your life, you invite distractions and detours. God will become less and less important.

Don't blame other people for your dysfunction. Take responsibility for where you are right now by forgiving yourself and then moving forward toward your purpose.

Eliminate toxic people and environments and situations from your life. To receive your gift and birth your purpose, you have to be consumed by God more than your dysfunctions.

When you are consumed with Christ, you will be ready for whatever the world throws at you. Everything will be new and joyful because you know you are His child.

Faith Activations

What truly delights your soul? What truly are the desires of you heart? Write the first five things, people, places, whatever, that comes quickly to mind.

Delights, Desires, and Dysfunctions

Do you delight in the Lord? Is your time with God the highlight of your day/evening? What steps can you take today to make your heavenly Father your first priority?

Write all of the ways your light may be dimmed because you are in dysfunctional relationships, an unrighteous lifestyle, holding unforgiveness in your heart, etc. Then write how you can (and will) correct each light-dimming aspect of your life. Take action!

Faithing It

SIX

Paralyzed?
Loose Yourself!

Ask, and it will be given to you; seek, and you will find; knock, and it will be opened to you.

(MATTHEW 7:7)

After we know the dream God wants for our lives, what do we do after that?

At times we can become frozen in desire. It's like we're paralyzed and can't move forward. Oftentimes, we are locked in position because we are not able to speak. This is because we have made ourselves believe that we have no power, but the reality is that the power to be free from the dead things comes from within us.

Labels can deplete your power and paralyze you! You don't have to live by the labels that others place on you—you can live by the labels you speak on yourself.

Has someone told you that your dream is impossible? If you internalize this negativity and make that your belief, then you will stop pursuing your gift and progress will be stopped. Believe in yourself and speak life over yourself, otherwise, you will remain in the chains that others spoke on you and you will not be able to loose yourself.

Labels can deplete your power and paralyze you!

Loose Yourself from Lies

So here it is! Are you ready for your first challenge in this chapter? I challenge you to stop living by what others said about you and start speaking God's thoughts over yourself. Don't cry out to people; cry out to God.

Oftentimes, we are paralyzed and unable to get the things we desire because we haven't spoken for ourselves. We haven't believed the power of life and death is in our tongue.

I am the children's ministry director of The Potter's House Church of Dallas now, but when I started I was not the director. I walked into the office with the desire for something bigger than the position I was in, but just as this book says, I had to go through a process. I had to evaluate my support system. I had to start faithing it, and I had to speak it.

So when I walked in the office, I spoke, "I will be the director of this ministry as I have seen it in visions that have been given to me according to God's perfect will and timing." I wasn't the director at the time that I spoke it, but I am the director now. What would have happened if I didn't speak it? I would still be in a mediocre position receiving mediocre praises and getting mediocre pay when God called me to a bigger position than that. I had to speak what I wanted and accept it and go through the process so that I could produce my purpose. Your purpose, power, and promise cannot be obtained without you opening your mouth to speak what you see. Speak out and loose yourself!

As the director, I find that our children believe that they are whatever you speak. So I hear kids tell me:

Don't cry out to people, cry out to God.

- I'm bad.

- I have anger issues.

- I can't do this.

The children truly believe these lies! So often children don't produce life because their parents don't speak life to them. So how does that pertain to who we are now? Whatever was spoken about you as a child will stay with you into adulthood. If your parents spoke life over you, then you experience more freedom than most. If your parents neglected to speak life, then you likely feel paralyzed in certain areas because you believe that what they said all those years ago is actually true. We have to loose ourselves from those lies! For the Bible says this:

> *People of Zion, who live in Jerusalem, you will weep no more. How gracious He will be when you cry for help! As soon as He hears, He will answer you* (Isaiah 30:19 NIV).

God will answer you and be gracious if *He hears you*, but God can't hear your cry unless *He hears your cry*!

If you don't believe in your dream, no one else will. If you don't believe you have a world-changing purpose, then you won't change the world. Instead, you will be swallowed up by the world that you were supposed to change! Why? Because you were too busy living in what somebody else said. Speak what God's shown you. Speak what you see and desire. If you don't speak up for yourself, then you will be submerged in the bottom of the barrel watching others take the world by storm. You don't want to sit, as the lame man did, on the side of the pool letting people step over you to gain something that could have easily been yours had you wanted it bad enough.

Loose Yourself from Worry

I want to talk to you for a moment about work over worry. Sometimes we can allow ourselves to be consumed by the worry of the timing of our promise, purpose, and power. We become worried about the "when" factor—*when* is God going to make it happen? Worry will rob us of our joy, our peace, and our dream.

Faithing it will take you over the temptation of worry. Let me explain.

You should not worry about when God is going to lift you out of your process and into your purpose. Just stay focused on your work at hand. Faith without works is dead—that's what the Word says! That simply means you have to work for what you believe God for.

My mother-in-law used to always say, "If you are going pray, don't worry. If you are going to worry, don't pray." I love that saying because oftentimes we will pray for something from God but not put effort into the work at hand. So far we've learned that everything we desire to obtain from God is given after we do something. So if you have asked God for something but you are not seeing it manifest, perhaps instead of thinking it's the devil, a spirit, or that you need to fast, perhaps you need to go to work. If you want to see the fruits of your labor, you have to do the work to plant the seed.

If you are going to pray, don't worry. If you are going to worry, don't pray.

Loose Yourself from Laziness

Asking God (prayer) isn't going to get a field planted. You have to go out there and plant the seeds. If you don't, you will look at your surroundings and everyone's field will be producing but yours. In that case, you cannot be upset if the people around you sowed and did the work and they are seeing a harvest, but your field is empty. If you are not willing to sow, then you will not reap. We can stand in our seedless field and worry why it's not growing. In fact, we worry instead of spending our time planting seeds in the field. If you don't want to work, then don't speak, don't ask, and don't knock. Everything you believe God for is going to come with some work, and if you don't want to work really hard to produce a big harvest, then you should not ask for a big purpose. You will receive a big harvest when you are willing to work hard.

The people you see being blessed are receiving an overflow blessing because they sow an overflow of seeds. Do not be jealous of others who are reaping more! Rather, question what you have sown.

The problem is that we often ask for more from God than we are willing to work for or give. So yes, we can worry about the harvest that we aren't receiving, or we can do something else. So here it is—I am giving you another challenge: I challenge you to match the amount of harvest you want to the amount of work you do. Then do as my mother-in-law says: If you are going to pray, don't worry, and if you are going to worry, don't pray.

Jealousy is deadly to the soul and it will stop you from moving forward. It's important that you stop worrying about other people's things and blessings and start working on yourself. A big part of declaring your promise is the understanding that even in declaring what you want you have to put in work. Yes, you want to pray, declare, and decree, but you also have to put in work when you want to obtain anything.

You and I have to put in time at our jobs in order to receive a paycheck. In a relationship, we put in work in order to be fruitful and multiply. Nothing is just handed to you—it is received through hard work.

Loose Yourself from the Past

We all have gone through something that makes us angry and shakes our faith. If we didn't go through something to shake our faith, then God would have never said that faith the size of a mustard seed can move the mountain. Things will shake your faith, but those things have come to bring about the strength in you.

All you have to do is press forward. Stop thinking about why He allowed the rape, molestation, abuse, divorce, abortion, fornication, pregnancy, and so on to happen. Start using the things you overcame to help you declare what is rightfully yours. If you don't go through anything, then you have nothing to talk about. If you have nothing to talk about, then what are you going to ask God for? The power to obtain your promise is based on your ability to embrace the process of the pain.

I know what it's like to be hurt, to be broken, to be bitter, and to be angry. But I decided to speak life to myself and to loose myself from the things that were hindering me. You may have been beaten and you may feel broken, bitter, angry, and hurt, but God has not forgotten about you. You will overcome this! It's time to speak life, and speak out.

When you can speak out about what you've overcome, then the enemy can't use it over you anymore. Your broken self, your bitter self, your negative emotions take power from you. Faith leaves, negativity enters, and you are hindered.

God may have taken you through the storm, but He still gave you a rainbow, and the point is that He took you through it. Start looking at your low points as an opportunity for God to show you His power to bring you out. You will not remain paralyzed at this low point forever! Don't allow your hurt to hinder you from reaching for power; let it motivate you to search for a healer. My dear friend, I speak to you and I say to you without hesitation, "You *can* heal while hurting."

Gain back your power! Overcome the things that are hindering you. When you are able to climb over the rape, the abuse, the humiliation, the embarrassment, the lies, and the hurt, then you will step into your promise.

Loose Yourself from Failure Feelings

I have seen God show up for me even when I didn't deserve it. I believe that you can still be elevated to a high level in Christ even if you don't feel you deserve it. I also believe that the people who stay in that humble vein are the ones who receive the most promotion. It's the people who are willing to withstand the fire who are met by God and then promoted.

Just think about Shadrach, Meshach, and Abednego. They were willing to go into the fire for God because they had faith He would save them. They received great promotion after they withstood the fire, and they were just doing what they felt God would have them to do. God brought them to high promotion because they remained humble and low in spirit (see Daniel 1–3). Your humility will open the doors that pride will close. Moses didn't believe he deserved it, but he stayed humble, and God used him, and God can still use you.

It's the people who are willing to withstand the fire who are met by God and then promoted.

No matter what happened to you, no matter what you went through, God can use you. You don't have to be whole in order for God to use and answer what you declare.

We allow the people who hurt us to take our power, and then we get upset when we are standing powerless, paralyzed, and without direction. Take your power back! Start declaring death on some things and speaking life on other things. What would happen if you were one declaration away from receiving your deliverance? What if all you had to do was speak death on that soul tie, speak death on that sickness, speak death on that past hurt, speak death on that past relationship, and start speaking life on your situation and your circumstances?

God can't bless you if you don't open your mouth. You must first be willing to let go of the weight that is keeping you from leaping into your perfect purpose.

To the people who didn't believe in you? Prove them wrong. You deserve to be at the top of the mountain, just don't get too busy concentrating on the people who have hurt you or surpassed you. Focus on where you are now and work to make it to the top. I am behind you!

God can't bless you if you don't open your mouth.

I want you to know that you *can* reach the top.

I want you to know that you *do* have a gift.

I want you to know that you *are* talented and necessary in the Kingdom.

Prayer—Get Real with God

Prayer got me out of my situation. I found true freedom when I communicated with God. I was real, open, and vulnerable with the only person who knows everything about me today, and everything about where I am going. Prayer allowed me the opportunity to talk to God—to speak to Him, to tell Him about my hurt, my pain, and my anger. If you can't be real with God about the things that hurt you and anger you, then you aren't having a real relationship. We always get in this stigma of saying we aren't supposed to ask God why. I don't know why we tell people that, because when Jesus was suspended on the cross, pierced in His hands and feet, He looked up at His Father and said something. The Bible says in Mark 15:34, "And at three in the afternoon Jesus cried out in a loud voice, 'Eloi, Eloi, lema sabachthani?' (which means 'My God, My God, why have You forsaken Me?')" (NIV).

Jesus was in relationship with God His Father. He felt connected to Him, and we too should have the same connection. God is your Father. If you don't know what's going on, if you want to ask your Daddy a question, then you ask Him. Don't sit in your anger and bitterness because you are afraid to ask God why. It is through our inability to connect with God in communication that the enemy is able to destroy us. Take your true self to God without hesitation! Go to Him in spirit and in truth, then you will have a breakthrough that will change your life for the better.

You deserve to have a relationship with your Father God. And if you know God better, in turn you will know *you* better. In fact, this is how you tap into the thing that makes you royalty! The God who healed the blind, raised the dead, and turned water into wine is the same miracle-working God in you. Also, while you're talking to your Father, ask Him for a strategy to help you produce your purpose. It takes more than just speaking it as you know, but you also need strategy, you need a plan, and you then need to walk it out.

You can get your power back! Go before the Lord with your anger and allow Him to heal you so that you are able to push forward in what He has for you.

Write a Letter to God

Are you carrying your cross and going through turmoil? Do you feel beaten and crushed? Even paralyzed? This is the perfect time to look to Him.

This is what I want you to do. I want you to write a letter to God, asking Him, "Why?" But listen to me, I want you to ask Him why from your hurt and broken place. When I went before God with my why it was, "Why would You make me go through infertility? Why would You allow them to hurt me?" I had several whys, but I ended my letter telling God my truth. This was my truth to Him: "God, I'm hurting and I'm angry. I love You and I want to trust You, but I am scared, and I need to know why I had to go through all this beating and all this crushing? I know You love me more than this, Lord. Help me to have faith in Your ability to give me everything I'm believing You for, even though I am hurt from what You allowed me to endure."

I received my answer, and I'm praying you will receive yours as well. God has a strategy and a plan for you, but you can't have access to the room until you are willing to address your situation.

What Am I Talking About?

God created the world all from the words that came from His mouth. God showed us that in order for us to produce greatness we must connect to the power that we have in our mouths. We can obtain whatever we speak while in relationship with God! How do I know? The Bible tells me so!

> *Ask and it will be given to you; seek and you will find; knock and the door will be opened to you* (Matthew 7:7 NIV).

We sometimes allow ourselves to stay in bondage and not have what is rightfully ours. All of this bondage is unnecessary. Speak to the mountain. Ask. Seek. Knock. If you want to obtain the thing that God has for you, speak it out. You have no more excuses! You have reached the point of knowing that you have to speak what you want to produce.

Ask and receive. Your purpose is of no value if it isn't spoken for. A lot of us have promises and purposes waiting for us, but we are unable to obtain them because we simply haven't opened our mouths. We haven't knocked on the door. We haven't declared our promise to come forth. So, what are you talking about? Are you wasting your words on something besides your God-given dream?

Everything that unlocks our blessings comes from our mouths. Let's look at another Scripture:

> *Again, truly I tell you that if two of you on earth agree about anything they ask for, it will be done for them by My Father in heaven* (Matthew 18:19 NIV).

To *ask* means "to say something in order to obtain an answer or some information." There it is again—*say something*. If you don't speak you can't obtain. If you allow yourself to be tongue-tied by the webs of the enemy, you will stay paralyzed—and you can't be upset when you don't have what is rightfully yours. Speak out! Don't allow people to speak for you. Speak for yourself. Part of bringing purpose back to life is to speak life.

Declare your promise, declare your power, and loose yourself from the entanglements of the world. Start labeling yourself according to what God thinks about you. Open your mouth so you can obtain your victory, promise, and power. It's in your mouth! Victory is in your mouth. If you don't decree and declare your vision, then it can't come to pass. In this moment you must understand that you are a child of the King, therefore you have rights to Kingdom blessings. But you must go through the pain of the process and embrace it and start declaring things over yourself.

Are you wasting your words on something besides your God-given dream?

You are linked to greatness—Jesus Christ. Therefore, you deserve greatness, but not without great struggles. Be delivered from your pain. Speak over yourself, address yourself, gain real relationship with Christ, and leap into your destiny and walk it out.

I Tell You, Arise

I am speaking to the scared you who is afraid to speak life because of the fear of what your success looks like in God's eyes. I speak to you, and I tell you, "Arise my king, queen, prince, princess. Arise. You were born to be great. You are an heir to the King of kings. You have a lot to offer, and you have a lot to give. You can do it. Pursue your dream. Press through. Whatever you do, don't let failure stop you—let it push you. Whatever you do don't let downfalls keep you from going up the hill. You are royalty, you own the light, and you choose whether you will rest in the light or settle in the darkness." So I take this time to speak and declare life over your purpose and your promise.

You are royalty, you own the light.

I pray that God places a heart in you that seeks Him with all that you have. I pray that God ignites the power within you to bring forth the things that He has spoken over your life. I pray that God restores you from the pain that you allowed to consume you. I pray God removes the weight that hinders you from being able to leap into your purpose. I pray that the pain of the past not be an issue for you, but that you use the past pains to press you forward. I pray that God would break every generational curse that you have accepted and that you haven't accepted, which has tried to bind you, and we curse it at the root. I pray that the fire of God seals every area of your life that is aligned with His perfect will and purpose for you. I pray that you would press forward and begin to speak life to the areas that need to be brought back to life and speak death to the bad areas that need to be dead. You are to be great in your purpose! I pray you begin to open your mouth and work and that the minute you do your harvest be plentiful and overflowing. I thank God that you are walking into your purpose with power, and that you are faithing it from this day forward. Thank you, God, it is so and so it is. Amen!

Scan this code for Cora's Chapter 6
PRAYER FOR YOU!

Or Visit

WWW.CORAJAKESCOLEMAN.COM

Faith Affirmations

This is one of my favorite Scriptures because it is a true examination of self and relationship with God. I find that we sacrifice unreasonable things before the Lord and expect Him to receive them. We become bound by our decision not to be free. I challenge you to be free in real life. Don't continue to carry the weight of the wrong things and wonder why you are weary. It is very hard to cast cares unto the Lord when you don't care for Him. It is very hard to trust a God you can't be vulnerable with. Jesus died for the things you keep trying to hide from Him. Give God your pain, be free from your perspective, and walk in the fact that you are loosed.

Faith Points

Believe in yourself and speak life over yourself—don't remain in the chains others wrapped around you.

Don't cry out to people—cry out to God. Believe what HE says about you, not how others perceive you.

You can become paralyzed where you are because you haven't believed in or accepted the power God has gifted you with. Speak your desires, then believe and accept. The power of life and death is in your tongue.

You must speak your promise, power, and purpose to obtain them. Speak out and loose yourself! If you are willing to withstand the fire, you will be met by God and promoted.

If you don't speak up and believe in your world-changing purpose, you will be swallowed up by the world that you were supposed to change!

Worry robs you of your joy, peace, and your dream. Faithing it squashes worry. Use the things you overcame to help you declare what is rightfully yours.

Faith without works is dead—you have to work for what you believe God for (James 2:10).

To see the manifestation of your prayers, you have to put effort into the work at hand.

Everything you believe God for will come with work; if you don't want to work really hard to produce a big harvest, don't ask for a big purpose.

Faith Activations

If you didn't write a letter to God when prompted within the chapter, write one now. Respectfully ask Him why this and why that. As you write, listen with your heart for His answers.

Picture in your mind and in your spirit walking up to a beautiful wooden door. You know the Person is at home so you ask Him for His presence. Then you peek into the windows, seeking His face. After that, you knock on the door—and He opens wide the door and invites you into His presence. Repeat as many times as necessary until you realize that He is waiting for you.

Tonight when darkness surrounds you, think about how the enemy would like to keep you and all people in darkness, feeling hopeless and lonely. Then get up and turn on a light, knowing and acknowledging that Jesus is the Light of the world and you represent Him. Shine!

SEVEN

Believe God

Surely God is my salvation; I will trust and not be afraid. The Lord, the Lord Himself, is my strength and my defense; He has become my salvation.

(ISAIAH 12:2 NIV)

*B*elief is defined as "trust, faith, or confidence in someone or something." *Trust* is defined as "a firm belief in the reliability of something." Why is this important? Because we must be able to put our trust in God. What happens with us is that we can rely on people to handle things, and we end up putting our trust in people instead of God. God wants us to trust in Him over our own friends, coworkers, and even our own thoughts.

Without trust in God you are bound to the trust that you place in man, and humanity will fail you every time. How do we know trusting in the Lord is so important? Let's go back to the Word. The Bible says, "Trust in the Lord with all your heart and lean not on your own understanding" (Proverbs 3:5 NIV). We must be able to trust in God over our own thoughts, theories, perceptions, concerns, and understanding. If I decide to believe God is bigger than me and better than me, and I allow Him to consume me, then my thoughts are His—and God has great thoughts about me! God sees me better than I could ever see myself.

God sees my ugly self and He still uses me.

God see the things I am embarrassed about and He still uses me.

God sees the times I didn't trust He was going to do it for me, and He still uses me.

And guess what? If God can still use me, then He can still use you. God is more reliable than any man or woman we know. On the other hand, there are relationships that God ordains and brings together. We carry a measure of trust with people that we know God brought into our lives. That's a good thing, and hopefully those God-ordained relationships will help us to stop putting faith and trust in relationships of the world. Put your trust in the relationships God has ordained and brought together. You are in charge of your fate and your faith. Push for it! Believe God for the things you want to obtain. You are powerful when you rely on God.

God has great thoughts about me!

Trust God First

You must be able to trust God first—that is the first step in our definition of belief in God. If you don't believe God is able to do more than you can, or more than humanity can, then you will not produce at a higher level. To trust people more than God is to allow yourself to have trust and belief in a flawed person and a flawed system. When you put your trust in a flawed thing, then you cannot expect that to produce a beautiful outcome.

The only person who can turn ashes into beauty is God. God is the Creator of all things, and He is the only One you can trust to turn your flaws into something that can be used flawlessly.

You may have broken pieces in your life, but let me encourage you to stop giving them to a person to fix. Start giving them to God so that He can turn your broken into beautiful. It's easy to give up, but I don't want you to give up. I want you to trust God to turn your ashes into beautiful. We must recognize that God is our artist and we just need to give Him our paintbrush. We must trust in the Lord.

The only person that can turn ashes into beauty is God.

Have Faith

The next step in our definition of *belief* is to have faith. We talked a lot about faith in chapter 2, but I want to talk to you about it on the perspective of the literal definition, not the biblical definition of faith. There is more to faith than just our biblical perspective.

When we look up the meaning of *faith*, it is defined as "trust or confidence in someone or something." What does that really mean—to have confidence in something? To have confidence in someone is the state of feeling certain about the truth of something. So if we have trust, we must now have faith, and in having faith we have linked up with confidence as well.

It's hard to understand that God can do more for you than you can do for yourself. To ensure the fulfillment of your purpose and promise, you must be willing to believe God even when it's hard. And in order to believe God, you must trust, accept, and have faith and confidence in His ability to get the victory over your situation. Without belief in God, we can't produce.

Faith in Me or Faith in God?

Now that we went over the definition of belief, I want to talk about your heart. We can't really believe God if we don't have a heart for Him, especially if we don't have a heart for His ability. Sometimes the way to show God we believe Him is to trust Him with the thing we have held in our heart and hands all along. The purpose and plan God has for us is bigger and better than what we could have thought. Ever since I was a little girl, I dreamed of my own little boy named Nehemiah, and I held on to him almost religiously. I began to write to him and dream about him. I brought life to my dream, and when I was diagnosed with infertility I just held on to my dream even tighter. I made myself the dream catcher by any means necessary.

Until one day God said, "Give him to Me." I had gone through two in vitro fertilization (IVF) cycles at this point. I was scared that he wasn't going to come. I had done all the fertility treatments, vitamins, acupuncture, teas, and herbs. I had a lot of belief in my ability, and I trusted my ability. I had confidence in the articles I read, and I was doing everything that the world told me to do, but I was too afraid to give God my dream. I felt like if I gave up the fight and I let Nehemiah go, then I had let the devil win. I didn't understand at the time that it was my belief in myself and confidence in me that caused me to continue to lose the fight.

I didn't understand that I believed more in the information I received from the world than I did in what God showed me. God doesn't give you a vision or a dream of your purpose for you to snatch it from Him and make it happen for yourself! God gave you the vision so that you could see what He was capable of—not what you were supposed to grab, but what He was going to grab for you. What if I were to tell you that the reason you haven't gotten your promise is because you have turned your dream into an idol over God, and God has become jealous? That is highly possible! You know, until you give God back His dream for you and take your hands off of it, you won't be able to get what was supposed to be yours a long time ago. Your belief in self is going to stop you from obtaining what God wants to give you.

Give the Vision Back to God

Here is your first challenge in this chapter. It may sound similar to ones we have done before, but this comes from the very soul and heart of you. This one may be painful and breaking, but it's going to bring you a release that is strong and necessary in order for you to walk in your calling. Here it is: surrender.

Believing God is not just something that you hear, it's something that you do. It's a release of self. This kind of belief comes with your ability to say and feel, "I surrender all." You have to be able to believe God is better, God is stronger, and He is your defense. Remember, "The Lord, the Lord Himself, is my strength and my defense; He has become my salvation" (Isaiah 12:2 NIV).

Let me explain how this worked for me. I had to give Nehemiah to God and stand on my belief in God over myself. I understand that if God said I would birth a son, then I would birth a son and it would be according to His perfect will and purpose for me. Even if He wasn't to give me Nehemiah, as I have dreamed, I recognize that whatever God has for me is better than anything I could orchestrate myself. Again, all of this brings me to the Scripture at the beginning of this chapter:

"I surrender all."

Surely God is my salvation; I will trust and not be afraid. The Lord, the Lord Himself, is my strength and my defense; He has become my salvation (Isaiah 12:2 NIV).

I Will Not Be Afraid

My favorite part of our Scripture is exactly what I was telling all of us before. Isaiah says, "I will trust and not be afraid." Let's stop there.

It's important that when you make a decision to believe (trust) God, you do it without fear. Oftentimes, we are not receiving the full promise and purpose that God has for us because we are too afraid to let go. We fear what will happen if we turn everything over to God. We fear what will happen if we don't keep our hands on our own vision. But this is God's vision! And God's vision doesn't operate by our own will and desires! What will happen if you stop believing in yourself and start trusting in God? If God gave you the vision, then He can create what He gave. Sometimes your promise is delayed because you won't deliver your vision back to God.

Now catch this—your true salvation comes in your trusting God without fear. True salvation means your deliverance from sin and its consequences, but also the preservation or deliverance from harm, ruin, or loss. This great salvation is ours—without fear.

God became Isaiah's salvation after he decided to trust in the Lord without fear. God needs you to trust Him without fear and without hesitation. Let go of what you have and give it to God. Your purpose and power doesn't belong to you, it is given through your trust and belief in God. That's what we have been talking about this whole time. You need to trust God again and develop a relationship and submission to God so that you can obtain that vision, dream, and plan He has for you. This is not the final step, but if you choose to take this step God will open the doors, and He will save you. You will learn the power of God's ability when you recognize how powerless you are without His ability.

Submission to the Holy Spirit can be hard, but I say to you: Don't be your own hindrance. Surrender! Don't spend any more time holding on to your life and operating in your own will. Hand it over to God. Surrender yourself to God's passion for you. I know you've been hurt and I know that you are angry. I know that you are afraid of letting go. Yes, it's hard to say, "God, even if You don't give it to me, I'll be satisfied." And I know the world's opinions and statements are trying to micromanage your faith.

I know it's hard to let go and trust God because you are trying to figure out where He is and why He hasn't opened the door and brought you what He promised you. The answer is simple. You can't believe in God's ability while making a backup plan in case He doesn't perform to your liking. You can't make a backup plan to God's timing because His timing is perfect. You are either going to operate in God's will or you will stand in your own will, but let me warn you: If you are not prospering in purpose it is because you are powerless, and you are powerless because you haven't allowed yourself to have an encounter and a trust in something that's bigger than you. If you aren't growing in God, it's because you have decided to grow in yourself.

You are either going to operate in God's will or you will stand in your own will.

I Am Responsible for Me

For your second challenge, I challenge you to stop resenting God for the pain you went through and release your hands off your situation.

Jesus endured the pain, suffering, and crushing, and He didn't complain. You have to understand that God is for you.

Jesus gave His life because He was *for* you.

Jesus was beaten because He was *for* you.

Jesus was nailed because He was *for* you.

And He didn't command them to stop tormenting Him because He was *for* you. If you don't stop blaming Him for your crushing and beating and start believing that He is for you, then you won't reach your full potential. Even when Adam and Eve sinned, He covered them up because He was *for* them.

We are spending more time complaining about the beating and not understanding that God never complained. We are more for ourselves than for God.

When we see that we aren't producing, we get mad. Really, all we need to do is believe that God is better at operating our story than we are. Therefore the enemy controls us because he discovers that we don't trust enough in God to believe that He is able to pull us through. We were never meant to fight the enemy, we were meant to resist him. We are to use our faith to defeat the enemies we have created within ourselves because we don't believe that God is greater than our weapons and more powerful than our floods.

You know what I mean—that thing you can fall into where everything that happens is the devil or a spirit. Yeah, you know what I'm talking about. It's that thing where you don't take responsibility for where you are, and how you ended up at a dead end in life. You simply make it the devil's fault so that you don't have to be responsible.

We must believe that God is better at living our lives and controlling our lives than we are. Otherwise, we will take the control and operate our vision, and we do everything on our own instead of believing God. This battle is not yours; it is the Lord's. It's time for you to take responsibility for where you are and turn it over to God and let Him navigate you through your obstacles of life.

It's simple, really. We can't do things the wrong way and expect God to bless it the right way. We can't trust ourselves more than we trust God. Here's a question: Where is your belief?

Have you been drowning and don't know why? Have you been challenging God and giving Him ultimatums and then getting upset when He doesn't pick the choice you wanted Him to? Believing God doesn't come with you giving Him ultimatums.

Here's an ultimatum for all of us: Believe God or don't believe God, but don't live your life one way and then expect God to make moves for you. You are responsible for how you are blessed, just as the Scripture says when you trust (believe), God becomes your salvation. In order to be saved from the hurts and damages of the world, you must trust God.

We can't do things the wrong way and expect God to bless it the right way.

Trust and Believe God in the Darkness

I know what you are saying—it's easier said than done. Let me share a story with you. I have a friend named Jada. She and her husband, Darryl, had been married for some time when naturally they wanted to start a family. They are both completely dedicated to God, financially stable, spiritually stable, and believing God with everything they had. They were ready and had everything planned and set up, but weeks turned into months and months turned into a year, and several negative pregnancy tests later they were faced with the devastating news from the doctor that they would not be able to conceive without a lot of help. So they began the journey of hoping and still believing God but also having to go to specialists and doing fertility treatments. They fasted and prayed. All the while they watched the people around them getting pregnant while they prayed and hoped for their child to come to pass.

Thoughts plagued their minds. *What did we do wrong? Are we being punished? Why is this happening to us?* They experienced the devastation of wanting to be happy for that friend who got pregnant but still desiring the same thing to happen to them. Though the weight of the pain got heavy and there were nights they cried, they never stopped believing God. They never doubted God's ability. They never left God. They trusted God. They were pushing for conception but continuously getting nos from God. Yet a year and four months later, when Jada was about to undergo another fertility treatment route, she'd always answer her phone by saying, "I believe God," instead of saying hello.

She was sitting across from her husband at her favorite restaurant enjoying some seafood when suddenly, after eating her favorite meal, she got nauseous. Her husband looked at her and he knew immediately their belief in God had finally paid off. He knew immediately that they made the right decision in trusting God. He knew immediately that although they went through the pain, God still covered them. It was in that moment he knew that he and Jada would be expecting their first blessing.

That day was the first time Jada took a pregnancy test and did not cry tears of pain. This time as the lines began to pop up on the test, she overflowed in tears. Her heart was full, excited, and indescribable emotions were inside her. Her husband, Darryl, makes this chapter and this story complete. When hearing the news he immediately fell to his knees and began to thank God. They went through the pain, they suffered the crushing, but they never stopped believing God. Even when they did not receive their promise, they believed God. And after they received their promise, they thanked God.

Previously, the doctors said they would never have children without medical help. Today they have three beautiful children all given to them through natural conception. God doesn't need outside sources to give you a blessing. Everything you need to accomplish your promise is in you. Your faith and trust in God, even when you aren't holding your promise, is the thing that brings your promise forth. Jada and Darryl believed God when they were breaking and hurting. They believed and trusted God, and because they withstood their storm they were blessed with the rainbow.

Faith in the darkness is very much like Daniel in the lion's den. Daniel was dropped into the den of lions by his enemies, yet he had no fear—only faith and belief in God's capability. Daniel believed in God more than he believed in his ability to fight the lions, and he was saved (see Daniel 6). So I say this to you: You may be standing in the lion's den and you may have been wrongfully thrown in, but if you will stand on faith, you will be saved.

The promise is coming! You are just in the waiting room. God is preparing your room and He is making the pathway straight. Don't complain in your waiting room; prepare yourself for what you are about to walk into.

Wait without Whining

Don't complain in your waiting room; prepare in your waiting room. There's no point in asking God to shift some things in your life and to make the crooked paths straight and then get upset when He says wait. Sometimes it's not God saying no to you, it's not even God saying it's not going to happen. Sometimes God is just sitting you in the waiting room while He is preparing a place for you.

Are you willing to wait without whining? I promise you, if you wait without whining your reward will be worth the wait. You are a treasure to God, and your promise and purpose can't just be given to you quickly, it has to be prepared.

Daniel had to wait for someone to open the door in the lion's den.

The woman with the issue of blood had to wait for Jesus to pass by.

Jada and Darryl had to wait for their baby.

None of these people complained. They believed and even worshiped God in their waiting. What you do while you are waiting is entirely up to you, but what you do while you are waiting will decide how big your room is. If you rush your blessing and push God's blessing, then you will miss out on lessons you could have learned while you were waiting. You may even miss out on the

Are you willing to wait without whining?

blessings that you could gain if you would sit down and wait on God instead of doing things the way you think they should be done.

The beautiful thing about waiting is that after you are done waiting without complaining, your reward is great. God wants you to hold your peace and wait for Him to claim the victory over your circumstance.

You don't have to be tormented.

You don't have to be bothered.

You don't have to worry.

You don't have to look around.

You don't even have to ask others how long they had to wait.

Your room may be bigger than the person next to you, so it takes more time for it to be prepared. So of course we aren't talking about a literal waiting room, we are talking about a spiritual waiting room. The way my father says it is, "A delay is not a denial." We can spend too much time on the denial and not enough on the delay. Just because you have been delayed in receiving your promise doesn't mean you have been denied. You are just being delayed.

Worship in the Waiting

Worship in your delay so that God can deliver your promise and purpose in a big room that has been specifically prepared for you. What is inside of you is extraordinary, and when you start understanding that then you will be able to recognize the beauty of the waiting. Quite honestly, the longer you have to wait, the bigger your room, the bigger your purpose, and the greater your promise. People who don't go through a waiting period have a smaller purpose. You have been called to something bigger than yourself, and with that comes a huge responsibility and you must take that seriously.

Your wisdom is in the waiting. Your knowledge, peace, and joy are in the waiting. Your strength to endure whatever you are about to be given is in the waiting.

Embrace your waiting room so that you can gain all the things you need in order to overcome the challenges of life. I've sat in the waiting room. God has opened the door in some areas, but in other areas I am still waiting. In some areas I am still gaining the tools I need to become great, but I have learned to be quiet, to trust the Lord, and be still in the waiting room.

God is a better friend and confidant than anyone. While you are waiting, pray and stay strong and seek God in all matters. You are in good company. God has His hands on you and He is preparing your room—all you have to do is wait. God will open the door and He is going to call your name. He hasn't forgotten about you; He was just preparing you and preparing your path.

Embrace your waiting room.

Walk forward, my dear. Believe in God. Be strong in the Lord and in the power of His might. Put on your full armor so that you can stand against the devil's schemes—you have the ability to stand against the tactics and plans of the enemy. The road has been tough, but do not be weary.

You've been broken, but believe God.

You've been waiting, but believe God.

You have felt alone, but believe God.

Your hope will birth your promise if you let God be your doctor. Trust in the Lord and have faith. Walk in your purpose. I know what it's like to feel lost and confused, but the answer is in your belief. May God strengthen your belief! Let me pray for you right now.

I pray that your faith be strong and that you believe God more. I pray that you leave the old you and trust the new you, and that your desire for God grows and flourishes in a way like it never has before. I pray that you are lifted from the bottom, and that you push for the top. You have all power in your hands when you are holding God's hand. I pray that you would take God's hand and that God would lead you to virtue and that you would rise to leadership.

I pray that you find strength in your sadness, and that you would build your happiness in the midst of your brokenness. I pray that the Lord would be your guide and your light in a dark place. I pray that God consumes you from the crown of your head to the soles of your feet, that God will strengthen your bravery, your wisdom, and your understanding.

I pray that the gifting in you that you have yet to discover would pour out, and I pray that God gives you a heart to forgive those who have wronged you knowingly and unknowingly. More importantly, God, I pray that You would heal the heart of my friend right now and that You would help them to forgive themselves and to understand Your heart for them. You are the author of our fate and in that we do trust. I thank You, God, for all You are going to do for this person and all that You have already done. Amen and amen.

Scan this code for Cora's Chapter 7
PRAYER FOR YOU!

Or Visit

WWW.CORAJAKESCOLEMAN.COM

Faith Affirmation

Believing God is the key to defeating the enemy. Everything you need from God is tied up in your ability to believe in Him. You could be who God called you to be, but you continue to let your past keep you from feeling worthy of your promise. God didn't choose you because of how great you are. He chose you because of your pain, your story, and your faith—your belief in His ability. If you stop believing now, you will become swallowed up in the enemy's lies, always trapped in fear and resentment, when God is trying to raise you in great prosperity. Believe God, not for you, but for who you desire and believe you can be.

Faith Points

It is imperative to trust God over your own thoughts, theories, perceptions, concerns, and understanding.

God will never let you down, He is the Great I AM who loves you unconditionally. People will always let you down, they are human.

You must be able to trust God first. He can turn your flaws into something He can use flawlessly.

God can do more for you than you can do for yourself.

You may not have received your promise because you have turned your dream into an idol over God—and God may be jealous.

Surrendering all of yourself to God brings release, blessings, and fulfilled promises.

The enemy can control you if you don't trust God and believe that God can pull you through each and every circumstance.

Your true salvation—deliverance from sin, harm, ruin, loss—comes in trusting God without fear.

You can't do things the wrong way and expect God to bless them the right way.

Wait without whining. Jesus didn't whine about the pain and suffering He chose to endure. You have been called to something much bigger than yourself—with that gift comes serious responsibility.

Faith Activations

Do you need to hand your dream over to God and trust only Him to bring it to fruition? Do that right now.

Write all the things—attitudes, relationships, thoughts, income, lifestyle—that you control but should be surrendering to God, realizing that He knows best. Pray that you can and will turn over every part of your life to Him.

What is your greatest fear? Why is that your greatest fear? Is that fear greater than God? Write your feelings about the fears you have. After each one, write a prayer to God, in the name of Jesus, that He will totally destroy each fear and replace it with His peace of mind and spirit.

Faithing It

EIGHT

There is Power in the No!

But He said to me, "My grace is sufficient for you, for My power is made perfect in weakness." Therefore I will boast all the more gladly about my weaknesses, so that Christ's power may rest on me.

(2 CORINTHIANS 12:9 NIV)

One reason why I wrote this book is because it gives me the opportunity to boast about my hard times and my weaknesses. Today, I want to share with you my hard places and brag on God's ability to take over and be strong in the areas where I am weak.

What's funny about being a Christian is that God can say no to you when you're doing everything right. For example, I was praying and in ministry and I asked God for something that I wasn't quite ready for. I thought I was ready, but God knew that I wasn't. And when He told me no, instead of facing my weaknesses I made excuses for my downfalls.

From my point of view, I was doing everything right. I made my checklist. I am a child of God, I delight myself in God, and I am daily delivering myself from myself. I wake up in the morning saying, "God, I am an open vessel for You to use for Your perfect will and glory." So even after doing all of that and living an "upright life," God still tells me no!

God can say no to you when you're doing everything right.

When I would hear no from God, it would make my flesh weak. My weaknesses came to the forefront and I swept them under the rug. I wouldn't talk about the fact that I had flaws and weaknesses. It was hard until I figured out why. I wouldn't talk about the hurts I was experiencing. I would live the life that everyone wanted me to live.

Instead of telling people the truth, I boasted about the things that made me strong and great. I wouldn't dare let anyone know that I was broken and hurting. I was leading but I was bleeding because I had never seen anyone great show me their weak areas.

Today I know I don't have to be perfect to help you achieve purpose.

I don't have to act like I am strong; I can share my weaknesses.

I don't have to be whole to help you reach your goal.

In fact, I gladly say that I have weaknesses because God has given me strength in my weaknesses. God has given me direction in my depression and power with my passion and my purpose. And though I may not have my promise in my hand, and though I may not have yet conceived, I know God has planted a seed in me. As long as I am real with God, then I can show some realness to you. Then I can bring life to this promised seed He has planted.

The Power of No

The concept of this chapter is very dear to my heart because today I understand why God said no at times in my life. God's no makes so much more sense to me now than it did when He said no the first time.

There are many ways God says no. God can say no, not now, absolutely not, no no no no, etc. It actually reminds me of a "no" button that my mother gave me for Christmas one year. It had many different ways to say no. I loved that button until I realized that I was hearing no from God in several different ways.

I am a weak producer without God. I don't have to worry about that now because God is my producer, my strength, my Father, my mentor, my disciplinarian, my leader, my everything. When I worship Him, I show God the weakest sides of myself in that moment. Still, He knows that He is my everything and I am faithing it in

I was leading but I was bleeding because I had never seen anyone great show me their weak areas.

all my weakest places. I show God my love, my faith, and my worship while I'm in the doctor's office, in the waiting room, in the bathroom, and on the floor in the closet. The only way I can be a faither is through God. I do not walk in my own strength; I walk in God's strength and power because I understand I am nothing without the power and blood of Jesus.

Here it is. Even if God doesn't do anything else for you, He has already done enough! When you acknowledge Him in all your weakest places, you show Him that He holds the power. This is about you showing God that you believe He can fix your broken pieces.

So here's your challenge for this chapter: I challenge you to begin showing God how much you trust, believe, and have faith in Him. I want you to do this by expressing your testimony even if He hasn't given you complete victory yet. I want to challenge you to share your story with the next person you see. Show somebody that God is the strength in your weakness.

Your Alabaster Moment

Another word for weakness is *vulnerability*. I want you to begin to show God that you want to be vulnerable toward Him, whether or not you have it all together or not. One day while Jesus was eating with friends, a woman came into the dining room with expensive perfume and lavishly poured out all of that treasure on Jesus' head. Let's look at the story in the Bible:

While He was eating, a woman came in with a beautiful alabaster jar of expensive perfume and poured it over His head. The disciples were indignant when they saw this. "What a waste!" they said. "It could have been sold for a high price and the money given to the poor."

But Jesus, aware of this, replied, "Why criticize this woman for doing such a good thing to Me? You will always have the poor among you, but you will not always have Me. She has poured this perfume on Me to prepare My body for burial. I tell you the truth, wherever the Good News is preached throughout the world, this woman's deed will be remembered and discussed" (Matthew 26:7–13 NLT).

And so it is. We are talking about her deed right now in this book. I think that this woman knew that she was opening herself up for rebuke when she walked into the dining room. I think that she knew she was making herself vulnerable to be attacked, but it didn't stop her. She brought to Jesus her most expensive gift and poured it out on Him. She wasn't looking for a blessing, she was looking to bless.

This is your alabaster moment. You need to pour out to God your hurts and bitter circumstances. Make yourself vulnerable to God and show Him that you believe that His power is the only power that can claim the victory over your finances, your relationship, your pain, your story, your household, your job, and your purpose. Show God that even if you have nothing, you believe He deserves what little you do have. If you have financial weakness, then stand before God in that weakness and boast gladly to the Lord, saying, "God, I may not have anything, but what I do have belongs to you. Even if I haven't figured out a way, I know You will make a way."

Give God Access

Sometimes God gives us a no because we gave Him a no to our money, a no to the foundation of our relationship, a no to our home, a no to our children, a no to our tithes, a no to our purpose, a no to our promise, or a no to our call.

Ask yourself this: Are you asking God for a yes to your prayer when you didn't give Him a yes to His call? Have you held your hands *out* for "more please" than you have held your hands *up* to say thank You? Are you personally giving your treasure, time, and talent into the house of God? Here's the big one: Do you give God money? If you are not giving your money, your time, and your talents into the body of Christ, then you are limiting your access to your power because you are limiting God's access to your life.

Are you asking God for a yes to your prayer when you didn't give Him a yes to His call?

If I walk into your house, will your life show me a life that God could say yes to or is your life for God just something people can see in church? If your life doesn't show a yes to God, then don't expect Him to show a yes to you. God's power gets all access to every door. You can't knock on the door and ask God to answer it when He's not in your foundation.

Listen to me. How dare we feel entitled to God giving us a yes when we haven't given Him a yes. Show your yes! Do more than act it—say it, show it, and prove it. If you say yes to God's call, then He will say yes to you. How do I know? The Bible says:

> *"Bring all the tithes into the storehouse, that there may be food in My house, and try Me now in this," says the Lord of hosts, "if I will not open for you the windows of heaven and pour out for you such blessing that there will not be room enough to receive it"* (Malachi 3:10).

When you give to God, He gives to you. When you reach for God, He will reach for you. Now catch this—God doesn't have to say yes to you. It's a privilege to get a yes from God. You are empowered in that. How awesome that you would say yes to God, and He would consider you enough to say yes back! Don't make God regret His yes, and don't get mad if He says no. You don't know why He said no, so wait and continue to share and make God the foundation and the truth in your weakness so that He can strengthen you and give you His power.

As children of the King, it is important to understand that we will have times where we will not be given what we want right away, and we may reach for something that looks exciting and fun for us, but God will say no because He knows more than we do. You can live life reaching for the things that aren't meant to be yours or you can heed to God's instruction. Sometimes our goals are not stronger and higher than God. Naturally we want to know why God doesn't allow us to have the things that we want when we want them. I am so glad to have the opportunity to give you some peace about God's no!

I'm Okay with No

We must realize that sometimes God will say no. And we need to be okay with that. We must be careful to not treat God as a genie whom we expect to perform every time we fall to our knees in prayer. Did your earthly father perform like that for you and give you every little thing you asked for? I hope not!

We don't ask God for things and expect Him to just say yes every time. Sometimes, you will ask God a question and He is evaluating whether what you asked for is better than what He has for you.

Imagine this: Your child asks you if she can go to the park on Friday, but she doesn't realize that you have a surprise trip to Disney World planned for her that weekend. She may be disappointed in your no but that's because she doesn't see what you have planned yet. If you complain because of the no then you won't be open to receive what God has, and what God has is always better than what you planned. When we delight ourselves in God, trust Him, go through the process, and embrace the pain, we will experience healing and naturally soar into the passion of our purpose. We can still ask God for things. The only thing is that now when you ask you are asking as a whole and healed person, someone who delights in God and is determined to walk in God's will, not your own will.

It may still hurt when you ask for something and God says no. You try to figure out why. You try to understand where He is coming from, but it's hard when you are awaiting His next move.

The worst part of walking in God's will is that you don't know His next move. But that's okay because when you are walking in God's will, His next move is always better than what you thought of without Him. I want you to be okay with your no. God doesn't just say no because He doesn't want you to have what you want, but God says no for several reasons. Let's look at those reasons now.

Why Does God Say No?

The first reason God says no sometimes is actually the hardest to accept. Even though we may be walking in God's will, we may not be prepared for what He has for us. We are quick to ask for things to fill the void and pain in our hearts, but we may not be ready yet for what God is going to give us.

It's possible that we have asked for a husband or a wife, but we aren't prepared to be a husband or a wife in return. Perhaps we ask for the management position, but we still have a low-income mindset. We can ask for a house, but we don't have income to manage the house. It doesn't matter what you asked for, what matters is if you are ready for what you asked for. Are you walking in faith? Does your life match what you are asking for? If I look at your life will I see that you are ready for what you are asking for from the Lord?

Let me put it like this. I was praying for God to bring me a baby and to allow me to be fruitful and multiply, but I wasn't taking prenatal vitamins, I wasn't working out, I wasn't drinking water, and I wasn't preparing my body to receive what I was asking for. So when I jumped in my own will to pursue what I wanted, God said no. At the time I got upset and I was hurt and angry, but I didn't realize that I wasn't prepared to receive what I was asking for.

I was crying out for a husband, but I wasn't learning how to cook, I wasn't enjoying cleaning, and I wasn't healed from my past relationships. So this is what I am saying: Show God that you are ready to receive what you ask Him for. Show God that you aren't just an asker, but you are a doer. You're not defined by what you say and ask for, but you are defined by what you do to get what you ask for. Your promise is given after hard work.

The second reason why God could possibly say no to our prayers is easier for me to understand. He has something better for us. It could be that you prepared and prayed and God still said no. The answer to this is hard to believe, especially for those of us who can be a bit controlling! God has written something better for you. Trust Him to write your book! There is no need to go into this big explanation here. God is for us, and He wants us to win. He wants us to have the victory.

Sufficient Grace

Trust God that when you are weak, His power takes over—which brings up our Scripture for this chapter. Let's break it down.

But He said to me, "My grace is sufficient for you, for My power is made perfect in weakness." Therefore I will boast all the more gladly about my weaknesses, so that Christ's power may rest on me (2 Corinthians 12:9 NIV).

We must understand grace. We have talked about faith, trust, belief, and even love, but we haven't talked about grace. Biblically, we know that grace is sufficient and it's new every morning, but what does it mean to really have grace? Well, let me tell you: Grace is a virtue that comes from God. Now, that is a bit vague, so let's go a little deeper. The word *virtue* means "a behavior showing high moral standards." So don't complain about your problems when you are weak. Maintain your high moral standards and yield your trust in God's grace—*God's* ability to bring His power and His strength into your weakness.

God beckons us to have grace in our hard times because His strength is made perfect in weakness. After God tells him this, Paul writes down that he will now boast about his weaknesses! Now isn't that crazy? Why in the world would anyone want to boast about their weakness? It's because in our weakness God's strength is made perfect. So maintain your morals and standards as you cry out to God for His grace so that you can receive power in your weakness.

Why is that important? When we go through storms in life and when things get heavy and we don't know what to do, we often begin to complain and ask Him to free us from our bondage. We want the ability to fight back, and we want Him to loose us, but if we will begin to boast in our weakness, then and only then will God be able to consume us with power. You have to go through your weakest points in order for God to give you power. So instead of us complaining about our weaknesses and wanting to be taken out of the weak areas, we must embrace them and boast about them. In doing so, we are seeking for strength that is higher than our strength.

You will be great! You will come forth and obtain the power you need, but don't run from the no. And don't be angry when God says no, trust His no so that you can gain His power.

I can remember model Tyra Banks saying that she received several nos from agencies before she got a yes. She didn't let the no stop her. She let the weakness and pain from receiving the no push her, and because she embraced the no and accepted it, she gained power. She gained promotion, purpose, power, and position. The position of your power comes at the level of your ability to boast about your weakness.

The position of your power comes at the level of your ability to boast about your weakness.

That's the thing about the no. When you have gone through the process, said your prayers, gained the relationship with God, and delighted yourself in Him, then when God says no it puts you in a weak place. But remember, God has answered your weakness and given you strength.

What I enjoy about our Scripture, is that if you go to chapter ten of Second Corinthians, Paul tells us how to feel about our weaknesses. He tells us what position we should rest in when we are going through ridicule in the world and others are being blessed and we aren't. Let's look at this:

> *That is why, for Christ's sake, I delight in weaknesses, in insults, in hardships, in persecutions, in difficulties. For when I am weak, then I am strong* (2 Corinthians 12:10 NIV).

So you will go through difficulties, insults, hardships, heartaches, and bothers of the world, but God is giving you strength to overcome—depending on how you choose to go through those difficulties. Will you delight in them like Paul did? Will you be boastful or bitter?

Boastful or Bitter?

I speak to you as you sit in the difficulties, insults, hardships, and bothers of the world. I tell you that you will come out of this! You were born to be great, and God has not given up on you. If you can trust Him in your weakest place, He can grant you power. If you can look to God when it is all falling apart, then He can lift you up and put it all back together again. He said no to weaken you, and He weakened you so He could give you strength. It's hard and it's heavy, but when you lay your weaknesses out, God will strengthen you.

You may feel alone, but God is not a man that He should lie. If He said He's going to do it, then you just have to stand on the fact that He will. Sometimes we can hear a no and it can detour us and we start to doubt God, but we have come too far to give up now! You are walking in great purpose, and you have to stay the course. When we have decided to trust God above all, there will always be obstacles and mountains, and we have to be able to be strong enough to faith it through those obstacles. I know it's not easy, and I know you want to give up, and I know it's not fair, but God gave you the no so that you would let your power go, and replace it with His power.

I am reminded of a story I heard of a woman who birthed twins. One survived and the other was pronounced dead after several attempts to resuscitate the infant. The mother and father wanted to say good-bye to their son and decided to hold him. The mother instinctively laid her lifeless newborn baby across her breast and was saying good-bye when the baby began to move. The doctor was called in. He responded by saying that the baby is dead, and those are just normal reflexes. They continued to hold the child and they began to see his eyes open. She tried to feed her son a drop of breast milk from her finger, and her son took it with excitement, and even after that the doctor didn't believe her and her husband. The doctor told her there was nothing he could do, and they needed to accept that their son was dead. She kept holding him, and he kept getting life (power) with every moment. She embraced the weak and scary spots and did not become bitter, and her child began to get more life.

This mother was in her weakest moment with a little bit of faith, wisdom, and understanding,

He said no to weaken you, and He weakened you so He could give you strength.

and God turned her weakness into His power. Two hours later, after holding him, he began to get color in his face and he started breathing. The doctor came back and was astonished to find out that the baby was breathing, responding, and he had a heartbeat. You may be holding on to a dead thing, and hoping it will gain life, but if you would hold on and let God turn your weak area into your most powerful moment, you can bring life to a dead thing. Your promise is worth the no because there is power in the no.

You may be facing your hardest, weakest thing, but if you can just hold on and allow God to consume you with His power, you will overcome in this situation. You will rise above this thing and you will bring life to something that you thought was dead. You are empowered to succeed.

There is power in the no.

Though the storms in life are raging, know that there is peace in your ability to embrace God's strategy. I have heard several nos in life, and some have shaken me, but none of them have broken me. I have gone through pain in life, but I have found that God has remained my strength—as long as I was able to embrace my weaknesses. So stop running away from the difficulties of life. Stop asking God to take away your weak spots and embrace them instead. It's okay to be weak as long as you realize that God is strong.

Now His Power Rests on Me

Wait! Our Scripture ends with the promise that God's power will rest on us.

Therefore I will boast all the more gladly about my
weaknesses, so that Christ's power may rest on me
(2 Corinthians 12:9 NIV).

You can have access to power, but it just hasn't rested on you yet. What are you allowing to rest on you? You can have weaknesses, difficulties, and even insults, but don't become the weakness. Overcome the weaknesses by embracing your weakest points when everything is falling apart. Look to the hills from whence cometh your help and you will overcome that weakness and receive power.

So now, let me speak to you. It's time for you to begin to show God that you are a good investment. God has planted something in you, and it's time for you to produce it. Stop brushing your pain and difficulties under the rug and start showing your scars. You are brought to strength in your ability to show your scars.

I had a lot of scars and a lot of pain. I walked in blame, which just made me even weaker. There were boyfriends who said they loved me and physically abused me. Then I was raped by someone who told me he loved me. Now that's a weakness, and I was afraid of facing that scar. That scar is there, but I'm still standing.

I was afraid of trusting that scar with anyone, but here I am trusting it with you because I've found strength in my pain. I found strength in the God who stood with me while I endured the pain. He was orchestrating my victory over the violence. I tried it on my own, and I failed every time, but when I sought God I found Him, and when I knocked on the door He answered. God called me to the door, and I said yes.

You have been chosen for such a time as this, to be bigger than what you think. God has called you to the door, and what's behind this door is bigger than what you think you deserve. He will give you the power to obtain your purpose, and that purpose is something that this world needs. There are hills you have to climb, but you do not climb them alone. And you don't climb them without power—you have obtained your power in the strangest spot. You have something that needs to be produced, and I can't wait to see you produce it. God may have said no, and you may have felt weak, but guess what? There is power in the no!

Start showing your scars.

Your scars are not a symbol of embarrassment, they are a symbol of power. You overcame, you survived. Often I hear people upset about their bruises, scars, hurts, and pains and they don't want to show them. I think to myself, do you know how many people went through the same thing you went through, and they didn't make it? Do you know how many people lost their battle because they focused on hiding their weaknesses over gaining their power? Your scars are not embarrassing, they are necessary, purposeful, and powerful. Yes, our scars show our weaknesses, but they are beautiful to God. You will become mighty because of your scars. You will join a movement of world changers because of your scars.

Stop running from the pain and the bleedings, because that's what makes you beautiful and identifies you as a world changer. Guess what? There was a man carrying a cross to Calvary. They beat Him, they crushed Him, they pierced Him in the side, they nailed His hands and His feet, and they mocked His position as King. They laid Him in a tomb and on the third day He rose again with all power in His pierced, nailed, scarred hands.

The thing that makes Him the King of kings and the Lord of lords is His scars. Do not spend one more day covering up your scars. Your scars are the crown of His grace!

> *I pray right now that you would come out of the darkness into the light. I plead the blood of Jesus over every pain, over every scar, over every weakness, and I pray, God, that You bring strength right now to the forefront. I pray, God, right now that You deliver my friend and show them the beauty in their scars and the power in their weakness. I pray, God, that You would demolish the pain that they have carried and that You create in them a clean heart. Lord, wherever they are and whatever they are doing, meet them where they are and comfort them right now. Take away the hurt, anger, and loss, for You are God and God alone. You are great and You have all power.*
>
> *God, crown them with grace and fill them with Your fire right now in the name of*

The thing that makes Him the King of Kings and the Lord of Lords is His scars.

157

Jesus. Align them in the spirit realm that they walk in that alignment. Lord, I pray that You clean their surroundings and cleanse their thoughts of anything that is not matching with Your will for their life. I thank You, God, that You are bringing restoration in their family's life, and that You are bringing healing. In the name of Jesus, it is so. And so it is. Amen.

Scan this code for Cora's Chapter 8
PRAYER FOR YOU!

Or Visit

WWW.CORAJAKESCOLEMAN.COM

Faith Affirmations

Saying "no" is often necessary for elevation. Being able to set boundaries for how you are treated is necessary in order to manage the hurt you encounter along this journey called life. We often place unreachable expectations on people for whom we don't set boundaries, and when they overstep our boundaries in order to meet our expectations, we get hurt, bitter, angry, and feel like we have been disrespected. There is power in your ability to stand up for yourself. Don't let yourself be placed in a situation where people get comfortable taking advantage of you because you didn't want to say "no." Examine your environment: be cautious in surrounding yourself with people who are always looking to give you a "yes," and set boundaries for how people treat you because of your "no." When we become more interested in pleasing man than pleasing God, we end up in pretty bad situations that leave us powerless. There is power in your "no." Practice makes perfect.

Faith Points

God can say no even when you are doing everything right. Don't get angry if He says no—you don't know why He said no. Always remember that God knows more than you do.

God gives you strength in your weakness, direction in your depression, and power to pursue your purpose.

To be a faither is to remember that you are nothing without the sacrificial blood of Jesus that allows you to walk in God's strength and power.

Even if God doesn't do anything else for you, He has already done enough!

Make yourself vulnerable to God; show Him that you believe He can claim victory for you in all areas of your life—financial, relationships, health, family, career, etc.

If you are not giving money, time, and talents to the body of Christ, you are limiting access to your power because you are limiting God's access to your life.

When you delight in God, trust Him, go through the process, and embrace the pain, you will experience healing and naturally soar into the passion of your purpose.

Why does God say no? You may not be prepared to receive or He has something better for you.

Grace is a virtue that comes from God. Maintain your morals and ethics as you cry out to God—His grace allows you to receive power in your weakness.

Faith Activations

If you haven't already, write your testimony about how God has changed your life. Memorize your testimony, and then share your testimony with every person God brings into your life.

Pour out to God all your hurts and challenges and fears. Pray that everything you are burdened with belongs to Him. Place your hands on your shoulders and then actually raise your arms up over your head toward Heaven, giving whatever is weighing you down to God.

To show God that you are a good investment, write down all your attributes that affirm you are investment-worthy. Of course God knows you intimately, but this exercise will confirm in you your value.

NINE

Considered Worthy for the Struggle

For everyone born of God overcomes the world.
This is the victory that has overcome
the world, even our faith.

(1 JOHN 5:4 NIV)

You are going to change the world with what God put in you. The world needs your message and people need to hear what you overcame. You have not been forgotten. You have been hidden for a long time, and God is going to shine a light on whatever you decide to touch. Whatever you ask for from God will be given to you in this season and window. Stop worrying if you are good enough. Stop doubting yourself. Stop doubting your ability and believe in yourself. Come forth. It's time for you to be great.

The world will miss what you have to say and what you have to produce if you stay focused on the "why me?" and not on the rewards after the pain. The rainbow is promised to you after the storm. Noah didn't focus on the storm; he focused on looking for land. He was faithful to obey God and not worry, and after the

*Come forth.
It's time for
you to be
great.*

flood God gave him the promise in the rainbow (see Genesis 9). Have you been concentrating on the flood? I'm here to tell you that God is going to give you the rainbow as soon as you stop looking at the flood. You are free from the wars of the world. Go forward in God's grace and peace.

Your Story for the Next Generation

It's time to push this baby out, but your unbelief can abort heaven's destiny for your life. It's time for you to believe in God and it's time to believe in yourself. You have been implanted with a seed of purpose and power, and it will erupt in the cities and in the fields. The harvest that you produce will overflow for every generation that lived before you and every generation yet to come. You are the manifestation of the hope of God. God's hope for you is prosperous, and you will be mighty in your area and in your call.

You are God's book—a best seller! And you will produce powerful works for God. Don't faint! Don't quit! He is still performing miracles for His children. God has considered you worthy because there is a gem inside of you that God needs, and He wants to see it come forth.

I'm thrilled that God considered me and wrote my story. So far I've lived that story and overcame in that story. Yes, I am still waiting for my Nehemiah. I am standing on God's Word and on my purpose. My passion for Nehemiah will produce my purpose, and he will come forth. I don't know what God is considering you for, I just know that He's considering you. I know that your birthing is just around the corner. You may have to go through some fire and some crushing, but God has chosen you to go through the struggle so that you can speak about the success when you come out of it. Think about it. Job was considered worthy of this great struggle that produced purpose. Moses was considered, Esther was considered, David was considered, Daniel was considered, and Shadrach, Meshach, and Abednego were considered. All of these saints had to withstand the struggle, and all of them received power, success, and promotion—but not without the pain of the struggle and the birth of the promise.

Your portion is worth the pain and the struggle that it will take for you to get there. Your portion is worth the pain and hurt of the process. Your portion is worth the obstacles that tried to stand in your way.

You have all power. Your position is needed in the Kingdom. Take your seat and stay there, no matter what you have to go through. Understand that your life is a testament of what you were willing to overcome.

God did not consider any of the people I listed above to go through pain. God considered them for their portion. He considered them worthy to impact the next generation. God has a specific plan and strategy laid out for your life, and all you have to do is walk through the storm with your head held high, without hesitation, and let God know that "though He slay me, yet will I trust Him" (Job 13:15). You have been designed to have the victory—all you need to do is walk it out. Your rainbow, your double portion, your crown, and your promotion are on the way. You have been considered worthy for this struggle because God sees your success just ahead.

You were born to overcome.

You Are an Overcomer!

I never really understood my struggle until I saw ahead to the success that was coming and the reward behind it. When you are in the moment, it's hard to see what God is doing. It can be a lonely place where you are looking for answers in a room where there are no answers to find, and God's voice is ever so silent. But I have learned that when God is being quiet, He is working on my behalf. I used to get angry at God's voice, but I understood that God was just orchestrating my success and preparing my portion. I understand that my life is the Lord's, and with that understanding comes the acceptance that there are times when I need to be quiet and let Him speak.

You are a natural overcomer because you are a child of God.

> *For everyone born of God overcomes the world. This is the victory that has overcome the world, even our faith* (1 John 5:4 NIV).

You were born to overcome. Everyone born of God overcomes the world. So let me ask you this question: Are you born of God? Are you pretending or are you really faithing it? Do you really believe?

There are a lot of people who adhere to the idea and theory of God, go to church, pretend to know God, and pretend to be a Christian, but aren't truly dedicated and born of God. You must first be born of God to birth the new promise of God.

Worship Him in Spirit and in Truth

We each need to know our own heart. Be honest with ourselves. Jesus said that those who worship Him must worship Him in spirit and in truth (see John 4:23–24). What if I could tell that you have been born of God only by the way I look at your worship? Are you a pretender or are you practicing truth?

I can remember as a little girl seeing people worship around me in church services. Some would have tears in their eyes, others would be on their knees and crying out to God. I could actually feel the compassion in their hearts for God. When I was little, I wanted to know what that feeling was like. I wanted to have that kind of passion for God, and even though I was a little girl I went toward God because of what I saw in spirit and truth. We don't have examples like that very much in church anymore, but you have the ability to grasp it.

I reached toward God and allowed Him to consume me. I chose God, and in my choosing God He choose me, and I became born of God. When God became my Father, my guide, and my director, I naturally became an overcomer and the victory of the world was placed in my hand. You can be of the world and born of the world, but that position will never make you an overcomer of the world. If you want to overcome and find the power in the struggle, you have to say no to the world for yourself. This chapter isn't just about the fact that God considered you for the struggle, but it's about whether you are going to make the decision to consider God.

I want to encourage you to humble yourself before God and say, "God, You are my Father. I worship You in spirit and in truth. I delight myself in You. I am Yours and You are mine."

It's Our Choice

We are all placed in the world with the right to make a choice to choose God or to choose the world. When you place God at the forefront of your choices in life, then you are officially placed behind God where He protects you and the seed He has placed inside of you.

Why do we put up walls? We put up walls to protect ourselves from getting hurt. We go through life and we shut people out of the real pain and weight that we go through. We become so good at it that we shield ourselves from even God being able to penetrate that wall. So we give God a little, but we hold back the real weight, the real truth of our being. We can get very good at protecting ourselves. You have been hiding behind your wall for too long. Remember, there is nothing behind your wall that is too hard for God to handle.

God can only be before you if you choose Him to be in that place—at the forefront of your life. When you are considered by God, you are considered for the struggle, just like Job. The hedge of protection around you is compromised when God considers you. Suddenly you find that you are tested and tried because God needs to at this point find out if you are really for Him. God needs to know if you really believe that He is for you. God needs to know if you will worship Him over your worry. If you are born of Him, you will overcome in your struggle.

Loved in Spite of Our Imperfections

I know you have lived a life with rejection, and you wanted someone to believe in you, and you needed someone to support you and walk with you, and every time you let someone behind your wall they would hurt you and take a piece of you with them. I know that you have spent nights crying for someone to love and accept you even with your flaws and imperfections. I know you're waiting for someone to see you as the person that you really want to be, and you want them to be okay with it. I know you've felt misunderstood and perhaps even felt dead looking for life.

It's time to trust God with all of that rejection. Bring the heartbreak, the pain, the sorrow, the shame, the humiliation, the devastation, the depression, the suicidal thoughts, the doubts, and the worry, and lay it all down before God. Break yourself for God's glory. God was crushed and beaten and humiliated for you. He did it all just for you.

He died for the purpose and the beauty that is in you.

He died for the things you are too afraid and embarrassed to show.

He died for the lost.

He died for the hungry.

He died for the sick and the hurting.

He died for all of that because He saw *you* worth considering. He saw what God had planned for you. He saw the power in your ability to give Him your pain.

You have been looking for someone to accept and consider you. Well, God says, "I have considered you. I have loved you. I have loved you without your mask. I have loved you while you were writing your suicide note, and that's why it didn't work—because I loved you in your weakness. I loved you when he or she left you. I loved you when you were alone. I loved you when you didn't love yourself. I loved you when you wouldn't dare take a picture. I loved you when I took your brother. I loved you when you lost your baby. I loved you when you buried your mother and your father. I loved you. I considered you. I love you and I just want you to pick Me—let me behind that wall of anger." God says, "I love you now even while you are angry with Me. I loved you when you are cursing your life because of the consideration of the struggle I am bringing you through. I love you."

It's hard to feel love when you are in so much pain, but God does love you. He loved you so much that He gave His only Son—not one of His sons, His *only* Son. And whoever believes in Him will not perish in his struggle (see John 3:16).

You will not perish in the storm.

You will not perish with the backlash.

You will not perish in humiliation.

You will not perish in abandonment.

You will not perish in rejection.

God gave us Jesus so that we will have everlasting life. God gave His Son's life for your life. It may not seem like it, and you may not feel like it, but He did. You have been considered just as Jesus was considered. You are royalty and you will get to your crown, but you must allow God to break down that wall you've put up so that He can build His purpose in you.

You have a legacy to fulfill and to leave behind. You are considered for a blessing of supernatural portions. You were created to birth the promise of God. You have no reason to be afraid. Do not be afraid for God is with you. Expect that now that you have accepted God as your Father, the enemy is going to come after you. Don't fight it, resist it and strengthen your faith. Stay close to God and continue to worship in spite of what you may be going through. God's got you. God is your Father now and that is different from accepting Him as your Savior. When you make God your Father, you are giving Him access to every part of you that is both pleasing and unpleasing to yourself. You are deciding to trust Him to direct, to discipline, to lead, to guide, and to love you unconditionally. You are entering into a relationship with God where He is not an outer entity—He is both an outer orchestrator of your life and inner orchestrator of your being.

Here is something for you to pray every day:

God, You are my Father. I am an open vessel willing to serve You however You would have me to. Give me the strength to walk through what You have considered me to accomplish today. God give me the strength to withstand the enemy's attacks. Protect, lead, and guide me according to Your perfect will, and I will be forever grateful. Amen.

You may not have it all together, and you may still need some help, but guess what? We aren't finished yet. We are still walking this journey together. We are still faithing it together. I promise you that the best is yet to come.

God in the Birthing Room—PUSH!

You were created to birth the promise of God.

Here's the question: Are you willing to push aside what people may say so that you can encounter God and gain His power? Are you willing to gain your heart's desires no matter what that means? Are you ready to make that sacrifice to press through, or will you settle for mediocre desires, mediocre life, with mediocre purpose? We cannot let what people say keep us from our encounter.

Without our own new birth, we don't receive the power.

Without the power, we can't obtain wholeness.

Without wholeness, we cannot birth God's promise.

Your success comes in your ability to surrender yourself to satisfy God so that He can consume the very essence of your being. Even if the road is bumpy, even if they are talking about you, even if they never understood you, and even if you don't understand yourself, you stay strong. In the middle of your doubt, reach for God with an ounce of faith and He will grant you His power.

The woman with the issue of blood fought through the crowd while she was bleeding, stinking, fragile, weak, humiliated, embarrassed, and passed the people who ridiculed her. She crawled through that crowd with just a little bit of faith that if she touched the hem of His garment she would be made whole. Your power comes when you reach for that hem. But your wholeness comes in your encounter with God.

Although she was afraid of what would happen, the woman with the issue of blood pressed through to encounter God, and because of this He made her whole. Some of you have allowed your humiliation, your embarrassment, and your "judgers" to keep you from your encounter. It is not until you allow yourself to walk past what people will say that you can encounter God and be made whole. Your healing and wholeness comes from your passion to encounter God.

You deserve to have your heart's desires, but God also deserves that you delight yourself in Him. Have you surrounded yourself with righteousness? Then prepare yourself now to let go of your past, failures, mistakes, hurts, angers, and losses. Don't allow yourself to be consumed by your past! Don't focus on the things you can't change. Instead, go after the thing that God wants. You must want more for yourself than to live your life in the bitterness of the past. Bitterness will produce a dead thing because you have self-sabotaged and committed intoxication of the soul, mind, and body. Don't go there.

Your power comes when you reach for that hem.

I challenge you to look beyond yourself so that you can birth your dream and grab hold of what truly matters. You deserve to know that there is nothing you can do about the past except walk past it. Ask God to heal you by faith, and desire more for yourself so that when you have your encounter with Christ you are able to gain power and wholeness.

It's important for me to let you know that you are better than this, and you deserve what God has planted inside of you. Don't let yourself be consumed by distractions. Just because it happens doesn't mean that God meant you to have it and to focus on it. The enemy will present a distraction every time you are about to walk into your purpose because it is a threat to his kingdom. Don't get distracted. Allow yourself the opportunity to be bigger, better, and greater than your distractions.

And don't assume that because you are personally discouraged with yourself that God is discouraged with you. God is not discouraged with you. God is delivering you!

Delivery Is COMING!

I am reminded of when my godsister went into labor with my godson. She was in pain the whole time, until she pushed my godson out. When God plants something in you, it's bigger than you! It's bigger than your comprehension! It's God's seed planted in you—a seed called purpose—and you have to reach for it. With every delivery there will be a process, pain, embarrassment, unbearable laboring, heavy breathing, highs and lows, changes of breath, people in your business, a lot of surroundings, detachment, and nurturing.

You are supposed to birth your purpose.

You are supposed be stretched.

You are supposed to be in pain.

If you concentrate more on the pain, then when it's time for you to birth (just like a real labor) you will be too tired, and you will feel like you can't do it. Some people push longer than others. Some people hurt more than others. The point is that they are all birthing! And God shows us in the birthing process that beauty can come from a painful thing.

There is beauty in your pain. Maybe you just haven't pushed it out yet, and you're still faithing for it, but keep faithing because if you don't you won't birth. Don't get stuck! Some of us stay stuck in the pain so we aren't able to birth and we aren't able to nurture because we have allowed ourselves to become consumed by the pain.

Meanwhile, your purpose (your baby) is waiting until you push. It's going to stretch you. It's supposed to hurt. Do not give up! PUSH!

Beauty can come from a painful thing.

PUSH!

I am your birthing coach and I am telling you, "Breathe!" Don't give up, it's time to start faithing. Allow it to happen, and *push* this thing out.

When they are in your business, push it out.

When people don't agree, push it out.

When you are all alone and tired to the bone, push it out.

It's time to rise! You deserve to rise. You deserve to come forth—you deserve to have your promise in your hand. You have to be willing to have an encounter in order to birth.

Deliver through the pain.

You don't get to the greatest part of having a baby until you have gone through the pain. After that long stretch of pain, you hold your beautiful newborn in your arms. When God places something in you, there are steps just like in a pregnancy. Once you identify you are pregnant, you must seek good counsel. You must follow instructions to keep the baby and the birth as healthy as possible.

If you are fighting and laboring, tired and weary, then you are in the process and that just means you are that much closer to your promise! The road is going to be hard, but in the end it will be worth it. Your destination to your desires lie in your ability to allow yourself to deliver through the pain. Fight the good fight of faith!

I realize that you can grow tired of fighting, but if you give up the fight then God will pass your purpose to someone else. Expect that the enemy is going to attack your purpose.

You are aligned with God.

You are connected with God.

You are in the lineage of royalty!

Anything that comes through you is stronger than what you could have thought of because you have connected yourself with Christ. Whatever you walk in is more powerful than you could imagine. If you truly walked in the full capacity of what God had for you and what you have access to, then you would change the nation. Make a decision to understand that you are royalty.

Your biggest success comes after your biggest sacrifice.

My challenge to you here is to work on learning about yourself so that you can recognize your value. If you believe in yourself as much as God believes in you, then you will walk in a confidence that is even more of a threat to the enemy.

God is not through with you—He is just getting started with you! Your delight is connected to your desires and you have the power. You deserve to pursue your purpose, and when you are ready to walk into your true purpose God will make a way, and He will make the crooked path straight for you. Your biggest success comes after your biggest sacrifice.

Hands Off the Windows!

My biggest sacrifice was my own will. I was so passionate about my heart's desire that I took over instead of letting God take over. I didn't allow God to consume me. Instead, I made myself God to everyone around me, and admittedly I had to deliver myself from pride and arrogance, thinking that I could do a better job than God could. I had to say, "Okay, I let go and let God."

When I surrendered and sacrificed myself and my will, it was very scary for me. But I did it to better myself. I was finally able to sacrifice everything I ever wanted and submit to the fact that whatever God gives me is bigger than anything I could ever desire.

When I took my hands off the windows, He was able to open the windows and pour me out a blessing I did not have room enough to receive.

> "Try Me now in this," says the Lord of hosts, "if I will not open for you the **windows** of heaven and pour out for you such blessing that there will not be room enough to receive it" (Malachi 3:10).

We have to move our hands off the windows so that God can open, and then and only then will we be able to receive what He pours out. When I took my hands off the windows and allowed God to orchestrate my blessings, that's when I was blessed with my daughter, my calling, and many other things.

Every day I am sacrificing myself to what God would have for me. Every day I am emptying myself of myself. Because of my ability to trust that God's thoughts are indeed higher than mine, I am able to say, "God, help me to see me the way You see me." At that point I am submitting my thoughts to what God thinks.

I let my thoughts center around what God sees. I allow myself, my life, and my story to be an open vessel for Him to write my story for me. If you allow God to write for you, when you allow Him to become a piece of you, then He directs and orders your steps.

Because of my submission, I know and believe that soon I will be writing about how God blessed me with birthing a son.

What do you believe God for? Are you holding on to the window? Are you ready to let go? Are you ready to let Him open it and pour out your blessings?

Or are you scared to trust Him because you are being consumed by past pains and hurts that He made you walk though in your process?

Come forward, dear heart, the nation needs you! It's time for you to let go of the hurts of your past, and begin to live in your process and reach for the hem of His garment. You're wanted in the birthing room. PUSH!

God in heaven, You are the Creator of all things and You have created something beautiful for my friend to receive. You have created something beautiful for them to birth. I pray, God, that You will leap them into their double portion. I pray, God, that You leap them into their rightful place and position in the Kingdom. God, I pray that You would give them a forgiving heart and that they be a forgiver to those who have harmed, hurt, and misunderstood them. I pray, God, You mend the broken relationships that You brought together and tear apart the ones You didn't.

Lord, I pray You instill them with passion for their purpose and remove their passion for pain. I rebuke every suicidal thought, every spirit of depression, everything that is not like You. I bind it up and send it back to the pit of hell from which it came. God, You control the order of their steps, so order them accordingly.

I thank You, God, for placing a crown on Your child's head and showing them that they have been considered by a man who has a double portion waiting for them. God, I thank

You for rebirthing them into You, for we know that if they are born of God they are overcomers. Thank You, God, for I believe it is done, and it is so and so it is in the name of Jesus. Amen.

God, I thank You that You are making a way where there seems to be no way, and God, I pray for a supernatural healing for my friend from the inside out. Every ailment, every problem, every curse that has tried to attach itself to this reader, we call it broken by the power of the Holy Ghost. You are God and God alone, and before time began You were on Your throne.

Lord, I thank You that You have considered them for the struggle, but that they are about to birth their promise. I thank You, God, that all things work together for the good of those who have been called according to Your purpose and will for their lives. We trust You for the divine timing and order of all these things, in Jesus' name. Amen and amen.

Scan this code for Cora's Chapter 9
PRAYER FOR YOU!

Or Visit

WWW.CORAJAKESCOLEMAN.COM

Faith Affirmation

I love the story of Job, and if you have been following me anywhere you know this. Job was the ideal man to show us how we must endure after being considered for both the beating and the blessing. Job reminds me of the trials he had to go through to get what God had for him. I think so often we get so consumed by the struggle that we can't see or hear the messengers God has sent to tell us about the blessing. We focus on what we lack and take advantage of what we don't lack. We place ourselves in a position to complain without truly understanding that nothing from God comes without having to work for it. Be it your faith working for you or you working your faith, there is work involved when you have been considered for a great blessing. The size of your endurance will dictate the size of your portion. We rush God's preparation and get mad when we get to an empty table when if we had listened to and obeyed God the first time, everything would have been prepared for us in spite of there being enemies. Stop being mad about your struggle and understand that the more you are willing to trust God, the more He is able to trust you with. You can't expect to receive more from God than you are willing to trust Him with. You can't trust God to give you a promise that you don't believe He has the capacity to accomplish for you. How can you live in doubt and expect God to deliver?

Faith Points

The world needs your message and the gifts God put in you. Stop doubting yourself, your ability. It's time for you to be great.

Concentrate on the rainbow that comes after the storm. Don't allow temporary situations to abort heaven's earthly and eternal destiny for your life.

Your seed of purpose and power will erupt in cities and fields—producing an overflow for every generation before you and after you. You are the manifestation of the hope of God.

God has chosen you to go through struggles so you can speak to others about the success when you overcame them all. God considered you worthy for the struggles because He sees your success just ahead.

Your life is a testament of what you were willing to overcome. You are a natural overcomer because you are a child of God.

There is nothing behind the walls you built that is too hard for God to handle. Trust God to take away your hurts, rejection, heartbreak, pain, sorrow, shame, humiliation, depression, doubts, worry, and suicidal thoughts.

When you make God your Father, you give Him access to all of you—both the pleasing and unpleasant parts of yourself. He loves you through and through!

Without your own new birth, you won't receive power. Without power, you can't obtain wholeness. Without wholeness, you can't birth God's promise.

Faith Activations

Considering yourself as a book God is writing, what do you think is the book's theme, the overarching premise of your life? If not the theme you would like it to be, what steps can you take to ensure an exciting page-turner with an eternally happy ending?

Have you built walls around certain areas in your life that you want to keep for yourself? God knows what is behind each wall. Take the sledgehammer from God's hand and use it to smash every wall, allowing the Light of Christ to shine and heal.

When you surrender yourself to God, you receive power. Explain that dynamic in a paragraph or two.

Faithing It

TEN

Covenant Relationship

Fight the good fight of the faith. Take hold
of the eternal life to which you were called
when you made your good confession
in the presence of many witnesses.

(1 TIMOTHY 6:12 NIV)

Y ou've been considered worthy by God to birth His dreams for your life and for the next generation. You are being trained for the fight by the best coach in the world—get ready! It's time to get into the ring. Every good boxer has to prepare for the fight, and God wants to prepare us in the same way. We are in a faith fight, and there is more to faith than just saying you have it. You have to be ready for the fight. You can get caught up looking to use what has worked for everyone else, but you need to use what works for you.

You can run into the ring impulsively, but I warn you to plan first. Everyone has a fight to fight, and their winning is specific to strategy. Be careful what you choose to fight with. You want to make sure that you face the giants in your life with no fear, full preparation, a good strategy, and most importantly, your coach.

When I was diagnosed with infertility, I had to go through IVF. When it failed in the first cycle, I went to God in devastation and heartbreak and said, "God, if You are going to make me go through this, You'd better make it count." At that time I also began to write to my promise (Nehemiah), and I told my promise, "I will fight for you…." Then I began to research to look up and find information. I sought good counsel and wisdom and understanding so that I could win.

It's time to get into the ring.

You will get the victory with God, but your faith must rest on substance. Hebrews 11:1 says, "Now faith is the substance of things hoped for, the evidence of things not seen."

If you have no substance, then you are only halfway in. You can't fight Goliath without a sling and stones. You can't fight your battle without substance—your wisdom and your weapon. Once you have everything in your hand, then you may get in the ring. I got in the ring with my faith, my coach, my wisdom, my understanding, and my armor, and I believed God for the impossible because I know with Him all things are possible.

I know that you have been ignited and you are ready to take on the world, but it is wise to get understanding and seek counsel before you take on your giant. You have to put on the correct armor that fits you. More importantly, you need to submit your fight to the power that God has already placed in your hand. No one ever won a battle without studying, practicing, and seeking counsel.

Know Your God

Now that you have been ignited for the fight, it's time for you to gain knowledge. Get in the Word of God and find out about what you are fighting so that when the giant rises you don't lose. I was thinking the other day about how much Word I have in me. Then I wondered about something. If I was only able to fight the enemy based on the Word that I have in my heart, would I win or lose? You can have God behind you and be consumed by God, but do you know about the God who is in you? Have you searched His Word? Do you know His capability? Do you have an understanding of just how powerful you are when you're consumed by Him?

Before you fight for the promise in God's hand, before you fight for the purpose that God has for you, before you step into the ring with the giants of the world, *know your God*. Know about Him, what He went through, and what He thinks of you. Trust me, you won't be able to know everything, but show God that this isn't a one-way street where you have become close to Him because you want to gain something from Him.

Show God your motives in this relationship. Tell Him that you want to think about Him more and more, and that you want to know Him personally. You need to become of God so that He can become of you, and you can become one. Your heart should be so into God that the people who want to be around you have to seek God in order to find you!

Stand Up for God

As Christians in the Kingdom, we have to take a stand for God. The media will shut us down, the radio won't want to hear from us. It's easier to conform to the world than change it. God is calling the anointed leaders of this generation to come forth.

Isaiahs, come forth.

Malachis, come forth.

Obadiahs, come forth.

Nehemiahs, come forth.

Esthers, come forth.

Marys, come forth.

Someone needs to speak up for God. We can spend so much time wanting God to stand up for us, but He needs us to stand up for Him too! We are Kingdom kids and it's time we start acting like it. If we don't make God's voice known, then His voice and His movement will die. He will be condemned again, and His crucifixion will mean nothing.

It's easier to conform to the world than change it.

He died for us. At the very least we can stand up for Him. Yes, this is what it's about. We stand for Him because when we take on this giant Goliath, we are going to have to be able to say that God and I are standing together. It is pointless to say that God is for you if you aren't for Him. Your relationship with God requires a level of responsibility. If you are unwilling to take responsibility in the world and in the spirit realm, then you will lose. You can stand for God and pretend, but the reality is if you deny Him in any element of your life, you will not be able to produce the power that is rightfully yours through relationship.

Can you stand for God in places where it's hard to stand? Are you willing to stand for Christ in public and in private? Is your relationship status with God complicated? Are you a God gold digger always seeking for what He can give you and unwilling to give back, or even say thank You?

Champions become champions based on the relationship and understanding that they have with the coach. A champion cannot win if he or she has a complicated, unyielding, rebellious relationship with the coach.

Check Your Relationship Status

So here comes your next challenge: Check yourself and your relationship with God. You are almost there. You are about to face your giant, but in order to win, you need a strong relationship with your coach.

It's all about relationship. Why? In order to produce, nurture, and nourish a seed, there has to be some type of relationship with the seed and the producer. You cannot produce a seed without a connection.

Production starts with a connection. You must get connected to God in order to produce and birth what He planted. When you are filled with the Holy Spirit, you are filled with a seed, with life. And it all started with your ability to allow God to connect with you and to fill you. Now you have to stay connected so that you can bring forth what He placed inside you, much like a baby. Just like a baby. You are connected with that child forever. You will always be that child's mother or father. If you aren't producing, you must ask yourself, are you connected?

Sometimes we get upset because we aren't seeing our fruit and we aren't seeing our promise, but we have to check ourselves. Have we become God gold diggers? Are we consumed with ourselves and with asking God for the things we want? Is our hand always out, ready to take, but not to give?

Put yourself in position to be a giver and a receiver.

You'll never be able to give more to God than He could give to you, but you must at least put yourself in position to be a giver and a receiver. For it is indeed better to give than to receive. If you give to God and you mean it beyond your own personal gain, and give in a pure heart, then He will give back to you.

When I started giving to God, that is when I started receiving from God. We need to stop looking for materialistic things all the time. Sometimes a day of peace is what God gives to you. Sometimes that calm in the middle of the day brought through a phone call is what God gives to you. Whatever God gives, be grateful because it is all connected back to the Word. If you are faithful over the few things, God will make you ruler over many things. The roads to promise and purpose are not easy, but when I am connected to God in spirit and in truth, I can't lose. How do I know? Well, I am glad you asked.

Covenant-Keeping God

One morning on a very hot day there stood a man over nine feet tall who tormented the Israelites and tried to start a war. He stood before the Israelites and challenged them to fight. First Samuel 17 tells us the story:

> *Choose a man for yourselves, and let him come down to me. If he is able to fight with me and kill me, then we will be your servants; but if I prevail against him and kill him, then you shall be our servants and serve us* (1 Samuel 17:8-9 WEB).

This nine-foot giant was named Goliath. He was large, loud, and obnoxious. Day after day Goliath came out and stood on the other side of the mountain and called to Israel. Goliath went so far as to defy God's army!

> *The Philistine said, "I defy the armies of Israel this day; give me a man, that we may fight together." When Saul and all Israel heard these words of the Philistine, they were dismayed, and greatly afraid* (1 Samuel 17:10 WEB).

The king of Israel, King Saul, and all of his armies were afraid of Goliath. He terrified all the Israelites—except one. There was a shepherd boy whose heart was for God. David was in a covenant relationship with God, and God gave him great power because of this. David's father asked him to leave his sheep to go see how his brothers were doing on the battlefield and to bring them some food from home.

David was just a teenager at the time, but when he heard Goliath shouting, he got angry. Why? Goliath had defied the living God. David said, "Who is this uncircumcised Philistine, that he should defy the armies of the living God?" (1 Samuel 17:26 WEB).

Circumcision was *the* sign of covenant with God in the Old Testament. All Hebrew baby boys were circumcised as a sign of the covenant between God and Israel. So when David said, "Who is this uncircumcised Philistine to defy the armies of the living God," David was pointing to the covenant God made with His people. David was saying, "This giant is big but he doesn't have a covenant with God—and God is bigger."

This giant is big but he doesn't have a covenant with God.

David stood for the living God because God had stood for him as a shepherd of sheep alone in the fields, and God hadn't failed him. David knew that God helped him defeat a lion and a bear as he watched sheep in the fields, and he was utterly confident that God would help him defeat this giant too. What I love about the story the most is that David didn't take credit for defeating the lion and the bear; rather, he gave the credit to God. We often get so locked up in trying to take credit for a battle that we couldn't even overcome if it hadn't been for the Lord. Give God the credit for the fight He helped you win before you got in the ring. You will defeat this new Goliath. So right now before I even continue, I want you to think of everything you overcame and thank God and give Him the honor for it.

David went before this giant with five smooth rocks and a sling in his hand. I love what David shouted back at Goliath. Just listen to the war cry of this shepherd boy:

Then David said to the Philistine, "You come to me with a sword, with a spear, and with a javelin. But I come to you in the name of the Lord of hosts, the God of the armies of Israel, whom you have defied. This day the Lord will deliver you into my hand, and I will strike you and take your head from you. And this day I will give the carcasses of the camp of the Philistines to the birds of the air and the wild beasts of the earth, that all the earth may know that there is a God in Israel. Then all this assembly shall know that the Lord does not save with sword and spear; for the battle is the Lord's, and He will give you into our hands" (1 Samuel 17:45–47).

And you know the rest of the story. David defeated Goliath that day. When we are born again, we enter into a covenant with God through the shed blood of Jesus Christ. When you are in covenant with God and you respect the position and the "bigness" of God, you face your giant fully equipped. You don't need anything but the Lord God Almighty.

For years David sang to God all alone in the fields as he watched the sheep. For years he had declared his desire and delighted himself in the Lord. In fact, David wrote that verse in the book of Psalms: "Delight yourself also in the Lord, and He shall give you the desires of your heart" (37:4). David stood for God and showed both the believers and the nonbelievers that there was a God.

So I ask you, what have you charged your giant with? Have you charged your giant with God beside you or God consuming you? Do you realize you are in covenant with God?

Time to Know God and Refuse Fear

Here's our second challenge in this chapter: How much time do you spend getting to know God and really consuming yourself with His Word and communicating with Him? If you spend more time on Facebook than you do fasting and talking to God, then when you are faced with your giant you won't win. Do you know more about your stats on your social media then you do about Scriptures? Come on now!

You can't expect success without the knowledge of the Scriptures of God. You must get to know God in order for Him to use you as an open vessel, and when you are an open vessel for Him, then He stands before you. He fights the battle for you and you are named victorious because He claimed the victory for you. You aren't victorious, the God in you that you choose to gain knowledge of is victorious. You aren't to be a God gold digger anymore. I teach my children in Destiny World that we must learn to say thank you to God before we dare open our mouth to say please.

Don't be someone who only opens your Bible at church or Bible study or when bad things are going on. Don't be someone who prays only when you want something or need God to get you out of something. Don't be the type of person who only praises God on Sunday and choir rehearsal, but let praise continuously be in your mouth. Seek the Lord daily. Read His Word daily and hide it (memorize it) in your heart. Like David, you are a winner when you attach yourself to God and to the Word of God. Remember,

God is older, wiser, and much bigger than any old giant that comes your way. Trust Him! He's the greatest and wisest coach in the world.

When my daughter was a little girl, she was afraid of monsters *in* her bed, *under* her bed, and around her room. After a few nights with us, she came running in the room to tell me and my husband that there was a monster in her room. I told her to go into her room and to pray and say, "Jesus." But before I said any of that, I told her that monsters aren't real. To her they were real, but the minute that someone more powerful, older, and wiser told her that they weren't real she believed it, and she isn't afraid of monsters anymore. She laughs now when she hears kids say they are afraid of monsters.

Learn to say thank you to God before we dare open our mouth to say please.

Why did I tell you this? It's simple. If someone more powerful, wiser, and stronger didn't tell her that monsters weren't real, she would still be afraid of the monster. God is more powerful, wiser, and stronger than you. You may be faced with what looks like a monster, but God says it's not real. You are seeing the flood coming, but it's not going to drown you, and He has built a standard against it. You are seeing the weapon form, but it won't prosper. God says, "Your enemy, this monster, is nothing. I am bigger and stronger and more powerful than he will ever be. Now pray and go to sleep, sweetheart, and believe that I have you."

When you have the word of someone more powerful and stronger than you, then you rest in that. You can rest with God and know that He will face your giant with you, for you, and within you. God wants to give you your power, love, and your self-discipline—you just need to let your fear go. The hardest part of a relationship is taking that risk of getting hurt and not recovering.

God wants you to take a risk on Him. Choose Him now. Really choose Him in all things and in every element of your life so that He can take control and work His power through you. You are almost there to the promise—it's right there. You will achieve, you just have to get to know God so that He can be of you.

I gave the Lord my heart and asked for His. I allowed Him to have access to me at all times every day. God produces beauty from my broken pieces and I want to be connected to that kind of flow. I want to be a light in the darkness of this world. In order for me to be a light, I must submit and let God consume me with the light that is Him.

Love God, Not Religion

It's easy to get stuck in religion and the rules of religion. God did not come for religion, He came for relationship. He came for love. To put God's relationship in the rules of religion is wrong because that's not what He came for. A part of the relationship challenge is that you loose yourself from religious rules and get connected to the relationship with God. That's what attracted me to God—not religion but the relationship that I saw He had with others. Religion can push people away, but God's love draws a crowd.

You can love God and not love religion. God wants your heart, not your long skirt or your nail polish or your tattoos or your cleavage or your panty hose or your makeup or your contacts. God came so that you would give your heart and soul to Him and that you would develop a love for Him that He had for you. He wants to show you His heart toward you, and in return you allow God to connect with you on an emotional level. He is your friend.

We are designed to have and pursue relationships. We need to make sure that the relationship with God is firm before we search for relationship with others. Make sure that you are having as many intimate moments with God as you are having dates and agendas with people. If you truly love God and you are spending time with Him above all others, then you are faithing it!

So guess what? Your faithing is in your hands now. Your promise is in your hands now, and all you have to do is speak to it. Everything you need is already in your hands. You have the victory. There is nothing left to do. Take hold, walk forward, for you are headed into covenant with Christ. God bless you and soar on!

God's love draws a crowd.

Single-Hearted Love

Let me take a moment now to speak to my single friends. If you are single, that's even better because you have access and more time than anyone else to develop a relationship with God that is true, dedicated, and real. Don't see your single life as a horrible fate, but enjoy this time together when you can have undistracted devotion to God. God loves you so much and needs you to fall more in love with Him, and He is giving you the time to do so.

Another wonderful thing about this is that when you allow God to be everything to you and the right person does come along, your relationship will be so tight in God that He will be able to tell you what's for you and what's not for you.

This is hard, but I'm going to say it. Don't fight for a relationship that God didn't ordain. Let go of it—God has something better for you. Stop feeling like you have a responsibility to hold on to every relationship for whatever reason. God severs those ties for a reason, and you don't have to hold on to it. Let it go. God is for you, so trust Him to lead you to the right person.

If you are tied in a relationship that has become a dysfunction, a disease, a hardship, or an unbearable and painful situation for you, let it go. God is for you. He is for your heart, and when you have a solid relationship with God, the people around you will love you the way that God would have you to be loved.

God is orchestrating everything for your benefit. When you seek Him, He will give you the answers and put everything in order. Clean up your heart so that you can rightfully receive the heart of God and see people for who they really are. When you force yourself onto someone who is trying to show you they don't want you, then you are raping yourself. Not only that, you are preventing someone else from the person that God is trying to give to them. Don't rape yourself and don't rape anyone else. Walk away before you become a poison to the people who are supposed to gain from your purpose.

It's hard to let go of someone when you have let them love you, be intimate with you, and you have given them more of your heart than you have even given to God, but understand destruction comes in a relationship when you love man more than you have shown love to God. You cannot expect your relationship that was planted in sin, rooted in sin, and guided by sin to work.

There will always be someone who doesn't agree with the decisions you make to go toward Christ, but if Christ is in your heart you need not worry or be concerned because He will fix the discords and the distractions. God loves you. Sometimes you have to let go of the damage in order for God to pull you out of a dead place. If you keep playing with damaged goods, then you won't be able to gain access to God's power, purpose, and promise for your life. You need high-quality love in order to receive a high-quality promise.

Your relationship with God is your most powerful weapon.

It's important that you understand that your relationship with God is your most powerful weapon. Whatever you are going through, your fight is God's fight.

Do you want the covenant relationships you're involved in to be right before God? Do you want to sever the relationships that God did not ordain and nurture the relationships that are of Him? Let me pray for you now.

I pray that God will instill you with the

right people in your surroundings. You are no longer bound by dead relationships. You are loosed! I pray that God will connect you to people who are for you. I pray that God would remove you from dead situations and give you the strength to let go of the things He needs you to let go of. I pray that God would make you great before the people of God and that your relationship with Him would become a natural and consistent routine. I pray that God gives you the wisdom and the words to release the relationships that are not meant for you. I pray that you have the strength to walk away and you do not look back.

I pray that you be healed from the soul ties of the enemy and that you rebuild a foundation of God's truth. I pray that He strengthens the relationships that He brought together, and that He releases the relationships that He didn't bring together.

More importantly, I pray God's peace would consume every relationship the enemy is trying to shake up. I pray supernatural miracles to come forth in every relationship that is under the umbrella of God's choice and divine connection.

I pray that anything that is in you that would cause your God-ordained relationships to sever, that God would remove that thing and make you the glue that holds you and your loved ones together. May you have the faith and strength to stand for God above all things, and may God open doors for you according to your obedience and diligence toward Him. And it is so and so it is, in the mighty name of Jesus. Amen!

Scan this code for Cora's Chapter 10
PRAYER FOR YOU!

Or Visit

WWW.CORAJAKESCOLEMAN.COM

Faith Affirmation

Only what you seek can be added unto you. If you are not willing to seek God's word, don't expect to receive the fruit from it. We can't be more interested in being penetrated by the things of the world than we are in seeking the power of God. Our covenant relationship must be tied to God before it can be tied to man. We can't expect to be ready for the scars in our husband if we are unwilling to address the scars in ourselves. We can't expect to be found by a man of God when we don't seek the God of man. We are often so focused on our vision that we don't seek the Lord's vision for our lives. We must position ourselves to be willing to be still and become intimate with God before we can ask Him to place us in a position to receive from a person. Your standard of self should call you to love yourself before you ask man to. Be confident in your foundation with Christ first, and let God provide for you in ways that make the feeling of loneliness go away. If you aren't willing to work hard on bettering yourself now, when you're on your own, you can't expect to be willing to work hard in a relationship later. Stop looking for someone to help you, and learn how to help yourself through the power and direction of God.

Faith Points

Fight the giants in your life with faith, no fear, full preparation, a good strategy, and your Coach—God Almighty.

Christian champions win based on their relationship with their Coach. A champion can't win if there is a complicated, unyielding, rebellious relationship with the Coach.

As a Christian believer, you have to take a stand and speak up for God whenever possible.

You must get connected to God to produce and birth what He planted within you through the Holy Spirit.

When you give to God and you mean it beyond your own personal gain, and give in a pure heart, God will give back to you abundantly.

The roads to promise and purpose are not easy, but when you are connected to God in spirit and in truth—you can't lose!

Give God the credit for the fight He helped you win, even before you got into the ring. You will defeat each new Goliath because God is in your corner. God is your most powerful weapon.

If you spend more time on Facebook than face to face with God, when you are standing before your giant, you won't win.

God will face your giant with you, for you, and within you. Let your fear go. Loose yourself from religious rules and connect with God.

Faith Activations

Do you really know your heavenly Father? Have you searched His Word? Do you know His capabilities? Do you have an understanding of just how powerful you are when you're consumed by Him? Start seeking today for answers to these questions.

Show God your motives are firm and pure in your relationship with Him. Tell Him you want to know Him intimately. Think about Him more. Pray more. Reach out to Him more with thankfulness. Stand up and speak up for Him at home, at work, in school, in the market...

Start tomorrow morning keeping track of how many minutes you are on Facebook, Twitter, and the Internet. Also, keep track of how many minutes you pray, read the Bible, discuss your faith, attend church services. At the end of a week, compare the two figures.

Faithing It

ELEVEN

Power Over Pride

What good is it for someone to gain the whole world,
and yet lose or forfeit their very self?

(LUKE 9:25 NIV)

You have a covenant with God Almighty and He has coached you and shown you how to faith it right into your promise. Victory is sweet, but you must know that when we get to the place of purpose that was promised to us, the enemy is going to come at us more now than he ever did before. God has given you the keys to the mansion—don't lose those keys because you aren't comfortable in your new position. Worse, don't lose those keys because you're *proud* of your new position. If the enemy can't get you tempted one way, he'll tempt you the other. He will try to make you feel uncomfortable in your placement and your position—a distraction you can't afford right now. If that doesn't work, he will feed your thoughts with how great you are and how there is no one like you.

What do you do? Keep your head held high and walk in this new place with a humble heart. Didn't God tell you He would bring you before great men and women? You are supposed to be here, so don't worry about what you have or don't have in the spirit realm. The truth is, you wear a victor's crown. You are now walking in faith like never before. You have been ignited, and you have fresh fire, and fresh perspective. All you need to do is keep ahold of this gift and don't lose yourself in yourself. You can't manage the gift of a mansion if your mindset is still in the projects or your old low-income apartment complex. And you will fall quickly if you think you are suddenly the best thing since sliced cheese. The Word of God tells us that pride goes before a fall. Stay humble.

Walk in this new place with a humble heart.

Don't Lose Ground

The good news is that when you are faced with these temptations or other tests, you are not alone. You have rekindled your relationship with God in spite of your pain, hurt, and anger. You have been held captive for some time, but God has not only unlocked you, He has given you the master key. As you go through the continued journey of faithing it, I urge you to stay close to God. Don't lose what you have gained in trusting and believing God. Do not lose the heart that you have toward Him. I urge you to stay focused on the blessings, not the bruises from the enemy. It's easy to lose the ground you've gained if you allow yourself to focus more on the battle and less on the blessing.

There is nothing left to fear and nothing to be bitter about now that God has orchestrated your purpose through this pain. You are going to be okay. You will go through battles, but you are not battling alone. Your purpose has made you productive. Your promise is beautiful and manifesting through your command.

Guard your faith just as David did. Do not let anyone sway you or allow your distractions and detours to control you. Control your distractions; do not submit to them. If you allow your mountains to destroy you or distract you, then you will easily lose your power. If the enemy comes to steal, kill, and destroy, then he has to do something that makes it easy for him to complete his assignment. The easiest way for him to do this is to bring forth a distraction. A distraction will make it easy for him to take the power out of your hand. If you get distracted, you'll be destroyed. Don't lose your power by taking the detours of life. Don't walk through every door in front of you because, as my mentor says, "Every door is not a God door."

Stay focused on the blessings, not the bruises from the enemy.

The Distraction of Looking Back

You may stand on high platforms and speak

about your testimony, but none of it will matter if you aren't moving forward. You can sound deep and you can sound powerful, but if you let the devil steal your anointing, then you will not be able to destroy the attacks that come.

You have a decision to make, just as Lot's wife did. You can choose to walk toward your promise or you can look back to see what you just left behind and be paralyzed into a pillar of salt (see Genesis 19). And that was the end of her purpose and even her life. She was destroyed along with the stuff behind her. If you spend too much time looking at the stuff burning up behind you, then you will not accomplish the assignments in front of you. I want you to know that you have been given a unique gift from God. Don't worry about the cost it took for you to get it, because you will never know the cost it took for God to give you the gift of His Son.

When God takes you to a new level in life, He changes your position, your name, and your title. You are royalty! You own the light, and if you learn to walk in that mindset, everyone else will follow. You are a leader and you have been placed in the front of the line because God felt like you could lead people. You can wait for the world to tell you you're ready or you can tell the world to get ready. You have gone through a transformation. Yes, it has been heavy, but you have come out, and God has given you a crown on your head and a scepter of power in your hand. You have been deemed a daughter or son of the Most High, so walk like royalty. Don't get distracted or you will lose your position.

Don't Lose Yourself

Now let's talk about the power in your identity. Luke 9:25

says, "What good is it for someone to gain the whole world, and yet lose or forfeit their very self?" (NIV). God has called you great and placed you in position, but it's important that you remain humble. One form of pride is trying to fit in with everyone else. If you try to pray like someone else, speak like someone else, laugh like someone else, then you are losing your personal identity in order to identify with someone you admire. Do not lose yourself and who you are by trying to fit in with everyone else.

Walk like royalty.

If you have yielded yourself to God through the process, stood up for God, let Him heal you, and you are walking in intimacy with Him, then your old mindset is gone. You aren't in the same mindset that you used to be. God has taken you to a new level, and not only do you personally see things differently, but the people around you will see *you* differently. That's a good thing. But let humility be your new identity. You walk with a different power now, but stay humble, solid, and don't lose yourself after all you have gained.

I know that I have power to achieve greatness, but that has nothing to do with me, and it has everything to do with whom I am connected to. Don't become arrogant in your access. This access and authority comes through your submission to God, whereby you allow Him to control everything. We don't deserve it, but He uses us anyway.

Walk Like Royalty in Your New Level

We can easily let our power become arrogance in the Kingdom of God, where we feel entitled to our position. But God has not called you there because you are entitled, He put you there because what He put inside of you deserves to be in a great position. It is a humble person in royalty who continues to get promoted and get blessings in the Kingdom. Your obedience makes God want to grant you the promises. Lot obeyed what God said, and he made it to the promise. Moses hit the rock in anger, and he wasn't obedient, so he didn't gain his promise. He was not able to obtain the riches of the world in its fullness because he wasn't obedient. Your obedience is truly better than whatever you could sacrifice, because in your obedience God works for you.

So here is your challenge in this chapter: I challenge you to stay humble even when it's hard—even when you are provoked. I challenge you to answer the distractions of the enemy with prayer and obedience. Be led by God in all things. If you are faced with a distraction, answer that distraction with a move of God. If God says don't respond, don't respond and don't worry about whether they are going to be taken care of. God will protect you and fight for you. Don't lose yourself because of the mindset of others.

You have a new mindset, a new position, a new name, and it's time for you to stop looking behind you at the stuff God is destroying and start looking forward so that you can continue to obtain the promises of the land. God has opened the door. Don't look back! Certainly don't take the credit for opening the door. Thank Him for opening it. Walk in it with your head bowed and continue to be obedient. I know that God can use a small door to give me something big, and I also understand that God can bring forth a huge storm just to show me that He has a rainbow. But the point is that God is the ruler of all things and He places me where He would have me to go, and I won't move unless He moves me.

Obtain the World or Be Swallowed by It

Walk in it with your head bowed.

Those who are born of God overcome the world, and they then gain the world. This is the transition that happens where you go from being faithful over the few things, and God making you ruler over many. This is the point where your relationship makes the decision of whether you are going to obtain the world or be swallowed up by the world. Put the past behind you and take a huge step forward. God just changed your position, and you have been transitioned into ruling the things that you desired. He has given you dominion in the situation. You are born to overcome. There is nothing the enemy should be able to present to you that you can't overcome.

What's important to note is whenever you gain the world and you don't operate and handle it the way that it should be handled, then you are at risk of losing it. You have power in your hands. If you fall because of pride, you will lose your power. Then you will have to start all over with gaining the trust of God back and showing that you can have power and will not operate in pride.

When you allow pride to control your power, then you are headed toward a fall. Do not abuse God's grace just because you are standing in a position of power. Do not play with your odds because you have been placed in position. You need to know that because you have been positioned in the seat of greatness you cannot get away with the stuff that you used to get away with. When God calls you to your promise and your purpose, you can't get away with looking back and entertaining the things that are behind you because that is how you end up losing your promise.

If you get distracted, prideful, or disobedient along the way to your promise, you will ultimately fall into destruction, and you will not be able to obtain the gift that awaits you. So you must lose your fleshly self, and your past self, but you must not lose the humbleness and gratefulness that God has placed in you. God has given you the world. You are new. Old things that were of no benefit have passed away, but you get to keep the genuine heart for God that you have gained along the way in this journey.

Your position and placement are new, but your heart for God is the same. Stay true to the person God has formed within you. He's called you to this journey. You are *new!* You may have a new position, a new call, a new purpose, and you may have to walk new, speak new, be new, and even see new. But in all of that, don't lose who you are deep inside. Stay solid and stand tall in your position with excitement and passion.

What good would it be for you to have the world in your hands and then allow people to manipulate you to do what they want you to do? If you cave in to the pressure of becoming what people want you to be, you will lose and forfeit yourself.

Keep Your Heart True

Let me explain it this way. My daughter watches *Sofia the First*, the Disney Junior television series. I love that cartoon! Anyway, let me tell you a little bit about Sofia. Sofia became a princess overnight, and she had to figure out how to do things right. There was so much for her to learn and see. She got access to a mansion (castle) and she was switched out of her public school to attend a school just for royalty. She was faced with adventures, but she remained excited to be Sofia the First. She gained the world.

Her name was changed, her position was changed, her title was changed, and she gained access to the world. Everyone did whatever she asked, but Sofia's heart was compassionate. She was loving and a good friend. She was a sweet little girl at her core, and she was humble, too. She was always trying to do the right thing. Even her gifts were different than anyone else's gifts. What am I saying? Although Sofia gained the world and was able to do things no one else was able to do, she didn't lose herself. She didn't forfeit her heart for the key to the world.

You don't have to forfeit who God has created you to be in order for you to gain the desires of your heart. You are uniquely and specifically made for God's perfect purpose in you. You're a light for your generation. You may have walked through the dark areas, but because you have decided to walk with God, your life will never be the same again.

That's what our Scripture at the beginning of this chapter is all about—the ability to gain the world but not lose yourself. It's time for you to accept your position and walk in it. Stop carrying the weight of the hurt from the past. No more! God has seen you as good enough, and because of that you can walk with your head held high and not worry about the hurts of the world. Stand in your power, not your pride.

It's been a long journey and we have overcome a lot of hurdles, but God is not done with us yet. God needs to know that if He gives you what you have commanded to manifest, that you aren't going to go on a power trip. God needs to be able to trust you with the power. Perhaps that's why we aren't seeing a lot of "the sick healed and the dead raised" moments. Could it be that instead of giving God the glory for the manifestation of power we, in our arrogance, and take the credit for ourselves?

Stand in your power, not your pride.

Keep your humility close to your heart so that you always have access. You don't have to tell people that you are royalty. God will speak for you. You don't have to defend your position or placement. God has put you there. You don't have to put disclaimers out for the power that is in you, just keep walking in it. When God is operating through you, He will speak for Himself. Walk in your gift and stay humble. Give God the credit and He will take it from there.

Stay Solid

I thank God that He is moving things out of the way so people can see the gifts in you. I thank

God that you have been chosen and called to pursue and produce your purpose and promise. *May you take up your bed and walk into victory in the name of Jesus. It is so and so it is by the power of the Holy Ghost. Amen!* Whatever you do, don't lose yourself, don't lose your faith, and don't lose your hope. If you have a little bit of hope, then you have something for your faith to stand on. If the devil can take your hope, then he can take your substance.

My husband, Brandon, has coined the phrase, "Stay solid." What this means is that no matter what the devil tries to do to shake who you are and who you are called to be, stay solid. I issue this phrase to you—stay solid. Don't lose yourself in trying to gain the world, and don't then gain the world and lose yourself. Stay solid in who God has called you to be and in the end it will work out just fine.

I have found comfort in my battle with infertility because I am in God's hands, and I have truly cast my cares upon the Lord. When I was a little girl I understood the revelation of these two Scriptures:

> *No temptation has overtaken you except what is common to mankind. And God is faithful; He will not let you be tempted beyond what you can bear. But when you are tempted, He will also provide a way out so that you can endure it* (1 Corinthians 10:13 NIV).

> *Cast your cares on the Lord and He will sustain you; He will never let the righteous be shaken* (Psalm 55:22 NIV).

I understood that no matter what I am going through, God will never put more on me than I can bear. In my heart I know that I will not have anything to bear if I will cast everything on Him. He said He will sustain me. What does *sustain* mean? *Sustain* means "to strengthen or support physically or mentally." So if God is standing for me and I cast all my problems, struggles, and hurts on to God, then He will physically and mentally strengthen me and support me.

So I say to you, whatever it is that you are carrying that isn't benefiting you, cast that weight on to God. Sometimes I hear, "Man, God said He wouldn't put more on me than I can bear, but honestly this feels too heavy." The only reason it seems unbearable to you is because you haven't cast the weight on to God. You have let pride overpower you, causing you to feel like you are strong enough to handle everything on your own. So you take on the world and you lose yourself because you continue to bottle up your weight instead of casting it on to God. What would happen if you would throw all that pride and all that weight to God and you walk in liberation?

Bow Your Head and Stay Humble

Let's talk about pride for a second before we close out this chapter. *Pride* means "a feeling or deep pleasure or satisfaction derived from one's own achievements." You may have gained the world, but it wasn't through your own achievement. Your accomplishments were achieved through God and your submission to God. What is fascinating is that God is able to use us for something bigger than ourselves.

Don't stand there waiting for God to clap for you and say you have done well. How about this? You turn around and clap for God because He allowed you to achieve what you did achieve. He helped you to gain the world so that you could access power. Now that you are walking in your purpose, don't stop praising Him for it. When you have obtained your power, when you have seen the gift of the promise, don't stop thanking God because it is in your gratitude that you are given more access. You can praise Him 'til the walls come down, but after they have come down praise Him because He did it! Praise Him because He's given you access to something great.

So what's the point? You have the power—don't lose it because of pride. When the doors open, walk through humbly and stay humble. When you reach your promise, and God actually gives it to you in your hand, don't take it and run and start showing people how shiny it is before you say thank You. Don't be a spoiled, entitled brat to the King of kings. Receive your gift in full understanding that He did it and you did nothing to deserve this gift. Recognize that He didn't have to call you to your promise and give it to you.

The biblical concept is quite simple and it goes a little something like this: "Give thanks to the Lord, for His love endures forever." The way that you do not allow pride to take your power is through having a grateful heart and staying humble.

It is in your gratitude that you are given more access.

I support you wholeheartedly and I am behind you. More importantly, God is behind you. Just walk with your head bowed before the King in order for you to keep your hands on your power.

Don't look back. Stop giving the people who hurt you in your past the power that is rightfully yours. Forgive those who have hurt you—not just for them but for you. If you need help mentally, physically, emotionally, and spiritually, walk to it. There is absolutely nothing wrong with needing help to get to your power, and there is nothing wrong with being afraid to succeed. Focus on your healing, physically and mentally, and search for the support and help you need to become great.

Has God convicted you of pride as you read this chapter? Conviction is a wonderful thing! Admit your sin to God and at your request He will cleanse you. Tell God right now that you humble yourself in your own eyes and He will lift you into His glorious light. Walk in your light and walk in your call, and push people into their destiny. Pick power over pride. You are a child of the King! Let me pray for you right now.

> *I pray that your life be a representation of what God is doing in you. I pray that you don't lose the gifts and power that has been granted to you since walking through this journey. I pray that you will be able to find the light in every dark place. I pray that God will strengthen your confidence in your power and purpose. I pray that you would humble yourself and see His glory in every success that He allows you to obtain. I pray that the strongholds of peer pressure be freed off of you, and that you walk in liberation as a leader and follower of Christ. I pray that you overpower the strongholds of pride. I pray that you always maintain your power according to God's will for your life. I pray that you start feeling you are good enough to be in your position.*
>
> *I pray that you stop living in the consequences from your past decisions and start living in the blessings of today. I pray you thank God that you have overcome those decisions, difficulties, and dysfunctions. I pray that you are lifted and God challenges you every day to become the person He has called you to be. You are stronger than you know. The enemy*

is trying to distract you. I pray right now that you would resist the distractions and walk forward without looking back. May God bless your heart to forgive those who didn't understand you. May God bless and soften your heart so that it remains humble enough to be able to ask for forgiveness to those you have offended. I thank God for the position He has placed you in during this season. And together we humbly say, "Thank You, God, for all You've given us." Amen and amen.

Scan this code for Cora's Chapter 11
PRAYER FOR YOU!

Or Visit

WWW.CORAJAKESCOLEMAN.COM

Faith Affirmation

Humility is key in order to elevate in God. Wherever there is pride there will always be failure. Whenever you get to a place where you can do this faith walk by yourself, you have allowed your direction to become more powerful than God's. When we start trying to lead God, we misplace ourselves. You cannot expect the blessings that come from God when you're always trying to go above His direction. You cannot expect for God to make you a ruler when you aren't willing to serve. You cannot expect for God to lift you up when you never bow down. Your power has been given before your title and position; you must now ask God to position you in humility because of the power He has called you to carry. You can never be too great of a man that you can't be a servant in the Kingdom of God. You must learn to lower yourself in the eyes and instruction of God so that He may see you and choose you because you were still, not because you were jumping. It's never the one waving his hand for the spot that gets picked first.

Faith Points

When you reach your place of purpose, the enemy will try and cause your downfall—perhaps through pride. Hold your head high as a child of God but keep a humble heart.

Stay focused on the blessings, not the bruises from or battles with the enemy. Your purpose has made you productive. Your promise is beautiful and manifesting through your obedience to God.

Control your distractions; don't allow anyone or anything to sway you. Don't lose your power by taking detours from the path God directed you to travel.

Do not lose yourself and who you are by trying to fit in with the world. Let humility be your new identity. A humble person in God's royal family continues to be promoted and receive Kingdom blessings.

Your obedience is truly better than whatever you can sacrifice, because in your obedience God works for you.

When you allow pride to control your power, you are headed for a fall. Don't abuse God's grace when He places you in a position of power. Stay true to the person God has formed within you.

When God is operating through you, He will speak for Himself. Give God the credit, and He will take it from there.

Don't lose yourself in trying to gain the world, and don't then gain the world and lose yourself. Stay solidly faithful.

Faith Activations

On a scale from 1 to 10, what number would you assign to yourself if 1 is humble and 10 is prideful. If you didn't choose 1, what can you do to move that scale toward 1?

What is the difference between pride and arrogance? Is there a difference? Can you name friends, acquaintances, or coworkers who fall into one or both of these categories? Do you fall into one or both?

Have you allowed your success to "go to your head"? Why is that a bad thing? Pray that God will forgive you and ask Him to keep you from falling and that you will remain His humble servant.

Faithing It

CHAPTER

TWELVE

This is a
BIG Deal!

Jesus looked at them and said to them,
"With men this is impossible, but with
God all things are possible."

(MATTHEW 19:26)

We've been on an amazing journey together! You're going to change this world because you are faithing it! You've surrendered, and God is proud to fight for you. God has desired your heart for so long, and at this point your purpose is ready to come forth. You have gone through the pain and the storms. You have embraced the hurt of the process so that you could make it to this moment.

I've been honored to join you in this chapter of your life's book. I've enjoyed walking together with you. I hope that after you read the last page, you walk away changed from the process we have both faced and conquered together. I pray that you are walking in purpose and accepting the changes in your life. You could have stayed where you were, but God has called you to the forefront. The power that

221

you were always searching for is now attainable through Christ Jesus living in you, through you, and for you. Your promise, your dreams, your purpose are all about to manifest because of the power and authority you have decided to tap into. You are now officially a threat to the kingdom of hell!

When you are walking in your purpose, you are a threat to the devil and there will be many trials and tests that you have to accept and walk through. Being a threat and a powerfully positioned person in the Kingdom comes with many obstacles. You have greatness inside of you and with that comes many mountains. But guess what? If you are in relationship with God and accountable to Him, you will achieve your position over your problems. You have gained the faith to overcome it all.

God has called you to the forefront.

You Are a Gift to the Kingdom

At this point, God has given you everything that you need for your journey to purpose. He alone is your keeper and all you need to do is trust Him completely. Keep faithing it! Let's walk together in liberation from this day forward, believing God will fulfill every promise that He has given to us. Stay focused, my friend. Don't lose yourself in the journey. Continue to have a heart to serve God above all and He will have a heart to serve you. Delight yourself in the Lord, and He will give you the desires of your heart.

There is a reward in the fire. God is with you while you stand in the fire. The power is gained in your encounter with God in that fire. Go low and humble yourself so God can use you to your full capacity. Again I remind you to let go of the hurt, let go of the anger, let go of the bitterness, and walk in the freedom and power of the Holy Spirit.

You are a gift to the Kingdom, so carry yourself like the prince or princess that you are. You have the power to command that mountain to move. Speak to it with authority. Speak over your desire, declare what you want, and watch God get it for you. You are empowered to succeed!

There is a reward in the fire.

Walk in Your Authority

We hear all the time about God's ability, but we have the same authority and ability living in us. Let's not forget that God wants us to connect to the Holy Spirit and His power resting in us. You are blessed by God to have the power to manifest your purpose. Walk in it from this day forward. God has promised you the land of milk and honey, so do not look back, and do not get distracted. Walk forward. The storms and floods of life will rage, but God is bigger than every storm. He has given you the power to walk through that storm and move that mountain through your faith. Believe God and you will tap into a realm that would have never been obtainable otherwise.

More importantly, you will reach a place of power that you would have never reached had you not chosen Him.

We have the power to make the blind see, to heal the sick, and raise the dead. We are no longer carrying around the bitterness from the cross we had to carry. We know what it is to believe God over our bitterness so that He has our true self. Glory to God! I am so thankful that we have time to live another day to faith our fights and be consumed by God!

My Last Challenge to You

So here it is. This is bittersweet, but here is the last challenge you will receive in this book: I challenge you to truly believe and receive the power of the Holy Ghost within yourself. I challenge you to overcome your anger from the story and life that you had to live in the past, and believe that God is going to do something better in your future.

You have the power to walk in greatness. All you have to do now is reach up and grab it. You are amazing! There is nothing too hard for God, and with Him living in you there is nothing too hard for you. The bigger your mess, the bigger your message! God has given you something to live through so that you have a testimony.

The Power of Your Testimony

I grew up thinking of my testimony as a test. God brought me through the test of a car accident because of my need for a healing. You may be in a test, but you are healed by the lessons you learn in that test. Don't get angry, now! Allow yourself to experience the test so that you have a story.

When you are faced with a test, start faithing it. Make faithing it a moral core value where you face your day-to-day life by faith. Command joy, peace, and harmony in your day and it will come to pass. We give too much power to the enemy. Now it's time for us to take that power back. Leap forward into your purpose, and allow God to manifest through you.

All this time God wanted your heart and the broken pieces. I am so proud of who you have become, and God is proud of you for choosing Him. Continue to walk in this thing called purpose. You are born to be a winner. Hopefully, by this point in the book, you have gone from a fighter who stands alone to faithing your struggles with God. I hope that you are no longer hiding your weaknesses, but you are boasting in your weaknesses and allowing God to be the strength of your life. Hopefully you are delighting yourself in God and gaining your true heart's desire.

The bigger your mess, the bigger your message!

You Are a Faither!

You are a faither! And you will accomplish great things for God through your faith. I am grateful for the gifts in you because your gifts make room for the next generation to follow and birth their gifts. I am grateful that you've tapped into God's power. Your power will give you the key to greatness, and you will be able to give the generation behind you the key to the power within them. You are not alone, for God is with you. He is standing for you, with you, and in you, and all you have to do is open the door to receive it.

Be able to receive as well as you give, and get in a habit of loving yourself the way God would have you to be loved. You know when you are mistreating yourself and not loving yourself enough. Love you enough so that you can love others, but also allow people to love on you. You are destined for greatness, so be willing to accept yourself as God sees you. If God calls you a ruby, stop acting like a cubic zirconia! If God calls you priceless and made in His image, stop living like you aren't good enough and feeling bad for yourself.

The Father Says to You...

The Father says, "Rise up, My daughter, arise My son, and come forth into the destiny that I have prepared for you. Cast your cares on Me. I am prepared to carry your weight. Do not worry about the weights of the world—I will figure this out, and pave the way for you. Reach for what you desire and it shall be yours.

"Walk in peace, for it is yours. Don't show the enemy your doubts, show him My authority. Trust Me as you have trusted yourself. Lean on Me as you have leaned on yourself. Depend on Me as you have depended on yourself, and I will shift your mindset so that you are able to tap into the true calling and authority that rightfully belongs to you. I am that I am, and I am all that you need."

It's Time to Go!

Go to God. Give that weight to God, give that pain to God. Don't give Him a little. Don't hold back because you think you can handle it better than He can. Give Him everything. You have a friend in Jesus, and He has planted someone in your life to be a friend of wisdom and guidance in the time of need. You are not alone.

God is the producer of purpose. Let Him control things or you are going to be left outside of the building of purpose wishing that you had the guts to go in and take what's yours. And while you are standing outside of this building, people are surpassing you.

God's output will always be better than your input because He is God and God alone. Will you continue to be okay with a mediocre position and blessings? Or will you open your mind to the possibility that there is someone greater and more powerful than you? I urge you to sit down so that God can stand up. I urge you to embrace the blessings of God that have been given to you. I urge you to search for God in every storm and not even concentrate on the rain. I urge you to be a supernatural dreamer so that you can obtain supernatural blessings and dreams from God.

Don't show the enemy your doubts, show him My authority.

God claimed your promise for you before the foundations of this world. He is holding it in His hands, and when you are in your perfect spot He will place it in your hands. Stop panicking, stressing, and predicting the worst because that is not going to happen. Release yourself to the will of God, and allow Him to move in you. When God is moving in you, then you have the authority through Christ Jesus. He is still moving things in order to bless you.

I am writing to tell you that your time is not running out. God is simply positioning you, and what He said will happen, will indeed happen. You are a testimony, and your storm must match where you are going. The bigger your storm, the bigger your ministry. Don't ask God for something big and think you will have little storms. He is positioning you to His perfect will so that you can receive what you asked for.

I've walked the road to purpose. I've walked the road to producing my promise, and I am still walking some of those roads. So let me tell you if you didn't already know—it's not an easy road. After my father told me that I couldn't stop fighting, I heard God tell me, "Nehemiah is coming, just not yet." I wiped my tears away, and I starting faithing with all my might, with everything I had. I became a faither—and I am still a faither.

The bigger your storm, the bigger your ministry.

Your Purpose Is a Big Deal!

Just because the storm comes doesn't mean that the promise is delayed. Your storm is telling you that your purpose is a big deal! Your storm is telling you that your promise is a big deal! It just means God is making your breakthrough bigger.

He is positioning you to His perfect will, and it won't be easy, but you are about to win. What you have been assigned to do in the Kingdom is a *big* deal, and that's why you are going through what you are going through. You will win if you don't faint and if you let God take control.

I am a faither. I may be crying, but I am not broken. I faced my infertility both spiritually and naturally, understanding that if I want to be a producer of great things, I must take responsibility for myself. I need to say, "I'm not producing because I am afraid of what will happen if I let this all go and let God really take over." I am daily looking for God to show me what He sees in me. I am daily faithing every trial, faithing every storm, faithing every struggle. I am faithing, and guess what? You can start faithing too. It's time for you to move forward. The reason why we are faithing is because the seed that God has planted within us is a big deal!

I told you earlier that I wrote this book because I love you, and I do not want you to feel alone or be alone. I mean that. God is for you, so rest in God's ability. You are ready now, and what God has spoken for you to have will come to pass because His Word cannot come back void. The enemy may be after your faith for what God promised, but no more! You have decided to start faithing it. If God is fighting in you and through you, then you cannot lose. You are a faither!

Are you ready to fight with your faith to produce your purpose? I am praying for you and supporting you.

My heart's desire is that you overcome your past and propel into your purpose. God placed us on the earth at this time so that we can become the generation of people who shift the world for God. May

God find us standing strong for Him and preparing the path for Christ's return. My heart's desire is that you are healed and that you walk in that healing and that you soar in spirit because you are faithing it!

The seed that God has planted within us is a big deal!

From this point forward, the enemy will not control your story, your win, or your life. This is *your* time to move forward with the zeal of the Lord and fight with your faith to produce God's purpose in your life.

Go, my friend. *Go.* You have the key. God has granted you access to His purpose—all He is asking is that you trust Him, and He will supersede your expectations. My friend, your purpose awaits, It's time for you to GOOOOOOO!

Please, let's join together in a prayer of agreement this one last time.

> *I pray you have boldness now to speak to your promise to manifest. I pray that the anointing that destroys the yoke is being consumed in you. I pray that the light of God is following you in every dark place. I pray that a hedge of protection is kept around your soul, mind, and heart. May God give you the strength to overcome the struggles of life, so that you begin to embrace yourself, and who you are in God. I pray you begin to see your surroundings, and God helps you to be a leader in every atmosphere He places you in.*

May God help you to birth your purpose like never before. May you be a healthy producer, and may God grant you the ability to do great works in Him. You are destined for greatness! May you begin to walk toward that destination. I pray peace consume the problems in your life, and God replace the struggles of your life with strategy. I pray that you begin to speak life instead of labels over your situations. I pray the glory of the Lord follow and keep you all the days of your life, and that God will begin to put the power in your hands that you need in order to achieve what is needed in the natural and spiritual realm.

I pray that your faith stand for you against the major and minor things of life. I pray you be great in your field, and outside of your field, and that God will grant you supernatural understanding in your mind. I pray that the things that used to be hard for you will now flow easily to you. I pray that God give you the kind of mind that you need to accomplish your purpose and that you will feel an urgency of purpose from the very depths of your soul.

I thank You, God, that Your child is coming forward right now. I thank You that the desires of their heart are being fulfilled. I thank You, God, that this child of Yours is no longer bound by their storms but they are now liberated in them. I thank You, God, for the purpose that You have placed inside of my friend, and I pray, God, that You put fire into his heart, put fire into her heart, so they achieve their dreams with the right mindset and goals.

Lord, I pray You put a thirst for You in our hearts so we don't forget You. I pray, Lord, that You show Your glory in every place that we ask for it. I thank You, God, that You are the Savior of all, and that You are walking with us.

I pray that my friend will have the passion to finish the things that they start, and the power to understand that they are good enough to finish it. I love You, God, and I thank You

231

for considering my friend for great purpose, and I thank You for placing the moral value of faithing into their heart. I thank You, Lord, that You are the power within us. Help us, God, to keep faithing it and to stay humble in that. I thank You, God, that You are great, and within us You will do great things, and manifest it for Your perfect glory. Amen and Amen. So be it.

Faith Affirmation

You could let yourself get swallowed up by the things of your past, or you could make a decision today to understand that it doesn't matter what bad you have gone through. Where God is calling you is bigger than your mistakes and failures. Where God is calling you is stronger than your heaviest burden. Lift up your head and understand that we all have had tears to shed, crushes to go through, and high mountains that we should have climbed instead of moved out of the way. Take your journey. Take it with strength and tenacity, knowing that God has given you power over the very thing that you won't free yourself from. Walk in freedom. Don't let guilt, regret, and mistakes be your driver anymore. Stop looking back and then wondering why you keep turning into a pillar of salt. Stop blaming others for the decisions you have made out of your own hurt, shame, and embarrassment. Take responsibility for your actions, ask God for forgiveness, ask those whom you have sinned against and hurt in your hurt for forgiveness, and move on. Stop beating yourself up over the sadness of rejection from people who don't have and never will have the capacity to forgive you. Stop being mad that hurt people are envying you for being healed. Walk in freedom, knowing that you made both good and bad choices and God still wants you. Don't be driven by your struggles, but let your struggles become your stars; and overcome every one of them so that you can cause someone else to shine. Some people will always try to break you because they see where God is taking you and they don't have the faith to believe God could do for them what He is doing for you. Be blessed, and keep on Faithing It.

Faith Points

You're going to change this world because you are faithing it! Your promise, your dreams, your purpose are all about to manifest because of the power and authority you have tapped into.

When you are walking in your purpose, you are a threat to the devil, but you have gained the faith to overcome it all.

You are a gift to the Kingdom; you have the power to command every mountain to move. You are empowered to succeed! You are blessed by God with the power to manifest your purpose.

Believe God and you will tap into a realm of power not reachable before connecting with the Power Source.

With God living in you, there is nothing too hard for you to overcome.

Your testimony has power to change lives. The bigger your mess, the bigger and more powerful your message!

You are a faither! You will accomplish great things for God through your faith. Search for God in every storm—don't even consider the rain.

God's output will always be better than your input—He is God Almighty. Be a supernatural dreamer so you can receive supernatural blessings and dreams from God.

Faith Activations

How will you put your faithing it into action? Write five ways you are going to move forward with the zeal of the Lord and fight with your faith to produce God's purpose in your life.

Write on a slip of paper or a 3x5 card: "I am daily looking for God to show me what He sees in me. I am daily faithing every trial, faithing every storm, faithing every struggle." Post the paper or card where you can see it daily and allow the admonition to seep into your mind and spirit.

Imagine that God personally asked you to write the last chapter of the book He is working on for you. Write the chapter as you believe He would, as He sees you. Include everything you have faith in Him to provide for you during the years before He calls you to your eternal home.

Daily Quotes of Affirmation

I wanted you to have 30 affirmations from thoughts that have blessed other faithers just like you. Pick one a day to encourage yourself throughout the day, and know that God is confirming Word in you daily.

1. The pathway to your faith is in the Word.
2. Sometimes God removes what has been distracting us to get our attention so that He can elevate us.
3. It's easy to get confused when you are leaning on what you understand.
4. Fear is a reaction from not trusting God.
5. Where there is fear, there is no power.
6. What you are doing right now—how is it benefiting you?
7. Have you prepared a room for your blessing?
8. You can't be friends with someone fighting for your seat.
9. Some of the ones you always thought you would keep God will call you to separate from.
10. You can't ask from your fruit something you are unwilling to produce in yourself.
11. Your forgiveness is a gift that should come with responsibilities.
12. You can't forgive someone you won't pray for.
13. It is easier to forgive than it is to carry the burden of unforgiveness.
14. Forgiveness is a position that you must stand in.

15. Where you can't believe God, you can't see from God.

16. You are standing in the evidence of your faith.

17. Believe Him more, and He will add more.

18. Stop fasting all the time, and just read your Word.

19. God didn't call you because you are great; He called you because He believed you would endure.

20. You can't expect to get anything from God when you are unwilling to serve in His house.

21. What you don't sow into you shouldn't expect bountiful harvest from.

22. Your confusion of God's voice will leave you undependable in the Kingdom.

23. Don't drag people into your struggle to fill your void of loneliness.

24. Don't expect people that haven't been taught how to love to love you with no problem.

25. Require a standard for yourself, and others will be taught how to treat you.

26. Don't require something from someone else that you aren't willing to give to yourself.

27. As long as you run from the enemy you will never have a footstool.

28. Your response isn't warranted for every situation.

29. You can run off the enemy better in silence than you can with screaming.

30. Stop making friends and family your assignments and then getting upset when they don't hold up to the position that you gave them.

It's been my honor to spend this journey with you and to share a bit of my journey and some of my friends' testimonies. You have the key to the door. Now I can't wait to see what faithing looks like on you!

God Bless You!

> Your sister and friend,
>
> Cora Jakes Coleman

WHEN
POWER
MEETS
POTENTIAL

DESTINY IMAGE BOOKS BY T.D. JAKES

40 Days of Power

Can You Stand to be Blessed?

Help Me, I've Fallen and I Can't Get Up!

Naked and Not Ashamed

Power for Living

Release Your Anointing

The Harvest

Water in the Wilderness

Woman, Thou Art Loosed

Why? Because You're Anointed!

WHEN
POWER
MEETS
POTENTIAL

UNLOCKING GOD'S PURPOSE IN YOUR LIFE

T.D. JAKES

DESTINY IMAGE₀ PUBLISHERS, INC.
P.O. Box 310, Shippensburg, PA 17257-0310
"Promoting Inspired Lives."

This book and all other Destiny Image, Revival Press, MercyPlace, Fresh Bread, Destiny Image Fiction, and Treasure House books are available at Christian bookstores and distributors worldwide.

For a U.S. bookstore nearest you, call 1-800-722-6774.

For more information on foreign distributors, call 717-532-3040.

Reach us on the Internet: www.destinyimage.com.

ISBN 13 TP: 978-0-7684-0431-9
ISBN 13 Ebook: 978-0-7684-0432-6

For Worldwide Distribution, Printed in the U.S.A.

1 2 3 4 5 6 7 8 / 18 17 16 15 14

CONTENTS

INTRODUCTION

I am absolutely convinced that God is extending an unparalleled invitation to every believer at this unique moment in history. It's an invitation to step into your identity, embrace your destiny, and fulfill your purpose. For too long we've settled for too little. I've written this book to excite your mind and expose you to some radical new normals. The old normal isn't working if you currently define your life as purposeless and powerless. It is downright illegal for you, a child of God, to live this way when so much has been provided, and so much remains still untapped and available.

Make no mistake, new realms of power and anointing are not reserved for the super-spiritual or superlative saints—promotion is for everyone. God's eyes are not roaming throughout the earth, zeroing in exclusively on pastors, preachers, and evangelists. The Scriptures give us a different story.

> *For the eyes of the Lord range throughout the earth to strengthen those whose hearts are fully committed to him...* (2 Chronicles 16:9 NIV).

Consider this verse for just a moment. There is no mention of profession or placement; *only* posture of the heart. The Lord's eyes are searching for hearts fully committed to Him and His cause on the earth. These are the hearts that will fulfill purpose. When they are invited into a new level, people with hearts like this have what it takes to sustain that dimension of glory. These are the people who catch the gaze of God.

Will you catch His gaze? In this verse we also see a promise of power to those hearts that are fully committed to Him. Understanding this is vital. Your wholehearted devotion and commitment to God is what actually positions you for the divine moments that call forth your potential, strengthening and empowering you to fulfill your divine purpose.

I pray the following pages would remind you of the journey you began the moment you were born. In fact, your purpose preceded your coming into the world. Just as God called Jeremiah in the womb, He has called you in the same way.

> *Before I formed you in the womb I knew you; before you were born I sanctified you; I ordained you a prophet to the nations* (Jeremiah 1:5).

Your journey began before birth. And now it's time for you to embrace it every day of your life. Apostle Paul gives us a glimpse of what this journey looks like, as he describes God's only desired travel plan for you—*from glory to glory* (see 2 Cor. 3:18). It's time for you to step into these new dimensions of glory, anointing, and power. It's time for you to recognize moments of divine visitation and run toward the supernatural promotion that's being presented your way. It's time for your potential to collide with God's power and release your purpose. That's what the world is waiting for—a people who actually step into their ordained assignment and fulfill their divine purpose.

You have untapped realms of ability, giftedness, and potential that are just waiting for one moment, one collision, one touch of God's power.

You have untapped realms of ability, giftedness, and potential that are just waiting for one moment, one collision, one touch of God's power. Too many people are running around searching for purpose, when in fact purpose is wrapped up in their potential. When your potential is realized and released, your purpose can be fulfilled. I want to help position you for these moments that change everything.

This book is for anyone who is hungry to experience a shift. A change. A transition. Elevation. Promotion. What you've always known and how you've always done life is changing. There's a meeting scheduled. Power is on its way. Elijah's getting ready to throw a mantle on you. You won't be able to keep plowing the field after you've collided with a prophet. Your moment is at hand, and this moment changes everything.

While reading the pages ahead, ask the Spirit of God to lead and guide you. Invite Him to give you clarity. Elijah and Elisha are examples. Most likely, you're not a plower being called to be a prophet. We're simply mining the multi-dimensional principles that are observable in this story. This is not your handbook on how to be a doctor on a new level, or how to be a plumper at a new level, or how to be a school teacher on a new level, or how to be a lawyer on a new level. I can't share out of what I don't have. You have a specific calling and purpose. I'm giving you basic principles that will prepare you to release your unique potential.

When you step into the new level, get the training. Pursue the instruction and teaching. Go after everything that will help you develop that potential. I'm here to coach you, equip you, prepare you, and arm you. I want to arm you, spiritually, to say "Yes" when power passes by. I want to sharpen your spiritual sight to recognize what is going on behind the *seen* and respond correctly on your day of visitation.

This book is all about the meeting of power and potential. I'll give you some glimpses of what this new level of living looks like, but my main goal is to help you work through the transition. When power comes, I want you to be ready. I want you to recognize your moment. Yes, there will be natural circumstances that set it up. But even more deeply and profoundly, I want to help tune you in to the spiritual dimensions of transition. You need to recognize what looks right, smells right, sounds right, and ultimately is your moment.

Above all, you must be ready to receive and run after the very touch that releases your potential: *God's power.*

PART I

KNOW YOUR PURPOSE

*...Then Elijah passed by him and threw
his mantle on him* (1 Kings 19:19).

CHAPTER 1

YOU ARE ON PURPOSE

For You formed my inward parts; You covered me in my mother's womb. I will praise You, for I am fearfully and wonderfully made; marvelous are Your works, and that my soul knows very well. My frame was not hidden from You, when I was made in secret, and skillfully wrought in the lowest parts of the earth. Your eyes saw my substance, being yet unformed. And in Your book they all were written, the days fashioned for me, when as yet there were none of them (Psalm 139:13-16).

For we are God's masterpiece. He has created us anew in Christ Jesus, so we can do the good things he planned for us long ago (Ephesians 2:10 NLT).

"For I know the plans I have for you," says the Lord. "They are plans for good and not for disaster, to give you a future and a hope" (Jeremiah 29:11 ESV).

YOU HAVE A PURPOSE

Your hands have formed me and made me... (Job 10:8).

You have a purpose.

You were created *on purpose*.

You were formed, fashioned, and knit together by a skilled Craftsman, not some arbitrary cosmic explosion.

You are not an accident.

You are not an incident.

You are not a mistake.

You are not just a glob of protoplasmic material that is the result of a reckless night or a weekend between two passionate lovers.

You are not just a mere mixing together of DNA.

You have a divine purpose. You were allowed access into this dimension of life by the nod of the Creator Himself, that you would be strategically placed at this time, at this age, in your gender, in your ethnicity, with your gifting, and with your talent for God's divine purpose.

Even the wealthiest person on the planet could not offer up any suitable form of tender that could purchase *purpose*. Surely they wish purpose could have a dollar value assigned to it, because then the relentless nagging of their souls could be silenced. They could rest easy knowing that the one unknown of life has been secured. Purpose is priceless, while purposelessness is very costly.

You can live in this world and make all the money you could ever dream of and be as beautiful as you want and be as educated as you please and accomplish whatever you want to, but if you die without accomplishing your purpose, you are a failure, a reject and a fool.

THE ROOT OF PURPOSELESSNESS

The fool has said in his heart, "There is no God" (Psalm 14:1).

The fool has said, "There is no God, there is no purpose, there is no meaning." He further adds, "I can do my own thing, go my own way, live my own life."

The fool who says in his heart, "There is no God" has essentially said, "There is no purpose." To divorce one's perspective from the reality of a Creator, a Master Designer, and a Purpose-Author, one is rejecting purpose and meaning as a whole. This is no small statement because it is no small action. The repercussions of saying, *"There is no God"* are far-reaching into every arena of our lives and society. It is downright deadly to reject the reality of a Creator, for it is that very Creator who assigns value and purpose to the created. If the created is without a Creator, then who or what assigns value or purpose to the created? There are no constants. There's nothing certain. We are without anchors. No one knows who they are, because they are detached from the truth of *Whose* they are.

> *The value of your Creator should cause you to reconsider your own worth and value.*

When Genesis 1 becomes a fairy tale and we are disconnected from the fact that we were created in the *"image and likeness of God,"* (see Gen. 1:26) that we were in fact hand-crafted in the image of the perfect Craftsman, purpose*less*ness abounds. Now, more than ever, we need this vision of the Creator and created; for as the Scripture says, *"Where there is no vision, the people perish"* (Prov. 29:18 KJV).

The world perishes because of the purposelessness of its people; people perish because they live without vision. I want to invite you to consider the vision of your Creator. As mentioned earlier, you are not some type of cosmic accident. You were hand-crafted and custom-made by a perfect Creator. The value of your Creator should cause you to reconsider your own worth and value. God did not make you in the image of an animal. He did not create you in the image of an angel. Rather, He created you in His very own image and His likeness. Time after time, Scripture invites us to consider the unlikeness of God.

> *Who is like You, O Lord, among the gods?...* (Exodus 15:11).

> *Lord God of Israel, there is no God in heaven or on earth like You...* (2 Chronicles 6:14).

> *Who is like the Lord our God, who dwells on high* (Psalm 113:5).

Because God radically stands out and above everything and everyone else in created order, consider the precious value that someone created in *His* image and likeness carries. *This someone is you.*

GOD CREATED YOU UNIQUELY

> *Then God said, "Let Us make man in Our image, according to Our likeness..."* (Genesis 1:26).

Once you realize that you were created on purpose, and created in the image of the Creator, you begin to recognize that there are secrets stored up inside you. These are the very secrets that must be discovered and unleashed to a purposeless planet and a purposeless people.

There are secrets inside you that God has planted, secret talents and secret gifts and secret wisdoms that have been divinely orchestrated. These gifts, these talents, these abilities, these wisdoms, these solutions, these creativities—these are uniquely *yours*. God the Creator is multi-dimensional enough to create you uniquely. Trust His design. The moment you start to embrace how you have been formed and fashioned is the moment you step into the very purpose you were created for. God is not the author of prolonged purposelessness; you are. One of the most prevalent enemies to you stepping into your purpose is the downright deception that "the grass is greener." In other words, something in someone else causes you to reject, and ultimately neglect the unique purpose within you. This keeps you exactly where the enemy wants you, and sadly, where the world cannot afford to keep you. You cannot make a difference sitting off in a dark corner somewhere, wishing that you were someone else.

Stop, stop, stop wanting to be somebody else. Do not insult your Creator by insulting His creation. You were fearfully and wonderfully made. Can you even fathom what the psalmist is expressing by using those words—*fearfully and wonderfully?* (See Psalm 139:14.) You were created with awe. God didn't just throw you together, stand back and say, "This looks good." Because God fashioned you in His very image and likeness, He has a right to stand back and actually awe His own creation. Why? It's simply God standing in awe of His own handiwork; God awe-ing God. This is how He looks upon *you*.

In fact, God considers you a "masterpiece" (see Eph. 2:10 NLT). God made you the way He wanted to make you so He could use you at a particular time in a particular way; and if you start trying to be like somebody else, you're going to miss *your purpose.*

People don't miss their purpose and bypass destiny because God decides to take it away; they miss purpose because they fail to invest in *their* purpose. One of the greatest ways we fail to invest in what God has wired into our DNA is through rejecting who we have been uniquely created to be and what we have been created to bring to this moment in history.

YOU HAVE WHAT IT TAKES

His divine power has given to us all things that pertain to life and godliness... (2 Peter 1:3).

You have everything you need to do what you've been designed to do and be who you were created to be. I repeat, you have everything you need to accomplish your purpose. If God needed you to be tall, He would have made you tall. If He needed you to be better looking, He would have made you better looking. If He needed you to have a voice to sing, He would have given you a voice to sing. Everything about you was designed with intentionality. In fact, your design is directly connected to your purpose. If you neglect your design and refuse to celebrate *how* you were made, you will never step into *who* you were made to be. We have no right to question the Potter about how He fashioned and molded the clay.

In Romans 9:20 (NIV), Paul directly confronts this issue of questioning the Maker about how the creation was made. He writes,

*But who are you, a human being, to talk back to God?
"Shall what is formed say to the one who formed it,
'Why did you make me like this?'"*

God knew what He was doing when He created you like He did. He gave you the right IQ and He gave you the right personality. He gave you the right temperament. Do not despise your design, for the Designer made you a certain way so that you could accomplish a certain purpose. Like I said, the more you disregard your design and continue to want to be like someone else, the more you distance yourself from stepping into your created purpose. You, *as you are,* have got what it takes to *be* who God has created you to be. Yes, get educated. Yes, get equipped and trained. Yes, pursue knowledge, learning, and wisdom. Scripture tells us to pursue these things, as anybody can have as much of these things as he or she so desires. Just don't despise who God has created *you* to be.

> *The Designer made you a certain way so that
> you could accomplish a certain purpose.*

Start believing this. You won't need as much counseling. You won't need as much therapy. You won't be as intimidated by other people. You won't be jealous of other people. If you understand your purpose, you will live in that purpose and you will discover your gifts and your talents and what you were put here to do.

Dealing with the Lie

Lead me by your truth and teach me, for you are the God who saves me. All day long I put my hope in you (Psalm 25:5 NLT).

And finally, whatever you've been through and whatever weaknesses you have, and whatever issues you've had—do not allow those weaknesses to abort your mission. Everyone's failed. Everyone messes up. Everyone's slipped, fallen, gotten up, fallen again, gotten up again, maybe wandered around in the dark for a season, moved on, etc. The devil is a liar, and he would love to deceive you right out of your destiny. One of the main tools he uses is reminding you of issues, hang-ups, setbacks, and sins. Your comeback should trump his lies *every* time. Your past is under the blood of Jesus. Your sins were dealt with at Calvary. God's not surprised by your weaknesses; this is why He promises strength! God's not caught off guard by your setbacks and problems.

> *It's never too late to get back on the path to purpose.*

Remember, it's not your weaknesses and failures that have the potential to abort your mission, it's how you see and respond to them. If you believe your weaknesses can abort your purpose, you will live in agreement with that lie. Nothing—absolutely nothing—can separate you from God's purpose for your life *unless* you start agreeing with lies. It's this type of agreement that causes you to veer off the path God has set for you. If you've been believing these lies, I encourage you to start disagreeing with the liar *today*. It's never too late to get back on the path to purpose.

I repeat—you have a divine mission to accomplish. You cannot allow *anything* to come between you and your purpose. In the pages ahead, we are going to look at the unique exchange that took place between Elijah and Elisha. As Elijah's time on earth was concluding, it was Elisha's turn to step up. If you need an example of someone who refused to let anything come between him and his purpose, this plowman-turned-prophet is your model. In fact, he is your mandate. I'm calling for a company of Elishas to rise up in this hour, recognize their moment of visitation, and start running toward the divine purpose God has ready to unleash to the world through their lives.

REFLECTIONS

1. In what ways is your design (how you were made) directly connected to fulfilling your purpose in life?

2. Why is it an insult to the Creator to question the way He made you?

3. How can your weaknesses and failures keep you from fulfilling your purpose?

CHAPTER 2

GET READY FOR YOUR MOMENT

So he departed from there, and found Elisha the son of Shaphat, who was plowing with twelve yoke of oxen before him... (1 Kings 19:19).

PREPARE FOR YOUR DESTINY-DEFINING MOMENT

Watch, stand fast in the faith, be brave, be strong (1 Corinthians 16:13).

Now we set out upon the journey to unlocking purpose. The first key to unlocking your purpose is preparing for destiny-defining moments. Be watchful, steadfast, and alert! It's in these moments when power meets potential, the power of God connects with the potential within you, and you are supernaturally catapulted into the pre-destined, preordained purpose that God has assigned to your life.

Throughout this book, we will be looking at the account of Elijah and Elisha and how their relationship is an example of what happens when power meets potential. For Elisha, it began with a *moment*. For you, it will be the same way. To step into our divine purpose, we need to recognize and steward our divine moments.

In this chapter, I want us to look at how Elisha responded to his moment of visitation. This gives us a powerful picture of how to respond when your moment walks up to you.

It begins in First Kings 19:19:

> *So he departed from there, and found Elisha the son of Shaphat, who was plowing with twelve yoke of oxen before him, and he was with the twelfth. Then Elijah passed by him and threw his mantle on him.*

Based on the text in First Kings 19, I want to share some vital keys to recognizing and stewarding your destiny-defining moments.

DESTINY-DEFINING MOMENTS HAPPEN QUICKLY

Then Elijah passed by him and threw his mantle on him (1 Kings 19:19b).

First of all, notice how quickly Elisha's moment happened. While Elisha was plowing, Elijah the prophet passed by, and *threw his mantle on him*. There was no ceremony or service. They did not sit down over a business lunch and discuss the logistics of what the mantle transference process would look and function like. There was no red tape. There were no emails. There were no phone conferences, Skype conversations, or cross-country travel reservations. Elisha was plowing, and Elijah—representative of Elisha's divine moment—*passed by him* and tossed the mantle upon him.

I know this example will probably mess up some people's thoughts. That's good. I want to mess you up, because it's in the process of messing you up when the Holy Spirit renews your mind. He's cleaning up your thinking and enabling you to accommodate His supernatural ways and workings. You see, I want to mess up your expectations of how you've got it planned out. So many of us are in bondage to preconceived ideas of how we assume God should launch us into our purpose and destiny. If your mind can comfortably wrap itself around a scenario, most likely, the Holy Spirit is going to uncomfortably remove the wrapping and invite you into an elevated perspective.

The main problem with our planning is that it discounts the power of moments—*quick moments*. Planning usually involves the image of a process. We consider the ideal process of how some certain result should come to pass. I say it again, God wants to radically mess up your process. This doesn't mean you stop thinking, cease dreaming, and quit planning. There is a difference between having a plan and being in bondage to your plan. Have a plan. Have a dream. Have goals. Have expectations. Have processes. Have a picture. Have an image. Have these things, but don't become yoked to them. Don't dare exalt your plan over the power of a God-ordained, destiny-defining moment. One divine moment orchestrated by the Master can shift things that have taken you a lifetime to try and change.

One divine moment orchestrated by the Master can shift things that have taken you a lifetime to try and change.

Going back to First Kings 19:19, it appears that Elisha's moment could have taken place in the blink of an eye. One moment he was plowing with twelve yoke of oxen; the next, he receives an invitation in the form of a mantle that would radically shift his destiny. The same is true for you. Your day of visitation is at hand. Your moment is waiting for you to be ready. Don't start getting paranoid, trying to figure out what your moment should look like. Elisha had no clue that his moment would look like some prophet throwing a mantle on him. In fact, it seems like Elisha recognized his moment, "after the fact." It was only after the mantle had fallen upon him and Elijah passed by that Elisha turned and ran after the prophet. Even if he was a minute behind his moment, he nevertheless recognized the power of his moment and responded appropriately.

Your key to being ready to run when your moment of visitation comes is simple. More than focusing on a moment, keep your eyes fixed on the Master. When the mantle hits, it is the still small voice of the Holy Spirit that will say, "This is your moment, son. This is your time, daughter. *Run after that prophet.*" We need to always be in a state of readiness and expectation, as we never know when those moments will happen when God's power collides with our potential.

DESTINY-DEFINING MOMENTS TAKE PLACE IN THE ORDINARY AND EVERYDAY

So he departed from there, and found Elisha the son of Shaphat, who was plowing with twelve yoke of oxen before him, and he was with the twelfth (1 Kings 19:19a).

Second, it is important to understand that destiny-defining moments take place in ordinary, everyday circumstances. In order to be trusted with a destiny-defining moment, we need to be good stewards of the unique moment we have been given *right now*.

Consider Elisha. He was simply being a good steward of where he was at his unique moment in history. He used his moments well, thus enabling him to be trusted with *the* moment. How we spend the sum of our everyday moments determines how we will respond to those life-altering, destiny-defining moments that come. I want to unpack this more, as I believe the secret to increase in the Kingdom has everything to do with stewarding what you have. How you handle the everyday shows God how you can be trusted with the extraordinary. Jesus notes this in His parable of the talents. The steward who was faithful receives this verbal recognition from his lord, *"Well done, good and faithful servant; you have been faithful over a few things, I will make you ruler over many things"* (Matt. 25:23). The "few things" for Elisha were his plowing. What are these "few things" for you?

> *How you handle the everyday shows God how you can be trusted with the extraordinary.*

When Elijah approached Elisha, the setting was nothing above average. There weren't heavenly beams and angelic choirs singing. Scripture tells us that Elisha was participating in something very common at the time. He was diligently plowing with the twelve yoke of oxen that were *before him*—the thing that was under his charge. He was faithful with what was before him, and this faithfulness positioned him to be in the right place at the right time when his moment came.

Too many of us want to chase after a destiny-defining moment; and as a result, we spend our entire lives running after something that should be running alongside us, ready to collide with our path. *Destiny-defining moments are like magnets to people who use their everyday moments well.* Do not despise where you are. Do not look negatively upon small beginnings. You are where you are for a reason, just like Elisha was exactly where he was for a reason—for that moment.

Also, too many desire a moment without recognizing that it is the sum of everyday moments that prepares a person to receive and run after their *moment*. Again, this should bring peace to our minds, which tend to fret over how and when our moment will come. This might sound backward, but the truth is those who become obsessed with seeking out *their moment* are actually ill-prepared for it and have the propensity to miss it when it presents itself. Why? God is looking for good stewards to trust with His greater works. He is looking for those who appropriately steward the lives they have been given before He promotes them into greater levels of glory, anointing, and power.

Many people seek after promotion from the usual, when in fact, God withholds the very thing they seek. He does not do this out of denial, but rather out of protection. Listen, God will protect you *from* your own promotion if that promotion has the potential to destroy you. If you're not ready for it. It's no mystery. Those who are faithful with the moments they have been given are positioning themselves for greater promotion; while those striving after promotion, but are neglecting the moments right in front of them, are being spared from a tragic downfall.

Keep in mind, it's everyday moments that prepare everyday people for extraordinary exploits. Character is developed in the moments. Integrity is cultivated in the moments. The fruit of the Spirit mature in the moments. Christlikeness, godliness, and holiness are birthed in the moments. God is examining your moments, for they gauge your preparedness for *the moment*.

DESTINY-DEFINING MOMENTS DEMAND A RAPID RESPONSE

And he left the oxen and ran after Elijah... (1 Kings 19:20).

The first thing we looked at was the swiftness of a moment's arrival. Scripture reminds us that *"Elijah passed by him* [Elisha] *and threw his mantle on him"* (1 Kings 19:19b). A quick moment demands an equally rapid response.

Before I continue, I want you to know that this is not some call to run after everything and make hasty decisions. There is balance. Elisha, no doubt, recognized that his moment was God-birthed and God-ordained. Before changing your life, switching jobs, moving across the country, marrying that guy, dating that girl, or doing something radical, the most important rapid, radical responses must always be to the One who authors your moment.

Let your heart be like Abraham's in Genesis 22, where he is brought into a destiny-defining moment. God instructs Abraham to sacrifice his son, Isaac, giving him up as a burnt offering before the Lord. Pay careful attention to how the scenario plays out. Before Abraham took his son up the mountain, prepared the altar, and yes, even raised the knife over the boy—only to be supernaturally stopped by the Angel of the Lord—Abraham offered a rapid response to God by saying "Yes" to His divine instruction. God set up the moment, and *"Abraham rose early in the morning and saddled his donkey, and took two of his young men with him, and Isaac his son; and he split the wood for the burnt offering, and arose and went to the place of which God had told him"* (Gen. 22:3).

> *Our rapid response always belongs to God first.*

Our rapid response always belongs to God first. He will reveal the specifics. He will provide direction. His Spirit will lead us and guide us. In order to position ourselves for divine guidance, we must offer a rapid, definitive "Yes" to what God is asking of us. Abraham did not wait around, giving himself time to talk himself out of the difficult thing God was asking him to do. God gave Abraham instruction, and we notice that *"Abraham rose early in the morning"* to begin this journey. He didn't wait around, pacing the floor, giving himself the opportunity to consider some other, user-friendly options. First thing in the morning, Abraham got up and began walking toward a moment that would not only define his life, but a prophetic moment that would set humanity up for *the moment* that would change everything. That moment would be the Cross of Calvary.

How did Elisha respond to his destiny-defining moment? *"And he left the oxen and ran after Elijah"* (1 Kings 19:20).

Moments happen *that* fast. In future chapters, I want us to look at *why* these moments are so powerful and how they unlock the potential inside of you. For now, we know that any God-orchestrated moment is worthy of our rapid response. Our "Yes" to God prepares us to say "Yes" to every decision we need to make in order to embrace the moment that is being presented to us. Likewise, our "Yes" to God emboldens us to say "No" to everything that would try to restrain us from promotion. Previously, we considered people who were ill-prepared for promotion. Just as bad as those who receive promotion who are not prepared for it, are those who *are ready* for promotion, but don't recognize its life-changing invitation that demands their obedient response. Run after it like Elisha did.

When your moment arrives, all bets are off. Running after a moment cannot produce that divine moment in your life. However, responding to a moment, *when the moment presents itself,* will bring your life into alignment with the power of that moment, and ultimately, God's glorious purpose for your life.

REFLECTIONS

1. What do you think a destiny-defining moment looks like? What did it look like for Elisha?

2. What are the three characteristics of destiny-defining moments—and how should you respond to them?

3. What is the difference between running after a moment and responding to a moment?

CHAPTER 3

EXPERIENCE THE GOD OF PURPOSE

There he went into a cave and spent the night in that place; and behold, the word of the Lord came to him, and He said to him, "What are you doing here, Elijah?" (1 Kings 19:9)

And we know that all things work together for good to those who love God, to those who are the called according to His purpose (Romans 8:28).

For in him we live and move and have our being... (Acts 17:28 NIV).

KNOW THE GOD OF PURPOSE

In him we were also chosen, having been predestined according to the plan of him who works out everything in conformity with the purpose of his will (Ephesians 1:11 NIV).

It is by God's divine purpose that power and potential intersect and meet. It is a mystery that I think is worth discussing. First things first. You need to know that the God you serve is a strategic God. He is the God of absolute purpose. He is the God who has a strategy, and according to Ephesians 1:11 (KJV), He *"worketh all things after the counsel of his own will."*

The God you serve is a strategic God—
the God of absolute purpose.

Nothing "just happened." Creation was not arbitrary. There are no cosmic blunders or mishaps. The God who created you is the same God who brought order to chaos, form to the formless, and purpose to nothingness. You may feel like that. You might feel like your life is formless, your future looks void of hope, and you have no purpose. Remind yourself, you were created by a God of Purpose. Nothing He made was created by accident—it was all sculpted with great skill and precision.

It was according to God's preordained purpose and divine design that He brought you into the world—and ultimately saved your soul. It was not your distress signal that brought God into your life. It was God who brought the distress signal that made you cry out after Him. Think about it. God is not just responding to your cry. He actually put the cry deep down inside you. He has put *eternity in your heart* (see Eccl. 3:11). He designed you in such a way that only He could satisfy the deep void inside your heart (see Ps. 42:7). In fact, the deep that *calls unto deep* was placed inside you by God Himself. He made it possible for you to even have a deep that could cry out to the deep of Himself.

God is not responding to you seeking Him. He put the seek down in you. This didn't just happen. You didn't just happen. God has a unique purpose and an essential role for you to play, and He's working everything, good or bad, in your life after the counsel of His own will. This should bring us great relief and freedom. Before we spend additional time studying how *our* potential is released and how we fulfill *our* purpose, it is foundational that we become acquainted with the God of Purpose. If we are confident in His nature as the One who is strategic and purposeful in all that He does, it will become much easier for us to trust that everything is in His most capable hands.

TRUST THE GOD OF PURPOSE

For the word of the Lord holds true, and we can trust everything he does (Psalm 33:4 NLT).

In view of this reality about God's purposeful character, we really ought to just stop the murmuring and complaining and sit back and let Him drive. Trust Him! His Word holds true, and everything He says, and everything He does can be trusted. He knows what He's doing. He will bring into your life who He wants to bring into your life. Conversely, He will bring out of your life who He wants to bring out of your life. He has a purpose and a strategy that defies human comprehension; and though many people don't understand why you are in the position or the role or the place you are in life, haters cannot stop your destiny. Their words, their slander, their accusations, their antagonisms, their doubts, their mockeries, their jokes—nothing any human being can say or do can restrain God's purpose from coming to pass in your life.

> *Nothing any human being can say or do can restrain*
> *God's purpose from coming to pass in your life.*

Consider the timeless accounts in Scripture of men and women persevering through their odds and experiencing their destinies. Mockers could not keep Noah from building an ark and saving the world. Egyptian armies could not keep Israel from leaving bondage and crossing the Red Sea. Insults could not keep Hannah from believing for her son. An insult-hurling giant could not keep David from securing a supernatural victory over the Philistine army. Persecution could not keep the Gospel of Jesus Christ from spreading throughout the known world. The seed of each monumental victory was everyday people trusting the God of Purpose in spite of what everything and everyone else was saying or doing.

Your job? Continue to agree with the God of Purpose. Remember, the enemy wants you to bow down to his lies. These lies come in the different forms we just looked at. He uses words. He uses memories. He uses something a parent said, something a teacher said, something a peer or student or co-worker said to try and deceive you right out of your destiny. Trust the God of Purpose, for the same God who is full of purpose is also full of power. He is also entirely sovereign. This means that He will make sure that your purpose is fulfilled, regardless what people say, regardless what problems come, and regardless how certain seasons of life treat you. Keep trusting the God of Purpose. The One who brings you *through* will also bring you *to.*

THE ENEMY OF YOUR PURPOSE

The thief comes only to steal and kill and destroy... (John 10:10 NIV).

Keep in mind, your purpose has an adversary (see 1 Pet. 5:8). This adversary, the devil, recruits a number of different methods of antagonism. These are the assignments aimed directly at your purpose. All of the mean things people have said, all of the mean things that they do, and all of the things that they set out against you are weapons of the adversary, targeted at your purpose. Stand on the truth that *"No weapon that is formed against thee shall prosper"* (Isa. 54:17 KJV). No weapon that the enemy aims at your purpose can dismantle it or defuse it. Why? Because God is going to see your purpose through unto completion. The One who *"began a good work in you will carry it on to completion until the day of Christ Jesus"* (Phil. 1:6 NIV). God's purpose for your life *will* come to pass.

> *No weapon that the enemy aims at your purpose can dismantle it or defuse it.*

Remember, satan is merely trying to steer you off course. He can't destroy your purpose. He also knows that you can't just lose your purpose, like someone loses a sock in the dryer or car keys in the sofa. He knows that his only formidable weapon against your purpose is securing your allegiance with his deception. When you start believing his lies over the truth of the God of Purpose, the devil beings to unleash his assault against your purpose. Again, it's not his tactics, tools, or terrorism that have any prevailing power against your purpose. What positions us for defeat is actually believing the enemy is more of a threat than he really is.

One of his main targets is your identity. He challenges your worthiness to fulfill God's purpose by using people to attack you. All of the lies, and the spirit behind the lies that are sent out against you, these are the enemy's attempts to distract you from purpose. The more you contemplate the negative things people are speaking against you, the less time you have to consider the greatness of the God of Purpose. He will surely bring His plans to fruition in your life and complete the good work He began. Your adversary knows that by getting people to spread lies and rumors and falsehoods about you, he is able to get you in that corner of distraction. It's like you are in the corner of a room, staring at a wall that is papered in lies. The lies try to consume your view, while God's truth is waiting just behind you, beckoning your re-focus.

If the enemy cannot distract you with lies, he will even try to use truth against you. He's desperate to distract you right out of stepping into your purpose by keeping your eyes off the God of Purpose. If you successfully stand your ground during his barrage of lies, the serpent will attempt another strategy. You see, the devil is an expert at digging up the dirt of your past and doing whatever he can to get you to stare at it—apart from the blood of Jesus. The Bible identifies satan as the *"accuser of our brethren"* (Rev. 12:10). You are his target, not God. He cannot accuse you before God because of the *"better things"* that Jesus' blood speaks (Heb. 12:24), but he knows that he can try to deceive believers right out of their status in Christ.

My goal here is not to make us overly conscious of the devil. Yet to defeat him and overcome his schemes, we must be aware of his tactics. Paul makes this clear, indicating that if we are ignorant of the enemy's devices, we can easily fall prey to his schemes (see 2 Cor. 2:11).

One of the enemy's greatest lies concerning your purpose is that *you are unworthy to step into so great of a purpose.* We just discussed the fact that he delights in trying to veer you off course by reminding you of your past, your sins, your setbacks, your failures, your issues, your obstacles, your bondages, your addictions, etc. Here's the truth—the God of Purpose will walk with you through each of these. He brings hope, healing, forgiveness, cleansing, deliverance, freedom—every solution to every obstacle. Listen to me, it's not the obstacle or the failure that keeps us from pursuing purpose, it's what we believe about the *power* of the obstacles that keep us in limbo. This is where the enemy works overtime, trying to convince us that our stuff has the ability to keep us from stepping into divine purpose. This is a flat out lie. Sin, hell, and death itself could not prevent Almighty God from reaching down into your mess, invading your life, cleansing you with Jesus' blood, filling you with the Holy Spirit, and setting you on a course for victory.

Just think about it, if the very power of death could not keep you from stepping into God's divine plan and design for your life, what could possibly hold you back? God has dealt with every possible barrier. However, there is one you will deal with throughout your life and you must learn to confront it appropriately should you desire to walk into your destiny. This is the boundary of belief.

What do you believe about your purpose and your potential to fulfill it? Don't let the devil distract you with his lies and deception.

THE GOD OF PURPOSE USES YOU IN SPITE OF YOURSELF

And He said to me, "My grace is sufficient for you, for My strength is made perfect in weakness." Therefore most gladly I will rather boast in my infirmities, that the power of Christ may rest upon me (2 Corinthians 12:9).

We need to stop focusing on ourselves so much. God does not use us because of us; He uses us *in spite of us*. Paul the apostle recognized this on several dimensions. He had weaknesses that should have disqualified him from ministry. These were not restrictive, though. God used Paul in spite of his weakness, and He will use you in the same way. Remember, it is not because of you that God chose you; it is because of His divine purpose. Just think about it for a moment. Why in the world would God choose David to be a king? He had no background of a king, he was not trained as a king, he didn't live in the palace, was not reared up in an environment of kingly order. He was a shepherd boy. He was a goat chaser; and yet God said, *"I have found...a man after My own heart"* (see Acts 13:22).

Did that mean that David was perfect, or even close to being perfect? Absolutely not. And it doesn't just mean that David was a God-seeker, though he definitely fit that mold. Truly, God looked upon young David and declared, *I have found the man that is after My heart, that is after My purpose, that fits the spot of My purpose and destiny. I have found him. He's out there in the wilderness. He fits right into the strategic purpose of what I have orchestrated and I will use him in spite of himself.*

> *It is not because of you that God chose you;*
> *it is because of His divine purpose*

Now you can sit there, read these words, and act like you don't understand that, but if you have walked with God at all, you have come to discover that God uses you in spite of you—not because of you! In fact, the conditions that seem to make you the least likely candidate for a God-sized destiny are the very factors that maintain your humility.

The devil is trying to use our own weapons against us. We need to know that our past is not a weapon against us, but an anchor—a pillar. Our past, our surroundings, and our upbringing reminds us where we came from, that God stepped in and chose us in spite of ourselves.

Once when I was being interviewed, the reporter noted that I exhibited a humility that did not match my circumstances, and then proceeded to ask me, "How do you stay humble, Bishop Jakes?" Here's my answer. I said, "Because I know me. I have no choice but to be humble. It is by God's grace that I stand where I stand. He uses me in spite of me. There are things that pulled me out of my comfort zone, that pulled me out of my insecurities and out of my inhibitions. *He* pulled me. I had no choice but to come. I didn't come because I was wonderful or better or perfect or superior or anything else. I came because He drew me by His right hand. He stretched forth His hand and said, *'I call you unto Myself, and I'm going to use you right there.'"* And the same is true for you!

YOUR PIECE IN THE PUZZLE

Though the Lord is great, he cares for the humble...
(Psalm 138:6 NLT).

You will never find your place until you find your purpose and you understand how we all fit together in the grand scheme of things. Remember, God is the One who assigns your greater significance. You may not see it. You may not comprehend it. It might not compute with your natural mind, but you have to trust the God of Purpose. He has a master plan to assemble the pieces together in such a way that from His divine vantage point everything fits together, everything makes sense, and there is a perfect image of all the parts working together as a whole. I repeat, in order to embrace the greater significance, you must trust the God of Purpose and not attempt try to do His work for Him. He is the only One capable of putting this great jigsaw puzzle of purpose together. In order to fit in, you need to humble yourself before His purpose.

Think of it this way. Everything fits together like a jigsaw puzzle. Have you ever tried to sit down and put one of those things together? I'm not good at those puzzles because I don't have the patience. It takes order. It takes time. It takes meticulous observation and precision on behalf of the assembler to fit one like-piece with its corresponding part.

With me, I want the stuff to fall into place *when I say so.* And so when I start working with those puzzles, I get angry. I get mad because there are too many of those little bitty pieces. You know how it goes when you are trying to put one of those things together. One of the pieces either fell down behind the couch and you can't find it, or someone walked off with one in a pocket, and the entire project goes on hold because of the gaping hole in the puzzle.

I get no joy out of putting puzzles together. The process gets on my nerves. My patience is not suitable for the puzzle process. Because of this, I try to improvise. This is where so many of us stray from safety when it comes to walking down the path of purpose. We step into uncertain territory because of our unwillingness to wait on the Master Builder's divine timing and precision, and we start trying to make things fit together.

You know you've tried it. When one of those puzzles gets on my nerves and I can't find the missing piece—or the right piece—I'll take a piece that's *close* to fitting and I'll try to jam it down into the spot because it's so close to fitting. But it doesn't work out. Even though it looks very similar to the right piece, it is still the wrong piece. In trying to make a wrong piece fit, you have to tear out something to make it become something that it is not in order to fit into the place that it really doesn't fit. Did you catch that? You need to celebrate who the Master Craftsman has created you to be, and not try to distort or disfigure yourself in trying to bring your purpose to pass the way *you* assume it should take place. Yes, there are growth areas. Of course we learn, grow, change, and develop. I'm not talking about that. I'm talking about who you are as the integral piece to God's glorious puzzle. I'm talking about how you have been uniquely designed, intricately wired, and purposefully positioned. Don't try to become someone else in order to fulfill your purpose. Why? As long as you strive to be someone you're not, you will never fulfill *your* purpose.

> *As long as you strive to be someone you're not, you will never fulfill your purpose.*

Remember, when you attempt to malign God's design by fitting yourself into a scheme or scenario where you don't fit, you have to tear something in who you are. What happens when you tear, or change yourself, to try and become someone else in hopes of trying to fit somewhere that you don't actually belong? Your little plan actually messes up the bigger picture of what you're trying to do, which is ultimately fulfill purpose. I repeat, the longer you tear yourself by trying to become someone else, the longer you will prolong your journey toward purpose. God curved you where you needed to be curved, made you straight where you needed to be straight, made you blue where you needed to be blue, yellow where you needed to be yellow, and as soon as you find and celebrate that place where you fit...*purpose happens.*

REFLECTIONS

1. How does the enemy try to distract you from fulfilling your purpose?

2. What does it mean that God uses you in spite of yourself?

3. What can happen if you try to bring your purpose to pass yourself instead of waiting on God's divine timing?

CHAPTER 4

ELEVATE YOUR UNDERSTANDING OF PURPOSE

Now when David had served God's purpose in his own generation, he fell asleep; he was buried with his ancestors and his body decayed (Acts 13:36 NIV).

One generation shall praise Your works to another, and shall declare Your mighty acts (Psalm 145:4).

YOUR POSITION IN GOD'S DIVINE PROCESS

But let him who glories glory in this, that he understands and knows Me... (Jeremiah 9:24).

Once we recognize that God is orchestrating a master jigsaw puzzle, we begin to live our lives very differently. Why? Because no moment is arbitrary. Randomness is not part of the equation. We don't just wake up to sleepwalk through our day, only to come home, go to bed, wake up and start the process all over again. God is elevating your perspective concerning your purpose, for there are seeds of fulfilling your purpose in every waking moment of your life. With every moment comes greater understanding of your unfolding purpose. You walk with a speaking God. This is your glory—that you know Him, and yes, understand His unfolding plan of piecing the puzzle together. I want us to study the process through which God begins putting the puzzle together. This intersection is where power collides with potential and pushes us toward purpose.

First, understand that there is a divine process for putting the puzzle together.

> *In the beginning was the Word, and the Word was with God, and the Word was God. He was in the beginning with God* (John 1:1-2).

The Word is the logos. In the beginning, we see that the logos was with God, and the logos was God. The logos in the beginning was the strategy, and the strategy was with God and the strategy was God, and on account of His divine strategy, He pulls you in to fit a particular place and time and destiny. He then calls you to meet who you need to meet right when you need to meet them to draw the picture, and start assembling the jigsaw puzzle of His purpose in the earth. Our God is the Master Strategist. Everything He does brims with intentionality. God is not the author of coincidence; He is the sculptor of divine providence.

> *God is not the author of coincidence; He is the sculptor of divine providence.*

You must keep your eyes on God's divine strategy. If you don't, you run the risk of adopting the Elijah perspective. Even though we are studying the transference that took place between Elijah and *Elisha,* during Elijah's final golden days on earth, this prophet of power experienced some deep moments of despair. Why? He redirected his vision away from his purpose.

THE GREATER PICTURE OF PURPOSE

But he himself went a day's journey into the wilderness, and came and sat down under a broom tree. And he prayed that he might die, and said, "It is enough! Now, Lord, take my life, for I am no better than my fathers!" (1 Kings 19:4)

Why did Elijah want to die here? Because something was missing, and he could not figure out what it was. His pain starts pointing him toward his purpose. At this point in the story, he has gone as far as he can go without meeting Elisha. It is in this same chapter, First Kings 19, where Elijah experiences some of his darkest moments, as well as his finest hour. One would think that the prophet's finest hour preceded this chapter, when he called down fire from Heaven, experienced a miraculous demonstration of the power of God, and executed the false prophets of Baal. God used him to dramatically impact the spiritual landscape of an entire region, all in a single scene. And yet in the following chapter, we see the same man who experienced an overwhelming victory suffer under overwhelming depression. How was this possible?

As incredible as the victory at Mount Carmel was, that was not the moment where power would meet potential. Don't be deceived. Some moments that appear the most suited for purpose can actually distract you from fulfilling your purpose. Don't settle on a high. Celebrate breakthrough and victory, but don't mistakenly assume that a single demonstration of God's power *is* your purpose coming to pass. Rather, it serves as a landmark on your road to fulfilling your ultimate purpose.

> *Some moments that appear the most suited for purpose can actually distract you from fulfilling your purpose.*

There was a greater picture of purpose in Elijah's life than simply experiencing a significant victory against the prophets of Baal on Mount Carmel. It would have been easy for Elijah to mistakenly assume that a victory of that size was, in fact, the fulfillment of his purpose on earth. Perhaps he did entertain such a thought process. However, when we settle for small when God has greater, the ache and groan in our spirits will begin to push us outside of our wildernesses.

Elijah was not only in a wilderness physically, he was also in a wilderness mentally. Elijah's life purpose was not fulfilled in simply calling down fire from Heaven and destroying the false prophets of Baal. Likewise, your purpose is not fulfilled through some notable exploit you perform, a mighty act, or some type of spectacular feat. Even though these are God-ordained and God-orchestrated, they are moments that ultimately fade. Displays of power are fleeting, but transferences of power *awaken* potential in others. This is what Elijah was waiting for; he just didn't see it at the time.

Remember, God's vantage point includes so much more than human eyes are capable of capturing. It's tempting to coast on yesterday's victory, when in fact, God has bigger prepared. He is the God of *Greater Works*. I repeat, God has better. His vision is not for something fleeting or forgettable, but rather something sustained and supernatural. This is what He was preparing Elijah for, and yes, even used some of the prophet's pain to position him to anoint his successor, Elisha.

THE MULTI-DIMENSIONAL NATURE OF YOUR PURPOSE

"For My thoughts are not your thoughts, nor are your ways My ways," says the Lord (Isaiah 55:8).

Your Mount Carmel victory should not be un-scalable. Why? Because your purpose is not wrapped up in a single event; rather, it's your active participation in an unfolding, lifelong process. There are landmarks along the journey, but we cannot confuse a landmark with ultimate fulfillment. Perhaps Elijah considered his fiery victory as ultimate purpose-fulfillment, when in fact, it was a piece of Heaven's divine jigsaw puzzle for his life and overall contribution to God's purpose in the Earth. Our problem is that we often mistake great victories for the entire puzzle, and then become disappointed when another major victory is not soon waiting in the wings to continue that momentum.

We start redefining our purpose, not by the divine orchestration of God's unfolding plan, but rather by the size and scope of our victories, miracles, and blessings. Remember, these are all integral, essential parts of the journey. However, when we assume that *part* of the journey has become the *whole* journey, we position ourselves to live perpetually disappointed. The very object of our purpose is reduced to something that happened in the past. Right after your breakthrough comes and right on the other side of your miracle, is an ominous future.

Consider it for a moment. What happens when we believe that our best days and greatest victories are behind us, not before us? We cease pushing forward, for we see no potential in forward momentum. That's the danger of believing that purpose is fulfilled in an event or a landmark moment. There is far more to your purpose on earth than one breakthrough or miracle, no matter how spectacular or significant it appears to be.

> *There is far more to your purpose on earth
> than one breakthrough or miracle.*

It's like believing that a piece of the puzzle is the entire puzzle. And yet, God is in His mercy gives us vision to see that the puzzle piece has interconnected edges longing for a complement. And you know that complement longs for a complementary piece, and so on and so forth. This is why I believe the puzzle analogy is most helpful in recognizing the flow and unfolding of God's purpose in our lives.

In other words, if we assume that a single victory or a significant event in our lives marks the complete fulfillment of our divine purpose, God is quick to remind us that what we assume is the whole is only a part. An essential part, yes, but still only a part. He gives us eyes to see the protruding edges on the pieces that are meant to connect and link with other pieces. He gives us the ability to see that what we perceive to be the be-all and end-all actually has missing portions. You know how a puzzle piece has missing ends and edges, purposed to be complemented by a corresponding piece? In the same way, your breakthrough has missing portions. Whatever it is—a breakthrough, a blessing, a miracle, a victory, a promotion, an increase—God's purpose is higher and bigger. One event is merely one piece of your puzzle of purpose. One victory helps complete the puzzle, but is inadequate to masquerade as the entire image.

Make no mistake, events launch us into purpose. Breakthroughs escort us from one level to the next. Miracles override natural law, and position us in places that we could not have gotten to by ourselves. We celebrate moments without mistaking them for the ultimate masterpiece of God's divine design. We steward every significant event that takes place as a push that takes us from one dimension to the next, one realm of glory to another. We don't camp out at Carmel. We don't build a memorial to every miracle—even the outstanding ones. Even the ones where fire falls down. We don't pitch a tent and try to live in yesterday, when in fact today is standing before us and we gaze, without purpose, into an uncertain future. Instead, we must see the catalysts for what they are and embrace their ability to move us along God's route for our lives.

THE MULTI-GENERATIONAL NATURE OF YOUR PURPOSE

For I will pour water on him who is thirsty, and floods on the dry ground; I will pour My Spirit on your descendants, and My blessing on your offspring (Isaiah 44:3).

In the same way assuming that a single significant event could capture the fulfillment of our purpose, we severely limit the expression of purpose when we simply focus on one person or a single generation. Purpose is beyond you, and it is beyond me. It is beyond our big breaks. It is beyond our successes. It is beyond our breakthroughs. It is beyond our victories. In the same way that purpose was beyond Elijah, so the expression and fulfillment of purpose is beyond a single generation. When you collide with God's power, the object of transformation is not just *you*. Even though you are being hit, and you are being marked, and your potential is being awakened, you step into the flow of something that was going on before you stepped onto the scene—and will continue when you are gone. He is the God who pours out His Spirit on *descendants* and *offspring*.

We miss the mark when we inappropriately elevate a single individual to a place of memorial without recognizing the *role* the person played in the continuing fulfillment of the purpose he or she served. We serve purpose, because we serve God. Remember, God is the God of Purpose. We are here to serve His purpose, not the other way around. Consider King David. Scripture tells us that he *"had served God's purpose in his own generation"* (Acts 13:36 NIV). Even the phrase, "served a purpose," carries the connotation that a purpose is beyond us. Purpose does not serve us; we serve it. We cater to it. We revolve our lives around purpose. We don't place demands on purpose. We don't dictate to purpose. Instead, we let it dictate to us and as we serve God's purpose in our own generation, we play a vital part in the great unfolding agenda of God. You serve a multi-generational God. He is God of Abraham, Isaac, and Jacob.

In serving God's purpose, we submit to His plan. Serving a purpose is not our invitation to celebrity status; serving a purpose is the call to lay everything at the feet of Jesus and say, "I'm in the King's service." The moment we take our eyes off the greater purpose of God and its multi-generational impact, we run into two dangers: 1) inappropriate focus on humanity, and 2) hindering the generational continuance of God's purposes.

When we take our eyes off the multi-generational nature of our purpose, we can mislead ourselves into believing that *we* are solely responsible for bringing our purpose to pass. This is both overwhelming and arrogance-producing. It's overwhelming to believe that saving the entire world is on our shoulders, but it is likewise arrogance-producing to assume that *we* have the ability to bring such a God-sized purpose to pass by ourselves. We must be careful to always see ourselves in the context of the greater picture, the larger puzzle. Each person is an interconnected piece, linked to other generations. When someone is divorced from his or her rightful place in the unfolding of a purpose, the person becomes elevated beyond appropriateness. The piece ends up receiving perverted recognition, for it is really the completed puzzle that solved the problem. The problem was incompletion; the process produced completion.

The process is beyond you, and it's beyond me. The process involves generations locking pieces to complete the puzzle. At one point, there was a puzzle that was missing pieces. However, as more and more pieces took their place in the puzzle, the purpose came to pass and was ultimately fulfilled. But think of how ridiculous it would be to assume that one piece, in and of itself, sufficiently completed the puzzle. This would be believing a lie and living in delusion. We play integral, interconnected parts in completing the most glorious puzzle conceivable—the puzzle of God's purpose being fulfilled in the earth.

> *You play an integral, interconnected part in completing the most glorious puzzle conceivable!*

God's great puzzle of purpose highlights two primary methods of interconnectedness between pieces. First, we are interconnected with each other in our present generation, recognizing what gifts, talents, abilities, and resources other people bring to the table in complementing who we are, and likewise what we bring complementing who they are. Second, we recognize how our generation is vitally interconnected with future generations. In Psalm 145:4, we are given one of many examples throughout Scripture revealing God's vision for interconnecting generations.

This was God's purpose in colliding Elijah with Elisha. The puzzle did not conclude with Elijah. It would be tempting to gaze through the annals of history and fix our eyes on this man of power for his hour. Many of us do, in fact. We look at the life of someone God used powerfully and place an unhealthy amount of emphasis on *that one person,* when in fact we should be looking into his or her *purpose.* The purpose did not begin with that one person, and it does not end with that one person. While we honor the call of God upon someone, we must take it a step further and decipher the piece of the puzzle he or she served as in that generation. Why? This gives us clues to how the purpose will continue to unfold.

God's ministry of breakthrough, power, miracles, and cultural-transformation did not conclude with Elijah; if anything, it increased in momentum when the mantle hit Elisha. The same is true for the work of God in this hour, in your life. If you wish to take your place as a carrier of God's purpose, you must recognize that purpose goes beyond yourself and beyond your generation.

REFLECTIONS

1. What is the "greater picture" of God's purpose for your life?

2. How does your purpose have many different dimensions?

3. Describe how you understand purpose to be multi-generational.

CHAPTER 5

FIND YOUR PLACE
OF DEPOSIT

So Elijah went and found Elisha son of Shaphat
plowing a field... (1 Kings 19:19 NLT).

MEETING THE CRITERIA FOR
CARRYING PURPOSE

We just explored how purpose is much bigger than you might have imagined. In the same way that purpose did not start with us, it does not conclude with us. It is multi-generational. We briefly looked at the example of King David, who *"had served God's purpose in his own generation"* (Acts 13:36 NIV). He recognized that purpose was bigger than his own piece of the puzzle, and simply served his uniquely assigned moment in history. Result? King David's life continued a momentum that ultimately birthed the Son of David, *Jesus Christ.*

In the same manner, Elijah sought to sow into a successor who would continue to carry his divinely assigned purpose. Going back in the story to where Elijah is discouraged after his Mount Carmel victory, the Lord informs him, *"I have reserved seven thousand in Israel, all whose knees have not bowed to Baal, and every mouth that has not kissed him"* (1 Kings 19:18). He was looking for soil to sow into, ready and fertile for the perpetuation of purpose.

In the following chapters we are going to switch gears and examine the process from Elisha's viewpoint. However, it is important to note the principle here. Elijah was searching for a place of deposit and could find none. He had a mantle. He had experience. He had wisdom. He had revelation. Elijah had so much to impart, so much to release, but it was reserved for specific ground.

Elijah's mantle was custom-sized for Elisha. Whether or not this is true in the literal sense, Elisha was the only one capable of wearing that mantle, for he was the designated place of deposit. The person of deposit is able to don the mantle. You see, none of the people Elijah had encountered or interacted with, up to this point, had met the criteria for the release of what he wanted to impart. Even though there were seven thousand in Israel who had not prostituted themselves with false gods, there was only one man suitable to be Elijah's spiritual successor. *Elisha* was Elijah's place of divine deposit. This is something we must learn to recognize if we are going to step into our purpose.

Don't waste your time trying to sow into unresponsive ground. It's got to be fertile. Listen, there is definitely a time for you to dig in, have resolve, and refuse to back up or back down. In these cases, your sowing is the very element God wants to use to supernaturally break up the fallowed ground (see Hos. 10:12). You need to exercise discernment, and evaluate whether or not the ground is worthy of your seed. What is your seed? It's your time. Your effort. Your passion. Your sweat. Your tears. Your intercessions. Your contending. Your laboring. When it comes time for you to sow and invest into someone else, identifying that person as a potential carrier and perpetuator of the purpose on your life, ensure that he or she is a suitable resting place for the deposit you carry. Otherwise frustration will overwhelm the process.

Likewise, you need to prepare *your* heart to be fertile ground for what power wants to impart. You really need to grasp both sides of this principle. Most of this book will focus on Elisha, and in turn, place you in the Elisha position. Elisha is the one being pushed into his purpose; in the same way, I believe God wants to set you up for those meetings with power that unlock your potential and set you on a whole new course.

For the sake of this book, you are Elisha. Got it? You are the one God wants to impart power into that will unlock potential. With that in mind, it's key to first study how Elijah chose a successor to sow into. This shows us *who* God is looking for to collide with His power.

THE PRACTICAL SIDE OF SOWING

And he who reaps receives wages, and gathers fruit for eternal life, that both he who sows and he who reaps may rejoice together (John 4:36).

Before we explore this principle any further, I want you to identify just how relatable it is to your life. I don't assume every person on the planet is a vagabond prophet like Elijah who just recently called fire down from Heaven. However, Elijah was a man marked by purpose. God had a purpose for Elijah in his generation prepared before the foundation of the world. In the same way, the God of Elijah has marked you with purpose. He has fashioned you for destiny. We reviewed this in the opening pages of this book. You're not a cosmic accident; you are the intricate handiwork of the God of Purpose. You have been placed in this moment, at this hour, in this season of history to fulfill your purpose in *your generation,* just as King David did.

What does this look like for the businessperson? The stay-at-home parent? The plumber? The accountant? The doctor? The coffee shop barista? The college student? The banker? Regardless what you are doing in life right now, you have been called to fulfill your purpose in your generation. Likewise, part of fulfilling your purpose is making an investment in other people and being one who is investable.

In the chapters to come, we are going to examine what it looks like for you to intersect with God's power, and how this power actually draws out your potential. This was exactly what happened between Elijah and Elisha—Elisha's potential was awakened and released when he collided with the power on Elijah's life and received Elijah's mantle.

> *Part of fulfilling your purpose is making an investment in other people and being one who is investable.*

I want you to have eyes opened for the divine collisions in your life—not only for those who collide with you, but keep your eyes open to the people God brings into your life to collide with. You have something to release, and you have something to receive. Yes, you. I don't care what you're doing right now. I don't care if you are a multi-millionaire or some broke college student living off noodles and peanut butter. Purpose is beyond your socio-economic status. Purpose is not thwarted by the kind of house you currently live in. Purpose is not intimidated by your situation or circumstance. If you are a child of God, you carry the power of God—and that supernatural power awakens potential. You carry this power, and at any moment this same power can collide with you and unlock possibilities that your mind cannot even fathom. All it takes is a single moment. One encounter. A single meeting.

The key is sowing where your contribution is valued and appreciated. Right now, the context is making investment in others. There will be times and places where what you bring is not appreciated, but it is something you *must do*. We can't go through life waiting to be appreciated before we do the right thing. That is not what I am talking about here.

Our context is mentorship. We're talking about the people you make an investment in and pour your life into. It's about being on the lookout for those who carry your DNA. Sure they might look differently, talk differently, act differently, smell differently, and dress differently. None of those externals matter when you see potential in that person. These are the people and environments where you are called to invest your pearls—the time, ability, gifting, talent, and wisdom of most precious value.

In the same way, I encourage you to be ready. Power is out there looking for you. Sowers are seeking those who carry the same DNA, same heartbeat, and same vision. You may look different, but that doesn't matter. If you are seed-ready ground, power is going to hit and awaken everything inside of you that needs to come out.

How to Identify "Seed-Ready" Ground

For he who sows to his flesh will of the flesh reap corruption, but he who sows to the Spirit will of the Spirit reap everlasting life (Galatians 6:8).

Keep in mind, you cannot give your pearls to pigs (see Matt. 7:6). No matter how tired you are of carrying them, no matter how much you're ready to release them, you cannot take the things of God and give them to people who are not ready. Wait and be looking for seed-ready ground. What does this look like?

One of the key characteristics is a lifestyle of one who frequently sows *to the Spirit* (see Gal. 6:8). Their lifestyle is marked by consistent spiritual investment. They are close with God—and you can see it. You see the fruit of their investment. Not everyone walks in this dimension, because not everyone stewards the seed he or she has received in the Spirit.

Think of all the believers out there. Yes, they are born again. Yes, they are washed in the blood. Yes, they have the Holy Ghost living inside them. Do you know how many people have this beyond-priceless inheritance living inside them, and yet live like spiritual paupers? They live in spiritual poverty because they sow to the flesh. Their spirit was transformed when they were born again, but they still live like the world lives. They still operate and think and respond and behave like everyone else. Something happened in the core of their being, *but*, hear me, they are not sowing into it. They are not stewarding the seed of God in their own lives.

God planted a seed in their spirit when you came to Christ. That's the seed of His Spirit—the Holy Spirit. He's not looking to simply hang out, unbothered, in our spirits for 70, 80,

90, or 100 years. The Holy Spirit is a Person looking for cooperation. He's seeking ones who desire total divine invasion of every realm of life. He's waiting for the ones who will sow into the Spirit and reap for themselves transformed minds, healed emotions, and God-ward wills. The ground must be spiritually ready. Are you?

Remember when Moses came down off the mountaintop with glory beams shooting out of his face (see Exod. 34:29-35)? He was ready to impart something to an Israel that was not ready. They were sowing into the flesh. They received this glorious invitation from Jehovah, and what were they doing? Impatience brought them to idolatry. Moses comes down and finds them dancing naked around the golden calf and actually has to cover the glory that he was ready to release. Why? The people were not ready to receive on the level that he was ready to release. Do you see the parallel? For the power inside of you to release the potential in someone else, there must be a readiness on their end.

> *Don't be caught dancing before the golden calf during your season of visitation.*

In the same way, for the power upon someone else to awaken your potential, you must be ready. For you to step into the things that God has purposed for your life, you must be prepared and seed-ready ground. You must be ready in season and out of season. Don't be caught dancing before the golden calf during your season of visitation. Too many believers give up just before their moment, either because they cannot find fertile ground to release impartation, or because they have been patiently waiting to receive the mantle of Elisha and are losing heart. They are waiting for Moses to come down off the mountain—and are getting impatient.

I encourage you to be ready for your day of visitation. Be faithful. Continue plowing where God has you plowing right now. You don't know what it will look like, sound like, feel like, or smell like when power comes. God's orchestration is perfect, and it is sovereign. Your supernatural setup will come in His divine timing. Those catalysts that catapult you further and further into your purpose by awakening greater dimensions of untapped potential—they cannot be setup by our scheming. They cannot be initiated by our own human devices. In fact, when we insert ourselves into the process, we start tearing up the puzzle pieces.

Think of the other examples in Scripture. Jesus came onto the scene and said, *"I still have many things to say to you, but you cannot bear them now"* (John 16:12). There were certain realities that Jesus restrained Himself from sharing with the disciples because the soil was not yet ready for the impartation. It would only be ripe and ready upon the coming of the Holy Spirit.

WHEN THE STUDENT IS READY, THE TEACHER WILL APPEAR

And let us not grow weary while doing good, for in due season we shall reap if we do not lose heart (Galatians 6:9).

When the student is ready, the teacher will appear. This was certainly true for Elijah and Elisha, and it is likewise true for your life. You have to be ready to receive on the next level and others have to be ready for your next level of impartation. By now you have probably noticed that all of us wear both hats at some point—teacher and student, Elijah and Elisha. All the while you are receiving from the teacher, you are releasing to students. All the while you are receiving as a student, you are releasing as a teacher. This is the process that Jesus described, *"Freely you have received, freely give"* (Matt. 10:8). As you receive more, more is able to flow through you.

When does the teacher appear on the scene? When the student is ready. You can't get the teacher to appear if the student isn't ready. The teacher has the power, and the student has the potential. Power needs to be released. It needs to express itself. It needs to reveal itself. However, potential needs to be ready in order for power to be recognized and have its full impact. Two of the key characteristics of readiness are not growing weary and not losing heart, as Paul wrote in Galatians 6:9. The one who has been faithful in the former season demonstrates the character that will sustain him or her in the new season. We will discuss this more extensively in the chapters ahead.

Consider Elijah again. He had no place to release this power. It felt like loneliness. Just think about the language he uses, *"I alone am left"* (1 Kings 19:10). He was in a wilderness, in a cave, and then on a mountain—in every place he seemed lonely and depressed. Why? Your loneliness, your agony comes when you have something to release and nobody is ready to receive it. He was looking for receive-ready ground where the seed of his impartation could find a resting place.

Take the conception process for example. Any creature will tell you there is nothing as laborious as trying to release a seed into a closed womb, a closed mind, an unreceptive audience.

For example, I sow the Word of God as I preach. As much as a pastor, teacher, or preacher would love to help regulate the receptivity of the audience, such is not the case. Instead, the audience largely regulates the flow of the Holy Spirit. No amount of hype and no amount of hoopla can fake a people ready to receive. When they're ready, they are ready. When they are not, they're not. Simple as that. We can press. We can push. We can sow and keep on sowing. Sometimes sheer perseverance starts to break up the ground, and then as one person starts getting hungry, others follow the lead. Generally speaking, though, it is the recipient who controls the flow of the Holy Spirit in his or her life. Power is looking for recipients who are ready. Who are faithful. Who are hungry. Who are pressing in. Who are persevering through.

> *Power is looking for people who are ready, faithful, hungry, pressing in, persevering.*

I'm talking beyond preaching. Whatever you offer, wherever you are, and whatever your unique gifting is, for the sake of stewarding it well and not wanting to bang your head against the wall, find ready ground. *Be* the ready ground! Ask the Holy Spirit to bring you into a collision with those who are hungry and receptive—those who will receive and benefit from whatever you carry. It does not matter who you are or what your gift is. If you're a businessperson, the principle is the same. Yes, there is a time for negotiation and salesmanship and marketing; but then there are people and companies that are just not ready to receive what you offer. Recognize this. Identify the relationships that are not ripe for your investment and discern the people who are ready for what you offer. You know what I'm talking about. There are people and situations that are just not ready for the glory that you bring.

On the other side, those who are receive-ready will actually draw the glory out of you. They will pull the revelation, potential, gifting, and anointing right out of you. This is what Elisha did for Elijah. Elisha was receive-ready, and Elijah—the teacher—showed up on the scene. There was a mutual recognition that each man was ready for what the other brought to the table.

There's another person inside you that the world has not seen yet. The time wasn't right before. You had to go through enough trouble, enough pain, enough agony, enough failure to get ready for this moment. But you're ready now. The teacher is appearing. The student is plowing. Remember, you are both the teacher and the student. Continue to sow; but at the same time, understand that to get to your next level, you need to be ready-ground.

Look for a place to make a deposit of everything down inside you while waiting for the deposit that's coming your way. Yes, you're going to talk to some people about it, and they're not going to be to even hear what you have to say. They're not ready for what you're discovering in these pages. Don't be frustrated when someone can't handle your glory, your gifting, you're anointing, your revelation. Don't get upset because the ground is not ready yet. What's the solution? Find someone who has been praying and crying out for what you carry. Make the deposit in his life. Make the deposit in her life. And when the power of what you carry meets the potential inside that person, *something supernatural will happen.*

REFLECTIONS

1. What is the "place of deposit?"

2. Why is it so important for the ground to be re-ceive-ready? How can you be that receive-ready ground?

3. What does the following statement mean to you: "When the student is ready, the teacher will appear?"

CHAPTER 6

IDENTIFYING UNREALIZED POTENTIAL

...Elisha the son of Shaphat, who was plowing with twelve yoke of oxen before him, and he was with the twelfth... (1 Kings 19:19).

UNSEEN POTENTIAL

Then Samuel took the horn of oil and anointed him in the midst of his brothers; and the Spirit of the Lord came upon David from that day forward... (1 Samuel 16:13).

You carry a glory. There's something deep inside you that requires a meeting with God's power in order to be released. Your potential is awaiting activation. Elisha remains unrealized, unknown, obscure, and unseen until his meeting with Elijah. This is what happened with King David. He was unseen—literally. While his brothers *looked* like royalty, it was the boy with the unseen character and unseen heart of worship and unseen victories over the bear and the lion to whom the prophet Samuel was drawn. He was the man for the mantle. God is looking to bring the unseen into the seen by using power to release your potential.

> *Something deep inside you requires a meeting with God's power to be released.*

Scripture is silent about Elisha *until* his meeting with Elijah. We don't get the privilege of learning his backstory. We're not told about his family life. We're left in the dark about his upbringing. Does this mean Elisha was unimportant before Elijah? No. Rather, the Bible gives us a glimpse into select moments where ordinary faithful men and women are launched out into their divine destinies. Before their collisions with power, they are still significant and valuable people. They simply carry unrealized and untapped potential. It's the intersection with power that draws out potential. It's the mantle that brings the unseen into the seen.

Scripture reveals example after example of those who experienced divine intersections with power, saw a release of potential, and ultimately stepped into the momentum of divine purpose.

Noah found favor in God's eyes. He had a family. He had a life. He had a concept of normal. And then God called him to build a boat that would ultimately save the planet. One intersection with power brought Noah out of the unseen into the seen.

Abraham had a story. He had a homeland. *And then God called him out.* Power met Abraham's potential, and he began a journey toward stepping into his purpose. He left his homeland, dwelt in tents as a nomad, and ultimately had a child at an old age through a wife (who was long-passed the age of childbearing) who would go on to establish a heritage for generations to come.

Joseph was unseen until Pharaoh heard that Power enabled him to interpret dreams; he asked Joseph to interpret his own dream and, in turn, made Joseph prime minister of all Egypt.

Moses was an unseen shepherd in the wilderness until Power met him at the burning bush.

David was unseen until Power anointed him and said, *"You're the King of Israel."*

Jesus was even unseen until He was 30 years old and Power opened the heavens and anointed Him.

A catalytic collision between God's supernatural power and your potential brings you out of the unseen and into the seen.

When I say *Power,* I am referring to One Power. I'm not making reference to some ambiguous mysticism. I'm not talking about some otherworldly force or energy. I'm specifically addressing the power of the Most High God. Apart from His power and ability, we can do *nothing* (see John 15:5). In every situation we read about, there is a catalytic collision between God's supernatural power and a person's potential that brings them out of the unseen and into the seen.

Until First Kings 19:19, we do not meet Elisha. He is unseen potential. Elijah hears about him. God gives Elijah instruction on meeting him and what this former plowman will ultimately accomplish. However, until his collision with God's power, Elisha remains out of public view.

Do you feel unseen? Do you feel out of public view? Are you living in that place of obscurity right now? Listen, I realize there are people out there who *want to be seen.* In fact, they *need* to be seen. Their grand pursuit in life is self being seen. They depend on being noticed and recognized and celebrated and catered to in order to maintain their self-worth. That's not what I'm talking about here. You have lived satisfied in the secret place, but you recognize there is something inside you that *you offer* the world. It has not yet been revealed or released. It has nothing to do with you becoming a celebrity or a diva; and has everything to do with you being receive-ready soil.

UNREALIZED POTENTIAL

Do not despise these small beginnings, for the Lord rejoices to see the work begin... (Zechariah 4:10 NLT).

Elisha was not only unseen potential, but he was also unrealized potential. As he plowed, surely he thought to himself, "I don't even know what I've got, but I know that doing what I'm doing is not my destiny." Plowing was a day of small beginnings, but it was the plow that positioned him for the mantle. Elijah found Elisha while he was plowing.

Do you feel like Elisha—that you've got something, maybe you don't even know how to define it, but you know there is something more than what you are currently doing? That ache in the very core of your being, constantly reminding you that where you are cannot define *who* you are and for what you have been created. What you're doing right now cannot shape your vision and expectation of what you will be doing for the rest of your life. We are diligent in our present season, all the while recognizing that the potential inside us is not merely reserved for where we are *right now,* but it's unrealized. In the same way we *realize* that we left our keys on the counter or the same way we *realize* that we left our credit card at the restaurant, there are moments in your life when someone *realizes* the potential inside you. The person recognizes what is there—maybe you don't even see it, but someone does. Power does. When you realize something, it compels you to act. When Elijah realized the potential inside of Elisha, it caused him to pass by and toss his mantle upon him.

> *Unrealized potential always involves your supernatural capability.*

Before this incredible transference took place, Elisha had been plowing in the fields. He was working in the dimension of the natural, praying through the pain. Unrealized potential always involves your supernatural capability. The things deep inside you are the very things that solve the deep needs and longings of humanity. This is beyond philanthropy, humanitarianism, and service. While these things are important, they are expressions of what's really inside you. There's supernatural potential burning in your natural frame. While there are gifts, talents, and abilities you have that are clear to everyone who sees you and knows you, Elijah calls out the deeper things. Power calls out the supernatural. Power commissions your ability to accomplish the impossible. Power summons you into the depths. Power invites you into the heights.

Elijah did not walk by Elisha, place his mantle upon him, and invite this plowman into a new dimension of natural work. In other words, Elijah did not summon Elisha into greater levels of plowing. Whether it was plowing in the field of a king, president, or prime minister, the natural act of plowing was not being called out of this man. In the same way, collisions with power, intersections with Elijahs, are not intended to simply upgrade what is already visible in your life. Elijah calls out the deeper things. He summons what's beyond the surface. He calls forth the things we didn't even know we had; and yet we somehow recognize that there is more to life than merely plowing a field.

Don't be satisfied settling for some type of natural upgrade and then calling it supernatural. Supernatural cannot be some term we assign to an extraordinary natural act that we are still capable of accomplishing through our own human effort, ingenuity, and skill. Many of us mistakenly assign the descriptive "supernatural" or "miraculous" to everything that requires just a little bit of extra sweat. I'm not demeaning the things we accomplish as human beings. God divinely knit us together with wisdom, skills, abilities, creative expression, fortitude, grit, gumption, and perseverance to do incredible things. Humankind has built skyscrapers, gone to the moon, painted, sculpted, and created. Because of *how* humans are created, we are capable of creating. We celebrate the potential of humanity. We cheer on what we are capable of doing simply by how we were assembled through divine design. That's not what I want us to focus on right now.

I want to to elevate your thinking little bit. I want to start a riot in your mind when it comes to your true potential. You have the potential to build a building of bricks and mortar, but you also have potential to transform the planet. You have the potential to fly to another galaxy, but also have the potential to change the culture to reflect the Kingdom of God. It might be unrealized right now, but it's there inside you. You have the potential to heal the sick, raise the dead, and set captives free. These realities are possibilities for you, even though they might be unrealized right now.

Unrealized potential causes us to ache to experience the supernatural power that ultimately unveils our true potential to the world.

LOVE THE ACHE AND KEEP PLOWING

Now may the Lord direct your hearts into the love of God and into the patience of Christ (2 Thessalonians 3:5).

I encourage you to love the ache inside that reminds you of what's available, but currently not in operation. Why? Too many of us suppress this ache. We downplay the ache. There's a cry within us for more, but we don't know what to do with it. So many of us try to push mute on this ache for more. It's relentless; but the fact that it is unceasing-until-satisfied should cause us to celebrate what's available rather than settle for what is presently accessible.

Plowing was Elisha's present-accessible reality. However, just because he was faithfully plowing did not mean he was ill-prepared for his moment of power. He was prepared because he did not run off and pursue some counterfeit version of what the deep of him surely longed for. I repeat, there are realities available to you that you are not yet walking in. Don't be disappointed that you are not walking in them...*yet*. Celebrate that they are available to you, and trust the God of Purpose to bring you into greater alignment with your supernatural purpose at His ordained time, through His methods. Remember, purpose is recognized, experienced, and realized through those moments and meetings with power. Patience is absolutely required if we want to protect ourselves from settling for an inferior alternative.

> *There are realities available to you that you are not yet walking in.*

This is what happens to those who are plowing—and grow tired. They become weary. They have not come to love the ache, but rather are desperate to silence its nagging noise. Day after day, night after night as they plow in their place of present assignment, the ache within reminds them that another reality is available. Rather than trusting the God of Purpose and waiting for His power, we give up. We kick the ox. We toss the plow aside. We leave the field—running. Our quest becomes to silence the ache, instead of waiting for God to satisfy it. As a result, we pursue counterfeit solutions to the ache for purpose. Every attempt to satisfy our ache with second-rate pleasures will prolong our true launch into supernatural purpose. We try to access our potential, not through God's power, but through our own pursuits. Our pleasures. Our passions. These things will never ultimately silence the ache within.

Patience prepares us for the power that unleashes our potential. Just as patience protected Elisha from second-rate pursuits and prepared him for Elijah, so our patience actually helps enforce the character and integrity necessary to sustain the power that satisfies the ache. Elisha must be ready in order to receive Elijah's mantle. One key readiness factor is maintaining patience in the process of waiting, while also celebrating the ache that prophesies to us:

"Elijah is coming!"

"Power is at hand!"

"Things you didn't even know you had living inside you are getting ready to come forth!"

I don't believe it was a mistake that Elisha was found plowing, because plowing teaches you how to break up the hard places. Plowing teaches you that you cannot put a good seed in ground that is not prepared. Plowing is a process dedicated to readiness. Plowing teaches you seed time and harvest, sowing and reaping. Plowing teaches you discipline and focus. Plowing teaches you how to follow. Plowing teaches you alignment.

Everything you have ever done has been preparation for what you're about to do.

There's a right kind of people for you to be aligned with, and a wrong kind of people. The ache cries out for the right people and will never be satisfied with the wrong ones. It has to be lined up. Your relationships have to be lined up. You can't go out and plow just anywhere. There's a strategy. There's a structure. There's a purpose. There's a plan. There's a seed. You think you've been doing something that's beneath your anointing, but everything you have ever done has been getting you ready for what you're about to do.

Plowing prepared Elisha for Elijah. Whatever you're doing right now is preparing you for the next level. Everything you have ever done, every job you have ever worked. Everything that you thought was a deadbeat situation, every relationship you thought was beneath you—all of it was training ground for the promotion that is about to break forth in your life. Elijah's coming, and he's looking for a plowing Elisha.

Where will you be found on your day of visitation?

REFLECTIONS

1. What is unseen potential? Unrealized potential?

2. What is "the ache" inside of you? How should you respond to this ache?

3. What are the dangers of impatience while waiting for your moments and meetings with God's power?

PART II

WHEN POWER MEETS POTENTIAL

...Then Elijah passed by him and threw
his mantle on him (1 Kings 19:19).

CHAPTER 7

UNWRAP THE GIFT
OF EXPOSURE

Then Elijah...threw his mantle on him (1 Kings 19:19).

THE KEY THAT UNLOCKS POTENTIAL

Potential was plowing in the field, all the while waiting for something. Someone. A moment. A miracle. A collision. A release. A deposit. An impartation. An encounter. Potential was waiting for something, not knowing *what* that something would look like. The same is true for you. You carry unseen, unrealized potential. There is an ache inside you, constantly reminding you that *more* is available than you are currently seeing and experiencing. All of the factors are in place. You are following Elisha's example and are faithfully plowing wherever you have been positioned. You are not looking to the right or the left. You're not allowing yourself to become distracted by other pursuits or counterfeit passions. With focus and fortitude you have made a resolution to move forward. You're not quitting. You're not stopping. You're not slowing down. You're not running off. You're not taking an indefinite coffee break. There's something *in* you waiting for something *out* there.

This brings us to the next step in the story of Elijah and Elisha. One day, Elisha looked up and saw Elijah. Potential looked up and saw power. What did power look like? The first expression power took was *exposure*. Exposure is a key that unlocks your potential. Power gives potential exposure. Power can take obscurity, and in a moment, in a second, in an instant—through exposure—bring its potential into full view. Don't ever doubt the life-shaping power of one moment of exposure. You can't buy it. You can't manufacture it. You can't make it happen. Anything you strive after in the realm of exposure will always be a second-rate copy of the exposure released through a divine collision with power.

> *Power can take obscurity and in an instant—through exposure—bring its potential into full view.*

Elisha could have spent his entire life, as many people do, pursuing exposure for himself. Many of us run after something that, once we get it, we only experience its true ability in minor measure. Think about it. Here we are, plowing away, doing what God has called us to do and being where God has called us to be. Again, because of impatience and because we assume we can make something happen more effectively and efficiently than God, we run out and pursue exposure for ourselves.

I'm not saying all forms of pursued exposure are wrong. We need communications divisions. We need marketing campaigns. We need to get our message and materials and products and services out there. But there's a difference between marketing and manipulation. Do you see where I'm coming from? Marketing is stewardship of our services, gifts, talents, abilities, products, and resources, exposing them to people who will benefit from their use—while manipulation is trying to *become someone* through manufacturing exposure.

You can market all day long, that's fine. But when you know that, deep down inside, God has created you for something supernatural and significant, the worst thing you can do is run out and try to manufacture the exposure that will launch you into destiny. Again, exposure through marketing and communications is normal and natural, but the pursuit of exposure to actually fulfill your destiny, become who you were created to be, and step into your purpose is taking matters into your hands that they are not fit to carry.

Remember, only God can set up the exposure that is the key that unlocks your potential and propels you into your purpose.

THE GREAT GIFT THAT POWER DELIVERS

But I have raised you up or this very purpose, that I might show you my power and that my name might be proclaimed in all the earth (Exodus 9:16 NIV).

One moment Elisha was a nobody out plowing fields. In the blink of an eye, he went from being a nobody to becoming successor to the greatest prophet in the land. Surely one of the greatest gifts you can give to anybody is exposure. God did this time after time. Again, reflect on Moses. One moment Moses was an obscure shepherd living in the wilderness; the next he is summoned to deliver a nation and demonstrate the power of God before the world's major superpower, Egypt.

One of the greatest gifts you can receive is exposure. Powerful people have influence, and influence is the foundation of exposure. Influence is what gives substance to exposure. Influence gives someone's exposure worth. Anybody can try to give you exposure. However, the only exposure that has the ability and power to unlock your potential is exposure that comes from a source of value. Again, this source is influence. Only a person with influence has the ability to bring you valuable exposure.

Elijah had something of value to offer Elisha. There are people out there who think they are valuable; but in the end, they are just empty suits. They want influence. They crave power. They pursue recognition. Unfortunately, they are in it for themselves. They are me-centric. You don't want what they have, because they have nothing more than a façade. They might be able to dazzle you for a season, but when the dazzle wears off, they are void of anything raw or real. They are without substance, and its substance that gives value to the exposure you receive.

Wait for the real; don't settle for the phony, the fake, or the flimflam. Impatience compels us to make some ridiculous moves. While waiting and plowing and waiting and plowing, we might see people who appear to "have it all." They look like they've got the power and prestige. You're looking at them, but they are not looking at you. In fact, nothing you do seems to get their attention. This is not God restricting you; this is God preserving you. He is protecting you from falling prey to people who would invariably over-promise and under-deliver. Trust His divine timing. Wait for Elijah. Don't go chasing after every prophet who comes to town. Don't make just anyone your mentor. Don't try to manufacture a meeting with power; when in fact, the person you think offers exposure has nothing to give you.

Elijah was the real deal. He delivered the goods. He had what could push Elisha into the next dimension. The exposure Elijah offered carried significance and weight. He carried true greatness; and when God exposes you to greatness, even for the briefest of moments, if you have potential inside of you, when power passes by that potential, there is a cataclysmic explosion that takes place. Both will always recognize each other. Powerful people recognize potential in people and people of potential know power when they see it. Whenever they pass by one another, potential says, "Now I get it! Now I see it! Now I understand it! Now I realize it!"

Then power says, "Do you know who you are potential? You are standing on the verge. You think you're impressed with this. There's twice as much in you as there is in me, and when we meet..."

Elisha kept plowing and Elijah found him. Depending on what God has called you to do, your moments of exposure *will come*. Not everyone receives the same exposure because not everyone is designed to do the same thing. And remember, exposure comes, not by you chasing after it, but by you remaining faithful in your season, in your moment, in your job, in your family, in your project, in your everyday life. Power that brings exposure is attracted to the faithful, for it is only the faithful who can survive the pressure and weight of exposure.

ARE YOU READY FOR YOUR MOMENT?

Now therefore, fear the Lord, serve Him in sincerity and in truth... (Joshua 24:14).

Faithful plowing reveals a heart that is ripe and ready for an encounter with power. Many people live in the waiting room, not because of God's unwillingness to promote, but because of their unwillingness to be faithful in their current life situation. Faithfulness and integrity are key qualities to promotion through exposure. God is seeking those who serve Him in *sincerity and truth*. He's looking for those who are hungry for the next level, but also understand that the key to stepping into that level is being faithful where they are.

> *Faithfulness and integrity are key qualities to promotion through exposure.*

Exposure is the greatest of blessings for the one who carries potential and stewards it well through a lifestyle of steadfastness, faithfulness, and integrity. This person is poised for the touch of power that releases the exposure needed for living in the next dimension. However, exposure can bring complete destruction and untold ruin to the life that is not ready for everything that accompanies it. God denies exposure for the sake of protection, not restriction. Anything that would hinder us from walking into our purpose is a red flag as far as Heaven is concerned.

Many have been crushed by pre-season promotion. They have pushed their way through the crowd, and instead of waiting for divine timing, they knocked down the door and did what they could in order to secure the object of their desire. A promotion, a blessing, or a breakthrough received before we are ready for it can crush us under its weight. This is not to say God expects perfection from those He blesses. Time after time, it's His blessings that invite us into new levels of maturity and development. At the same time, I am not referring to a deliverance from bondage or healing from a disease right now. I am talking about a promotion that takes you into a new level, a new dimension, and a new season of life.

If you don't have what it takes to stand strong in your new season, then the very thing that was meant for your blessing, could harm or even destroy you pre-season. This is why patience cannot be emphasized enough. Elisha did not find Elijah pre-season. That mantle could have killed him before that divine moment. The responsibility would have been too much for him. He needed to plow more. He needed to learn the value of hard work, time management, and discipline. Elisha was not perfect when Elijah found him, but he was prepared. He was ready for his moment.

Are you ready for yours?

I assure you, as you continue to faithfully plow in this season, God Almighty is faithfully preparing you for the next. Every moment you continue in the natural, faithfully plowing, faithfully working, faithfully going to school, faithfully serving, something supernatural is taking place behind the veil. Your lifestyle of faithfulness attracts the gaze of Heaven. Every moment you stick to the plowing process, you are becoming more and more fit for your meeting of power and moment of exposure.

You don't even know what's going on inside you. You are gloriously clueless to what the Creator is working on and weaving behind the scenes. You may feel like you're sitting in the back. You might feel unnoticed and unrecognized. You may even feel like saying, "If I have to plow one more day, one more time, one more moment, I'm gonna throw that thing in the ditch." Yet there is something pushing you. Someone is compelling you to keep going. Keep plowing. Keep reading. Keep studying. Keep working. Keep giving. It doesn't matter if no one knows your name. You may have no recognition whatsoever.

The truth is, you are potential ready for action. There's potential energy inside you just waiting for that push of kinetic power. You are stationary until that one bump, one push, or one spark comes along and launches you right into the next dimension.

Your moment is at hand. That's why you can't be satisfied. That's why you can't sit back and look around. You are potential waiting for power to release you into your moment. You're just waiting for the hookup. And as soon as you get that hookup, you're going to go up. You're next in line for the hookup. You are not forgotten. You are not on some shelf somewhere. The eyes of the Lord God are upon you. His favor surrounds you. His glory is within you. His power is around you.

You've been plowing in the field waiting for the right time, waiting to be in the right place, and waiting for the right mantle to pass over you. Get ready. Power is coming that will expose your potential and unlock your purpose.

REFLECTIONS

1. How is exposure valuable when it comes to releasing your potential?

2. Is it possible to pursue false exposure?

3. What happens if you experience exposure before you are ready for your moment? Why would God deny exposure to you?

CHAPTER 8

RECOGNIZE YOUR MOMENT

*And he left the oxen and ran after Elijah, and
said, "Please let me kiss my father and my mother,
and then I will follow you..."* (1 Kings 19:20).

ARE YOU READY?

*No one, having put his hand to the plow, and looking
back, is fit for the kingdom of God* (Luke 9:62).

When Elijah shows up, everything changes. When our moment
comes, we must be ready. Elisha recognized his moment. He was
ready. This is why God denies moments of power to those *before*
their moment is ready. We just saw how a moment that transitions you from one season to the next can actually be deadly if
you are ill-prepared for the moment.

I want to help you get ready, so that when Elijah shows up,
you can recognize the arrival of the moment that changes everything. Because let me tell you, when that moment comes, you
can't go back to who you were. You won't be able to. *When you
catch a glimpse of what you have been called into, what you're being
called out of will never satisfy you again.* To return to what you
are being called out of would be living beneath what has become

available. I believe God does everything in His power to make this type of regression impossible. Does it happen? Sadly, yes. But not to you. Don't let it happen to you. Be the one who embraces the journey. Go from glory to glory and strength to strength.

Look at Elisha's moment:

> *Elisha left the oxen standing there, ran after Elijah, and said to him, "First let me go and kiss my father and mother good-bye, and then I will go with you!" Elijah replied, "Go on back, but think about what I have done to you"* (1 Kings 19:20 NLT).

Elisha was ready for his moment, absolutely. When he tells Elijah that he is going to back and kiss his father and mother good-bye, he is not behaving like the example Jesus gives us in Luke 9:61, who says,

> *"Lord, I will follow You, but let me first go and bid them farewell who are at my house."*

There are two different perspectives here. Let's contrast these two accounts. Elisha was ready for his next season, but still returned to his household, while the people in Luke's Gospel account are obviously *not* ready for their next season.

NO TURNING BACK

In Luke 9, Jesus gives examples of those who would be crushed by the weight of discipleship if they had continued on with Him while maintaining the attitudes and paradigms they demonstrated. Read what happened:

Now it happened as they journeyed on the road, that someone said to Him, "Lord, I will follow You wherever You go." And Jesus said to him, "Foxes have holes and birds of the air have nests, but the Son of Man has nowhere to lay His head." Then He said to another, "Follow Me." But he said, "Lord, let me first go and bury my father." Jesus said to him, "Let the dead bury their own dead, but you go and preach the kingdom of God." And another also said, "Lord, I will follow You, but let me first go and bid them farewell who are at my house." But Jesus said to him, "No one, having put his hand to the plow, and looking back, is fit for the kingdom of God" (Luke 9:57-62).

Even though the situations each of the people in Luke 9 discussed seemed valid—from the one who wanted to bury his father to the one who wanted to bid farewell to his household—context is what assigns meaning to what was taking place in this text. It was not a parable. It was not a story. It was reality. Jesus was journeying on the road, and came across at least three different people who wanted to follow Him, but also wanted to go their own way. They wanted a mixture. It had little to do with just burying a father or saying good-bye to family members. Hearts were divided. They did not recognize the power that was passing them by, power that could unlock their potential and push them into their next seasons. Jesus had this power; sadly, the three examples we read about were ill-prepared for their moments of visitation.

Even though Jesus was asking them to make some significant sacrifices at the same time, He was inviting them to journey along the same road He was traveling. There is no greater fulfillment to the question, *What's my purpose in life?* than to be one who journeys alongside Jesus.

> *The Kingdom of God does not offer a two-for-one special.*

The three individuals in Luke 9 wanted both Jesus *and* their way. The Kingdom of God does not offer a two-for-one special, where we get the best of God and the best of mediocrity. The best of the Kingdom and the best of the world. The best of the holy and the best of the vile. The best of the glory and the best of the profane. In fact, there is no room for God's best and second rate to take up residence together. They will not peacefully cohabitate. One will rule the day. Our hearts don't have the capacity for dual-surrendering. We either yield to God, or we turn back and go our own way. Jesus recognized this, and knew that these individuals did not recognize their moment. If they truly knew who was standing before them, inviting them into a lifestyle of journeying the same road as He, the attachments that they ended up listing would have been non-issues. Why? Because when potential recognizes its moment of power, it responds appropriately. This reveals the maturity of the one carrying potential.

Excuses reveal immaturity. Remember, immaturity demonstrates that we will not hold up under the weight and pressure of promotion. Perfection is not required for promotion, but there is a degree of maturity that is required in order to sustain us during the period of transition into a new season. Jesus gives us three examples of immature people who had potential, but were not ready for their intersection with power.

WHAT'S ON THE OTHER SIDE?

Think about it. These three people in Luke 9 *could* have been disciples. They could have joined the ranks of those who turned the world upside down (see Acts 17:6). Their hands could have been used to heal the sick, diseased, leprous, and maligned. They could have been mouthpieces touched by the fiery words of Heaven to preach the piercing and powerful truth of the gospel. They could have trampled upon all the works of the enemy (see Luke 10:19). They *could* have released their potential and gone down in history as those who were *"with Jesus"* (see Acts 4:13).

We have just reviewed what these people *could* have done with their potential. So what happened? They did not recognize their moment standing right before them. They did not have a vision for what was on the other side of Jesus' invitation.

> *A divided heart delivers the wrong answer when power walks up and invites you to join Him on the journey.*

I encourage you, be ready for your moment. There's nothing for you back there. You know where "back there" is. I'm not telling you to leave your family. I'm not asking you to go overseas. I'm not saying sell the dog, trade in the car for a jalopy, and completely rearrange your current living situation. Jesus was more focused on their hearts than He was their externals. Family is not bad. Attending funerals is not wrong. Rather, it's a divided heart that delivers the wrong answer when power walks up and invites you to join Him on the journey.

Be sure that your heart is undivided when power reveals itself. So many of us want the perks of power without the anchor of responsibility. This is not possible. For power to be released, and ultimately sustained, it requires a suitable resting place. In order for your potential to be released, you must be a willing and obedient vessel that power can touch and make demands of. Power knows better. Power is touching you because it knows where it can take you. However, power requires your cooperation. It will not drag you kicking and screaming, spitting and clawing. Power is looking for those who say will say "Yes" to its invitation.

What could have happened to these would-be disciples along the road if they responded to their moment? I believe Luke gives us a glimpse of what would have been possible for those who said "No" to Jesus because they wanted their next season on their own terms. The concluding verses of Luke 9 transition seamlessly into Luke 10, where we are given a vision of what would have been available to the disciples who settled for second rate when power was beckoning them.

Let's briefly look through Luke 10:1-9:

> *After these things the Lord appointed seventy others also, and sent them two by two before His face into every city and place where He Himself was about to go* (Luke 10:1).

After *what* things? Jesus identified those ready for their moment and positioned for their next season. It's amazing how quickly this season was coming. Think about it. Those who said "No" to Jesus' invitation said "No" to a whole new way of living that was just around the corner.

Those who recognized the cost and responded to their moment were commissioned as the "seventy others" who become sent ones. To become a "sent one," we must respond appropriately to the moment standing before us. Power stood before these disciples, ready and eager to call out their potential. Power would not have even approached these individuals if there was no potential. In the same way, power wants to visit you. Power wants to unleash what's inside you and turn someone who was walking along the road of life into a royal ambassador sent to announce the advancing Kingdom of God. Power takes ordinary plowmen and turns them into anointed prophets.

We read on:

> *Then He said to them, "The harvest truly is great, but the laborers are few; therefore pray the Lord of the harvest to send out laborers into His harvest. Go your way; behold, I send you out as lambs among wolves. Carry neither money bag, knapsack, nor sandals; and greet no one along the road. But whatever house you enter, first say, 'Peace to this house.' And if a son of peace is there, your peace will rest on it; if not, it will return to you. And remain in the same house, eating and drinking such things as they give, for the laborer is worthy of his wages. Do not go from house to house. Whatever city you enter, and they receive you, eat such things as are set before you. And heal the sick there, and say to them, 'The kingdom of God has come near to you'"* (Luke 10:1-9).

This was the lifestyle that Jesus was summoning people into; and ultimately this is what they were saying no to. Jesus was calling forth laborers who would heal the sick, raise the dead, and destroy the works of the devil. He was commissioning disciples to step into their purpose as spokespeople for an eternal, unshakeable Kingdom.

Your response to power's invitation has enormous implications. If those walking along the road would have said yes to Jesus, they would have been immediately launched into the Luke 10 lifestyle we just read about. Unfortunately, their moment walked right up to them and they were not ready.

Are you ready? I want you to be. That is why we are going through these stories. This is why we are looking at these examples. I want to overwhelm you with information and truth and revelation that positions you to be on the ready line when your moment of power arrives.

ELISHA'S RESPONSE

On the other end, we notice Elisha's response to Elijah. At first glance, how Elisha reacts does not seem all that different from the would-be disciples of Luke 9. Look again, because it's all about context. The difference between Elisha and the disciples who never made the cut was that the plowman was ready. It's ultimately not about saying good-bye to your family or friends. It's not about giving a funeral or having a wedding. It's not about whether you go back to your town and throw a party and pass around meat to all the townspeople. It's about being ready for your moment when power meets potential.

Power hit potential when Elijah tossed his mantle upon Elisha. The man got hit, and he could not go back to normal. Something inside him changed. Even though he went back to kiss mom and dad good-bye, an allegiance had been broken inside him. In Luke 9, the soul ties were still there. Those people were unwilling to follow Jesus and respond to His invitation because their hearts were knit to something, someone, or some life. Elisha got hit with a mantle and was messed up. He was ruined for old ways and the old days. Even though the text tells us that he went back, his heart never went back. In fact, going back was Elisha's test. We'll look at this in more detail toward the end of our time together, but God has different tests for different people. They are custom-made, for He evaluates us on an individual level.

I think that as Elisha prepared the farewell feast for his townsfolk, people were asking him, "Elisha, what are you doing? Where are you going? Why are you going off with that prophet? Why are you throwing your life away? Why don't you settle down? Get married. Have some kids. Get a good job. Work on your portfolio. Build up your retirement. Go on vacation. Carry on the family business."

Something kept Elisha's heart ready and receptive for transition. It was Elijah's response. After Elisha told his new mentor that he planned on going back home to say good-bye and throw a party, Elijah did not deem it a deal breaker. Elijah did not call him unfit for the new dimension he was being called into. It was obvious that Elisha was ready for his moment. All Elijah said was, *"Go on back, but think about what I have done to you"* (1 Kings 19:20b NLT). That's all Elijah *needed* to say.

When Elisha went home in the natural, his heart was still with Elijah. His allegiance was still with his invitation into the next season, new dimension, and greater glory. He was ruined and wrecked. I have to believe that during his trip back home, after crossing paths with Elijah, the former plowman was thinking:

> I can't go back to being who I was. I can't act like it didn't happen. I can't ignore this whole new level of glory. I can't sit in that same place, even though loving

hands pushed me there. I can't stay there, Mama. I love you, Daddy, it's been real. I know you had a plan for my future, and I hate to mess that up, but I've been exposed to power on another level, and I've got to go into the next dimension.

> *One collision with power and you will*
> *never go back to normal again.*

Get ready to step into your next dimension, into your next flame of glory, into your next supernatural release, into your next realm of the power of God. Like Elisha, you're being set up for an encounter with the glory of God. You're on track to getting all messed up. One collision with power and you will never be able to go back to normal again. There's no normal anymore. Normal has been redefined, upgraded, and supercharged. Your normal is now a whole new level!

REFLECTIONS

1. In Luke 9:57-62, what prevented the three people from recognizing their moment and responding to Jesus?

2. What's on the other side of correctly re sponding to your moment?

3. How was Elisha's response to Elijah different from the examples in Luke 9?

CHAPTER 9

RESPOND TO YOUR MOMENT

Then he [Elisha] arose and followed
Elijah... (1 Kings 19:21).

RUINED FOR THE OLD LEVEL

Do not remember the former things, nor consider the
things of old. Behold, I will do a new thing, now it
shall spring forth; shall you not know it? I will even
make a road in the wilderness and rivers in the desert
(Isaiah 43:17-19).

Elisha had a meeting with power that redefined and reori-
ented his entire life. That's what power does to potential. When
potential is ready for its intersection with power, and the two
collide, there is no going back. There is only one travel option—
forward. Onward. Upward. The first thing we see is that Elisha
"arose and followed Elijah" (1 Kings 19:21). It's time for you to
arise and respond to your meeting with power.

In the previous chapter, we saw how Elisha's collision with
power rendered him utterly useless in his old season. When your
potential is called out by one moment with power, you become

wrecked for living in your former season. You arise. You lift up your eyes. You see things on a new dimension. You see what you had not seen before. When you're ready for that new season and your moment comes, and power touches your life and releases what's inside you, there is no going back. You can try, but your plan will be foiled.

Someone may call and want you to come back, but the level of anointing that's been released over your life cries out, "No, I won't settle for the old times, the old ways, the old fun, the old games, the old talk, the old hangouts. That satisfied me in my old season. That met some need inside of me while living in my former level. But you don't understand, I've been touched by power. Power was waiting all along. While we were having fun, the Maker of Heaven and earth was arranging a meeting. When we were hanging out, God Almighty was orchestrating a divine setup. He was getting ready for my new glory. When we were on the golf course, in the hair salon, having a cheeseburger, something was happening in the unseen realm. You didn't see it, and I didn't know it, but something inside me was getting restless. Power was getting ready to come on the scene and show me who I was and what was inside me. Now, I just can't go back!" Surely thoughts of this kind consumed Elisha's mind as he walked through town and around his old neighborhood.

Elijah recognized that the touch of power would utterly ruin Elisha for everything that was back home, in his old version of normal. We read that on Elisha's trip to say good-bye to his old season, his old life, his old ways, his old routines, his old normals, his old friends, and his old job, he must have taken Elijah's instruction to heart. When Elisha asked permission to go back home, Elijah did not scold or condemn him; he just left him with something to ponder. Elijah said, *"Go on back, but think about what I have done to you"* (1 Kings 19:20 NLT). I have to think that this one thought kept him ruined for the old while still interacting with the old.

This is not some call to isolate yourself like a hermit. There are people and places that will not change, even when you are touched. Those collisions with power call out *your* potential; they do not call it out for others. Each person must experience his or her own moment where power touches that person's potential. It's an intimate experience. Elijah's mantle was ready for Elisha—no one else. Even though there were 7,000 who had not bowed their knees to Baal and played the harlot before false gods, Elisha was the man who got the mantle.

As you come into contact with certain elements of your old level, don't belittle them. Don't shame them. Don't elevate yourself into some "above the rest," superiority position. God ordained you to make a transition from the old to the new for His purpose at this season according to His will. If others aren't there, just remember what took place in your life. If they try to invite you into their ways and activities, which were *your* old ways and old activities, smile and decline. You don't need to condemn others for not making the transition yet, just as others did not condemn you in your previous level. God is patient with His people. He has a plan. Some just cooperate with it easier or more quickly than others. Rather than making anyone feel poorly about where they are, simply *live* at your new level. Speak at your new level. Operate at your new level. Don't flaunt it around. It's normal. It's natural. It's seamless. It feels right. It sounds good. This is just how you live now.

Normal for you is the next level for somebody else. Live at your new normal, keeping in mind that your lifestyle is calling other people up higher. They see your potential released and something starts stirring within them. They see you operating in your gifts and talents, and they start wanting to steward what they have been given. Just encourage them to be faithful. That was the key factor that positioned you for the mantle transference.

Remember, Elisha faithfully plowed. He didn't run around looking for his moment. He didn't go to every service, conference, crusade, seminar, and motivational talk seeking out his moment. He was faithful in his old season and this positioned him to respond correctly at the most significant transition of his life. Most likely, Elisha had to deal with some of this thinking when he went back home to say good-bye to his old level. There was a whole town of people who were living in Elisha's old level.

Maybe there is a whole workplace of people living at your old level. Maybe you're in a house filled with people living at your old level. Maybe you are roommates with someone living on your old level. The best way you can summon them upward is by living at your new level as *normal*. It's no longer your next dimension—it's your normal dimension. It was the next level when you were living at the old level. It was an upgrade when you were out in the field, plowing. But that was no longer the case for Elisha. The mantle was placed upon him. The next level quickly became his new level. The same is true for you!

HOW TO BE LAUNCHED BY A MOMENT

The Lord was with Joseph, and he became a successful man, and he was in the house of his Egyptian master. His master saw that the Lord was with him and that the Lord caused all that he did to succeed in his hands. So Joseph found favor in his sight and attended him, and he made him overseer of his house and put him in charge of all that he had (Genesis 39:2-4 ESV).

Now I want us to look at what it means to live in this new dimension we have been launched into. There are people who get launched, but never learn how to live. They experience success, but they don't become *successful* like Joseph. They don't embrace a perspective where the touch of power transforms their entire mode of living. There are people who do experience a legitimate touch of power. It shakes them. It rattles them. It shifts stuff around. It heals. It delivers. It releases. It gives freedom. It makes them feel all good inside. Quickly, they were exposed to another dimension. The invitation was issued.

Now it's time to learn how to function at this new capacity. An experience is great, but it must be the gateway into something. It's one thing to stick your finger into an electrical socket and get shocked, but it's something else to learn how to live with a finger stuck in that socket. That's what I'm calling you to do. No, you're not always going to feel some zing, but you're going to recognize that what you felt, sensed, and experienced launched you into a new dimension of living. Going back is not an option. I want you to have eyes that not only recognize your moment, but learn how to move forward *after* the moment.

Look at Elijah. All he did was pass Elisha by and let his mantle pass over the plowman. This was the moment when true power was exposed to true potential. Something happened in that moment that was undeniable and crystal clear. In fact, it was as if potential responded before power did. Power passed by potential, but potential dropped everything and ran after power. Again, potential recognized its moment. Potential quickly responded when power passed on by. Read it again, *"Then Elijah passed by him and threw his mantle on him. And he left the oxen and ran after Elijah"* (1 Kings 19:19-20). Elijah was ready for the next dimension. Not only did he recognize power's arrival, but he responded. He ran after it. You've got to want it that much.

God sovereignly sets you up, but you have to want it. You have to respond. You have to choose it. You have to run after it. When He brings you into a moment of power, don't fall down, spin around, jump on your head, and think to yourself, *Wow, that was a powerful touch!* The touch is never designed just to touch—the touch of power is designed to release you into the new level. Your moment is not about a moment, it's about a dramatic collision that will set the course of a whole new trajectory for your life.

Too many receive the touch, but don't follow the Teacher. Therein lies the test. Those who will not steward their moment are ultimately unable to step into a new season at that particular time of life. It doesn't mean God is done with them. It doesn't mean Jesus has passed them by. It just means there is more plowing to do. It just means that maturity, integrity, steadfastness, honor, and character need to be developed before people start living and functioning at a new dimension as a new normal.

You see, many are content to set up camp on the outskirts of a new dimension. They are fine fishing in the shallows when His voice beckons them into the deep. They camp out on their moments of power, believing that the moment was all there was. Your moment was never designed to be sufficient—it was purposed to be a launching pad. Consider how a diving board is not the final end, the pool is. People can jump up and down on a diving board all they want, it does not mean they are going to be launched from one level to the next, from land to water, from air to pool. Too many people live their lives jumping up and down on the diving board. Some moments might take them very high where they have dramatic encounters with power.

Just because you jump up does not mean you jump forward. Just because you go up does not mean you go out. I've been assigned to call you up and send you out.

This "up and down" thought process reveals that the person is not yet fit to go beyond the moment, jump forward, and step into the lifestyle. Imagine if Elisha had responded the way so many people today do to their moments of power. If you can, try to re-imagine the account in First Kings 19. Elisha could have been plowing, caught the mantle, fell down, rolled around, did some back flips, and then gone right back to plowing the same way he had always done it. He could have kept on jumping up and down on the diving board—his moment with Elijah just adding some spring to his step.

Let's never reduce encounters with power to something that adds spring to our step. This is laughable. God does not bring Heaven's electricity into your life to simply give you a thrill, but rather to give you a glimpse of what a new dimension of living looks like. The shock of the collision wakes you up to new levels of glory, anointing, power, realized potential, and activated purpose.

RESPOND TO YOUR MOMENT

The key is response. We must respond to our moment in order to live at another level. In order for potential to become released, we must respond to our moment of power. In the previous chapter, we discovered how important it is to recognize your moment of power when it's standing before you. Elisha recognized Elijah and ran after him. Even after going back home and tying up some loose ends, Elisha still *arose* and followed him.

On the other side, the three people mentioned in Luke 9 did not realize the power of their moment, for they all responded poorly to their meetings with Jesus. They encountered Him, but they did not follow Him. They had a moment, but the moment did not change or transform them. They were still clinging on to the comfort and safety of their former level of living. That's what they knew. That's what made sense. That's what they understood. The new level of living Jesus was extending their way was unsafe. It was radical. It was upside down. It was supernatural. They met Power as He walked down the road, but ultimately, they did not allow their moment with Power to launch them into a new dimension. That new dimension would have likely meant their inclusion among the disciples in Luke 10 who were commissioned to transform the landscape of the known world. They were sent out as laborers, purposed to preach a new Kingdom and release the power of God. Truly, the 70 people in Luke 10 responded correctly to their moment of visitation, while the three nameless individuals in Luke 9 did not.

> *You have got to know when it's your moment—and do something about it.*

You have got to know when it's your moment—and do something about it. You've got to want it. Blind Bartimaeus knew when it was his moment, and even though they told him to shut up, shut up, *shut up,* he said, "I can't shut up! This is *my* moment!" The man had an obvious impediment—his blindness. This could have been his excuse to bypass his moment. This could have been his easy out. This could have been his license to wallow in his old level and continue to be defined as *Blind Bartimaeus.* He decided to take another route. He used every faculty available to step into another level. Even though he could not see, he used what he had available—his hearing—to respond to his moment. In Mark 10:47 we read how the story unfolds, *"And when he heard that it was Jesus of Nazareth, he began to cry out and say, 'Jesus, Son of David, have mercy on me!'"* He responded to his moment.

Even though Bartimaeus had a physical handicap and although he experienced some significant resistance, he still used what he had to step into this moment. Why? He recognized what was on the other side of his collision with power. People told him to shut up, but he took that as fuel to cry out all the more and all the louder.

What are people telling you? Are they trying to keep you from stepping into your new season? Are they wanting to restrain you from launching into a new dimension, only to maintain you at their level? Press through. Recognize your moment and run after it like Elisha did. Silence the crowd by crying out louder like Bartimaeus did. Press through the crowd like the woman with the issue of blood (see Mark 5:25-34). They saw their moments and responded. They were not content to let power pass them by. They weren't after a fleeting touch or a mere experience. They recognized that the touch of power was simply a transfer point that would launch them from one dimension to the next. From plowman to prophet. From blind man to disciple who could see (see Mark 10:52). From woman with a non-stop flow of blood to a daughter of God, healed and whole (see Mark 5:34). On the other side of each collision of power was a transformed life that still speaks to us today.

REFLECTIONS

1. What does it mean to be "ruined for your old level of living?" What does this look like for you?

2. Is it possible to experience a touch of power but not see your life changed? What would this look like?

3. Can you identify examples of people who correctly responded to their moments of power and stepped into a new level?

CHAPTER 10

SEIZE YOUR MOMENT

...and [Elisha] became his [Elijah's]
servant (1 Kings 19:21).

THE VALUE OF YOUR MOMENT

Elisha did not just receive a touch of power—he allowed that touch to transform his very identity. In First Kings 19:21, we see the result of Elisha's encounter with Elijah. He allowed the touch to transform him from plowman to Elijah's *servant*. This is why your meeting with power is so vital and valuable. The key was *how* Elisha responded to the moment. He was not casual or cool about it. He was not lazy. He was not idle. Rather, he *seized* the moment and allowed it to transform him. We seize what we recognize as valuable and transformative.

> *You seize what you recognize as*
> *valuable and transformative.*

A moment of power is never given simply for the purpose of thrills and emotionalism. It is a transfer point. Don't be content to simply camp out on the outskirts, when your moment has the power to call something out of you that *only* functions at a new, higher level. This is why stuff inside of you has not come to the surface yet. It's not that you don't have what it takes; you do. However, what's inside you is prepared and positioned for another level. If it came forth now, it would be destructive. If you started imparting and offering and sharing and releasing what you currently have stored up inside, no one would get it. You'd be written off. They'd call you crazy. You've gone off the deep end.

I understand that with the release of potential, levels of persecution and resistance do come. However, there is also resistance that comes when we try to step out into our next season too early. What's inside of you requires an intersection with power. The meeting is divine. It is sovereignly staged. But remember, God does not set up these meetings just so you can get some type of spiritual high off the flowing current of His power. Your moment is intentional. It's designed to launch you into a new level where everything inside you will have its place to come forth.

Bartimaeus needed the divine intersection with the power of Jesus in order to become who he was created to be—a healed, seeing follower of the Lamb of God. He could not have made that happen in his own strength, nor could he have received any benefit from just seeking a touch without transformation. Every touch is designed for transformation. In Mark 5, the woman with the constant flow of blood reached out and touched the hem of Jesus' garment. Power proceeded out of Him and ushered that woman into a transformative moment where her identity shifted. No longer was she the woman with the *"issue of blood"* (see Mark 5:25 KJV). Her moment changed her into one Jesus called *"Daughter,"* whose response to that moment *"made thee whole"* (see Mark 5:34 KJV).

Both these individuals pressed their way into transformation. They recognized the immeasurable value of a moment. Don't be content to simply receive a touch, when in fact God desires to release transformation. Bartimaeus would not have risked greater ridicule and cried out among the crowd if he did not expect a touch that transformed. In the same way, the woman with the constant blood flow would not have left her home, crawled out into a very public place—where crowds were gathered around Jesus—and pushed herself through the people to simply touch the edge of his robe if there was no expectation of transformation attached to this touch. She was not looking to feel good; she was looking to receive wholeness. She didn't want to live in her current level with some bells and whistles added; she wanted to step into a whole new dimension of living. The value of these moment compelled each person to press through to Jesus.

Bartimaeus would not shut up. The woman didn't care if she had to crawl through the dirt in order to touch Power. This must be our attitude when stepping into our new level. We should have no other approach to the transformative touch of power. I can't repeat it enough. A zing won't change you. Running around the building won't escort you to another level. You can touch the fire, feel the wind, and taste the rain, but if the extraordinary feelings that a touch of power brings are not accompanied by an extraordinary transformation, you're simply staying where you are with a good memory of how, one day, Elijah threw something on you and it made you feel good— but you didn't do anything with it. You'll daydream about the exciting moment when Jesus came through town, and you didn't run, push, crawl, wiggle, bicycle, or skateboard to get through the crowds and receive the touch that transformed everything. Why didn't you push through and receive from Him? You will never benefit from a moment of power if you do not recognize its value *beyond* a temporary feeling. You won't risk everything for a temporary feeling, but you will for a transformation.

VISION PRODUCES RESOLVE AND TENACITY INSIDE YOU

Where there is no prophetic vision the people cast off restraint... (Proverbs 29:18 ESV).

Your moment is valuable because it has the ability to draw out your potential, and in turn completely transform your identity. This is exactly what happened with Elisha. He responded correctly to his touch of power by following Elijah; and as a result of properly handling his moment, he went from plowman to prophet. The same is true for you. When you have a vision for what your moment has the ability to produce in your life, you become tenacious. You have relentless resolve. You're not only going to get touched by a moment, but you are going to step into your moment.

People often experience a moment without ever stepping into the potential of that moment. This is what gets you from one level to the next. When you begin to visualize the other side of your moment, you become like the people in the Gospel accounts who cast all inhibition aside because they knew their moment with Jesus would change everything. They seized it at all costs.

Is this you?

When your moment comes, don't just stand around. Start running. Your moment of power is an invitation into a lifestyle of unleashed potential and realized purpose. That's beyond valuable! People spend all their lives chasing after these things. The wealthiest individuals on the planet would gladly surrender their entire fortune for the very thing that presents itself to you in the form of a moment. Why? That moment unlocks the door to a greater release of your potential and greater fulfillment of your purpose.

Whatever it takes, go after it.

Whatever it takes, go after it. If you have to crawl, resolve to crawl into your moment. If you're knocked down on your knees, it doesn't matter. You're still coming in. This is tenacity. This is resolve. This is the grit that demonstrates whether or not you value what your moment has unlocked. Greater levels of living are not for the faint of heart. God protects people from greater levels if they don't see the value, and in turn don't exhibit the vigor to walk upon these high places.

Think about the exchange between Elijah and Elisha. Elijah, the teacher, doesn't even realize the magnitude of what took place by exposing potential to power. He kept on walking. Was he ignorant? No. At the same time, he was waiting to see what would happen. Did Elisha, the student, value the touch? How was this plowman going to steward the mantle that was tossed upon him? Was he going to celebrate the touch and go back to plowing, or was the plowman going to receive the invitation to become a prophet.

Think about what happened between Jesus and the woman with the flow of blood. Many people were touching Him, but there was a touch that produced transformation. In fact, when the afflicted woman touched Jesus, Scripture tells us that *"power had gone out of Him"* (see Mark 5:30). Jesus turned around and asked, *"Who touched My clothes?"* The disciples surely thought to themselves, "What is He hollering about?" They explained to Jesus, *"You see the multitude thronging You, and You say, 'Who touched Me?'"* (Mark 5:31). But there was something special about this woman's touch. Scripture does not give us any additional clarity as to whether or not all of the other people who were thronging and touching Jesus were actually receiving from Him. Maybe they were, maybe not. Vision is what caused this audacious woman to step into her moment. She had a vision for what touching Jesus would produce in her life.

Even on her way to meet the Miracle Man, she was filled with vision and expectation. We read that *"she said, 'If only I may touch His clothes, I shall be made well'"* (Mark 5:28). In the Amplified Bible we are given a greater glimpse of how this woman responded to this vision. We read that *"she kept saying, 'If I only touch His garments, I shall be restored to health.'"* This was not some type of mantra. This was not a positive confession. This was not "put your mind to it, envision the outcome, and poof—it just happens out of the blue." This woman was driven by a very clear vision. She knew the touch of His power would unlock her potential. Her potential was wholeness. Her potential was receiving healing. Her potential was living without the incessant flow of blood that plagued her for twelve long, hard years. She had a vision for how the touch of power would unlock and release her potential so that, ultimately, she could fulfill her purpose. Power unleashes potential—and potential enables us to do what we have been designed to do.

This woman was restricted by her affliction. Her obstacle held her back from stepping into new levels of living and ultimately, hindered her from fulfilling her purpose. Power destroys restrictions. It breaks through the chains that have held our potential hostage. The key is recognizing and responding to power when it shows up on the scene. When it walks in the door, something inside you will start leaping. What's happening? The potential inside you recognizes that the power that just walked in is the power that will draw potential out.

DON'T LET YOUR TRANSITION PASS YOU BY

He who has a slack hand becomes poor, but the hand of the diligent makes rich (Proverbs 10:4).

Don't have a "slack hand" when it comes to seizing your moment. Proverbs 10:4 is a key for putting this principle into proper use. You have to grab it when it comes, and you have to hold on to it. If you don't seize it, you become poor. I'm not just talking about money. There are people with more money than they know what to do with, but they are still poor because they refuse to seize their moment.

Let's go back to Blind Bartimaeus. While the woman with the issue of blood took hold of her moment, Bartimaeus refused to let his moment pass him by. He knew that the power Jesus carried would unleash his potential and transition him to a new level. Jesus was passing through town, and this man responded. Let's look at the context and note the similarity between Bartimaeus and Elisha.

> *Now they came to Jericho. As He [Jesus] went out of Jericho with His disciples and a great multitude, blind Bartimaeus, the son of Timaeus, sat by the road begging. And when he heard that it was Jesus of Nazareth, he began to cry out and say, "Jesus, Son of David, have mercy on me!"* (Mark 10:46-47)

Just as Elisha could have missed Elijah, so Bartimaeus could have missed his moment with Jesus. Bartimaeus responded to the fact that Jesus was coming through town. He started to cry out. People tried to shut him up, but this became fuel for the fire. He upgraded his cry. He got louder. Maybe he got a bit wilder. He did whatever he could to get noticed—and he was. We see that *"Jesus stood still and commanded him to be called"* (Mark 10:49). This was Bartimaeus' moment. And yet, it seemed like there was the possibility that he could have missed it—even now. Follow the rest of his story:

> *...Then they called the blind man, saying to him, "Be of good cheer. Rise, He is calling you." And throwing aside his garment, he rose and came to Jesus. So Jesus answered and said to him, "What do you want Me to do for you?"...* (Mark 10:49-51)

It was his turn. It was his time. It was his moment. In excitement, Bartimaeus got up, tossed aside his garment, and came over to Jesus. There they stood, face to face. Power locked eyes with blind potential. Jesus was getting ready to start fishing in this man's heart to see if he was ready for the transition. Even though Bartimaeus was blind, Jesus still asked, *"What do you want Me to do for you?"* Why such a question? It should be obvious—right? The man was blind, and he needed to see.

Jesus was evaluating whether Blind Bartimaeus actually recognized the moment he was in. Jesus wanted to release potential, but He wanted to make sure that both He and Bartimaeus were on the same page. Jesus didn't want to just touch the guy; He wanted to heal him. Jesus didn't want to pat him on the back and comfort him in the affliction.

There is a chance that the blind man could have responded incorrectly to Jesus' question. He could have given Jesus an answer that revealed a heart not capable of presently carrying a new dimension of glory. He could have simply asked Jesus for a touch—and no more. He could have thrown a pity party, elevating the status of his affliction above the power that Jesus had available to release and unlock Bartimaeus' potential. I know this sounds ridiculous considering who was standing before the blind man, but this example speaks volumes to believers today.

So many of us stand before power and give the wrong answer. We give wrong answers because of how demanding, how outlandish, how supernatural, and how impossible the right ones sound. We give wrong answers because we want to be safe rather than seize the moment in front of us. But if you don't seize it, it will pass you by. I don't care how wild it sounds. If you heard that Jesus had the power to heal blind people and you were Blind Bartimaeus, you would seize that opportunity no matter how "out there" the prospect of a miracle sounded. If you had to stand on your head and turn cartwheels, it wouldn't matter. Power is standing before you, and that power is the only catalyst that can release your potential.

The key is, you have to want it, and that intense want has to exceed your mind's tendency to rationalize. Jesus was familiar with the natural mind. He knew that Bartimaeus might have been in a wrestling match with logic and reason and common sense. "Miracles don't happen." "That's impossible!" "Blind people don't see—they are blind!" We don't know what transpired in his mind. All we know is that he heard Jesus had come into town, and he seized his moment. He knew that regardless how impossible it sounded, Jesus was the only One who could release his potential.

Bartimaeus gave Jesus the correct answer. In responding to Jesus' question, he said, *"Rabbi, I want to see"* (see Mark 10:51 NLT). The result? *"Instantly the man could see, and he followed Jesus down the road"* (Mark 10:52 NLT). It was more than a touch. It was more than a healing. It was more than a miracle or a moment. Bartimaeus was launched into his purpose because he seized his moment, experienced the touch of power, saw potential unleashed, and was propelled into purpose. His ultimate purpose? Although healing was part of his purpose, the end result of his healing was that Bartimaeus could now become one who *followed Jesus.*

REFLECTIONS

1. How should you appropriately respond to the divine moments that God brings into your life? How did Elisha respond?

2. What does it mean to recognize the value of your moment? How will a vision of its value change the way you respond to it?

3. What stands out to you from the example of Blind
   Bartimaeus—how he responded to his meeting
   with Jesus?

CHAPTER 11

NO RETURN TO THE ORDINARY

And he left the oxen and ran after Elijah, and said,
"Please let me kiss my father and my mother, and then
I will follow you. And he [Elijah] said to him, "Go back
again, for what have I done to you? (1 Kings 19:20)

GET MESSED UP FOR THE USUAL

I now want us to look at *what is produced* when power meets potential. Even though it's a brief moment in time, it is a moment that is absolutely pregnant with purpose. Remember, it's the divine intersection of power and potential that bring us into purpose. Your meeting with power is your God-extended invitation into a life that is messed up for everything it used to be.

> *The divine intersection of power and*
> *potential brings you into purpose.*

Let's rewind a little bit and go back to when Elijah tossed his mantle onto Elisha. The plowman knew what had taken place. It didn't demand a discussion. He knew that the mantle Elijah threw upon him demanded *everything*. This is why he told Elijah that he wanted go back home to kiss his father and mother good-bye. He did not go back home because his heart was still aching for his old season. Elisha went home to say so long and "goodbye" to everything that defined him up until his moment with power.

Likewise, when you have been bleeding for twelve years, and then because of the power you experienced in a single moment the bleeding stops, the mere notion of going back to the bleeding is repulsive. There is nothing back there. Nothing in the plowing. Nothing in the blindness. Nothing in the bleeding. Each of these people experienced a different set of circumstances, but each had a single common denominator—they were invited into a new level. Each one had a collision with power that brought them into a new dimension. Each individual experienced a most unique promotion.

Your promotion makes the plow work of yesterday highly unsatisfying. The very thing that positioned you for promotion can actually rob you of the blessing of promotion if, like Lot's wife, you look back. Jesus tells us to *"Remember Lot's wife"* (Luke 17:32). What's so important about this woman and her decision to look back? As Lot and his family were fleeing the city Sodom and Gomorrah, which the Lord had marked for destruction, they were given a very clear set of instructions: *"Do not look behind you nor stay anywhere in the plain. Escape to the mountains, lest you be destroyed"* (Gen. 19:17). Why? There was nothing back there for them to look at. It was a city in ruins.

Lot and his family had an intersection with power. God paid them a visit in the form of two rescuing angels (see Gen. 19:1). Power was delivering these people out of a dying city. Power pulled them out of a dark place where who they truly were would never be recognized or realized. There was potential inside Lot and his family that remained untapped as long as they remained in the depravity of Sodom. The problem was, something inside Lot's wife was still connected to the old life, the old ways, the old friends, the old places. Something inside her was still deeply attached to how things used to be—so much so that she directly disobeyed the angelic instructions they received. When she looked back, she turned into the very thing that the city became, a *"pillar of salt"* (see Gen. 19:26).

> *God is calling you out of what you have known and is inviting you into the deep waters.*

Maybe Lot's wife thought she could enjoy the best of both worlds. God was calling Lot and his family into the high places. He was calling them up, into the mountains (see Gen. 19:17). Lot's wife was trying to save something that was infinitely inferior to what she was being invited into. In some way, Lot's wife was in bondage to her old life. The prospect of stepping into something new might have been overwhelming. Maybe she was terrified. She had known Sodom. This was her stomping ground. She knew the streets. She knew the city. Maybe she was friends with the neighbors. She knew that Mr.

Jones came out every morning at 8:30 and watered the plants. She knew that Mrs. Jenkins walked the dog after dinner at 6 o'clock. She had a schedule. She had a system. She had a routine. Do you see where I'm going with this? God is calling you out of what you have known and is inviting you into the deep waters. You are being beckoned to abandon the familiar and the comfortable and the safe, and step out into an entirely new dimension of living.

Sadly, many never actually take this step because the familiar and comfortable restrain them.

THE EXTRAORDINARY IS CALLING

So Abram went, as the Lord had told him, and Lot went with him. Abram was seventy-five years old when he departed from Haran. And Abram took Sarai his wife, and Lot his brother's son, and all their possessions that they had gathered, and the people that they had acquired in Haran, and they set out to go to the land of Canaan... (Genesis 12:4-5 NIV).

Sometimes the comfort of an old season tries to keep us from embracing the new thing God wants to launch us into. We prefer the ordinary, because the extraordinary has too much uncertainty attached to it. The ordinary is what we are being invited out of. The ordinary was all fine and good for its time, but now the God of the Extraordinary is calling. Your name is up! Let's not be like Lot's wife who ultimately rejected the summons to step out of her old season. She responded just the opposite of Lot's uncle, Abraham. When his moment came, *Abram went as the Lord had told him* (see Gen. 12:4). He moved toward the unknown and unfamiliar. This was his pathway to promotion.

It's amazing how even if the place where we are living is destructive, like Sodom, or idolatrous like Haran, we still stay because it's familiar. Abram did not, but Lot did. Why? There's comfort in what has become our ordinary. Even if we're blind, even if we're bleeding, some are content to stay in the comfort of their pain instead of stepping forward into the unknown of their purpose. Purpose is only unknown because we have not stepped *in* yet. When power calls us, we must respond, for it's in our response where potential is realized and released.

> *Some are content to stay in painful comfort*
> *rather than stepping into perfect purpose.*

For some of us, our pain and problems became a source of perverted comfort because they give us something to fall back on as we are being summoned out into the unknown. Hear me out, I'm not that saying pain, in and of itself, is comfortable. It's not. It stings. It hurts. It restrains. It withholds. It debilitates. It harms. It hinders. Pain is not comfortable; but for some people, they have chosen to identify themselves with their pain. Blind Bartimaeus was recognized as "Blind Bartimaeus." Maybe people identified him by his condition like a nickname. Perhaps this is why Jesus was asking him, "What do you want Me to do for you," when it seemed like his need was quite obvious! But as I mentioned earlier, I think Jesus was searching for something. He wanted to see if this man was really serious, not just about receiving a touch, but getting a name change. Jesus wanted to see how deeply blindness was ingrained in Bartimaeus' identity.

In the same way, Elisha was faced with a choice. His situation was different, although the principle is the same. Even though he was not caught in a debilitating situation, he was nevertheless living at a former level. He was plowing when the invitation to purpose passed him by. Was Elisha going to stay "Elisha the plowman," or would he step into the role of "Elijah the prophet?" Consider the ramifications for just a moment. If Elisha did not respond to the mantle of Elijah and just kept on plowing because plowing is what he knew and plowing was his safety net and plowing was familiar, the prophetic calling assigned to his life would never have been realized. On the other side of each power-filled moment is a release of unlocked potential that completely changes your life. Blind Bartimaeus got healed and became a Christ-follower. Elisha became a prophet who walked in a double portion of the anointing that was upon Elijah. Consider the result of Elisha saying "Yes" to the unknown and unfamiliar.

On the other side of each power-filled moment is a release of unlocked potential that completely changes every life.

Elisha stepped into a realm of miracles that even Elijah had not experienced. These miracles, and the lives they impacted, would have never been realized or demonstrated if Elisha kept on plowing. If he stayed behind in his old realm, in his former glory, in his previous position, he would not have been privileged to participate in the extraordinary exploits that were only activated when he stepped out. If he decided to keep plowing, his eyes would not have seen the Jordan River divided (see 2 Kings 2:14). If he chose to remain a plowman and forfeit his opportunity to become a prophet, he would not have performed a creative miracle that healed the waters at the spring of Jericho (see 2 Kings 2:21).

Understand, all of this potential was available to Elisha. *This* is exactly what was unlocked at the moment of the divine meeting, when Elijah's power awakened Elisha's potential. Maybe his eyes didn't see it all right there when he caught Elijah's mantle. And in your moment of power, you probably won't see the entire plan. Every detail, every stop along the road, every blessing, every meeting, every breakthrough—your mind would not be able to handle it all right there in a single encounter with power. You don't need to know. All you need to understand is that the moment of power activates potential to do things your imagination cannot even conceive.

Second Kings tells us that Elisha went on to miraculously provide oil for the widow woman (4:1-4), raised her son from the dead (4:35), purifies food (4:41), multiplies bread (4:43), heals Naaman's leprosy (5:10), causes a metal ax head to float (6:6), and heals blindness (6:17). Even a dead man is raised to life because his body came into contact with the bones of Elisha (13:21). Even after Elisha was dead, buried, and decayed to the point where only his bones were left, the power upon that man's physical frame was so strong, so potent, that just by coming into contact with it, healing broke out. *This* is what that one moment of power released Elisha to do, both in his life and after he had died.

I wonder what God is getting ready to release inside you!

Yes, in the stepping-out process there is mystery. One moment Elisha was plowing and the next he felt a mantle hit his shoulders. There was mystery in what all of this entailed. Elisha didn't have all the answers. He didn't get some instant download of the complete course of action that would follow his collision with power. He just knew something was shifting. He was ready, he was willing, and in turn he responded. Don't dare settle for the comfort of some old, worn-out season when you are being beckoned and brought into the unknown. It's only unknown because you haven't experienced it yet. You haven't touched it. You haven't tasted it. You haven't smelled it. You haven't seen it. It's unknown because it's not the familiar. It's not the ordinary. It's not what you've always known. It's not where you've been. It's something fresh, something new, and something that's going to shake everything.

> *Don't settle for worn-out known when you*
> *can step into His glorious unknown.*

CHANGE YOUR IDENTITY

The problem for some of us is that the old season, even though it was destructive, is something that we are familiar with, and by continuing to live in that old season of familiar pain, we prevent ourselves from stepping out into the new season of unfamiliar purpose. Somewhere along the line, we identified self with a season.

Good or bad, we cannot identify ourselves by a season, for when the season changes, we get worried. We start shaking. We're nervous. Why? Because who we were is changing. We need to celebrate. If you were Blind Bartimaeus in your former season, I've got good news. You're about to become Healed Bartimaeus. You're about to become Blessed Bartimaeus. You're about to become Bartimaeus, the disciple. Don't ever hold on to some identity you embraced in your former season, because it might have been wrong.

You need to know who you are, absolutely. You need to know who you are and what you have in Christ. You need to know your strengths and weaknesses. You need to be familiar with your faults and foibles. You need to know what you're good at, what you're wired for and how you've been programmed. Those are healthy identities that carry you through any and every season.

There are unhealthy identities like Blind Bartimaeus, when you become identified by your plight or problem. When your addiction labels you. When your bondage becomes a badge. When your name is determined by your enemy.

Embrace the shift. When power meets your potential, God wants to break that false identity and build a fresh one.

Beyond unhealthy identities, there are simply old-season identities you need to deal with. God has called you to be faithful where you are, doing what you're doing—*for now*. Elisha was a plowman, and he faithfully fulfilled this assignment and identity. However, when power unlocked his potential, his profession shifted. His identity changed. What was right yesterday would be wrong today if he tried to continue in that same identity. If

Elisha sought to remain *the plowman* while trying to step into his identity as *the prophet,* he would be stepping right into a nervous breakdown. The plowman made it possible for the prophet to emerge. Remember, Elisha was faithful as the plowman and then he was elevated. Promotion was the byproduct of faithfulness in the previous season. But when the moment comes and the mantle hits, you have to think on your feet. Don't hang on to a past identity when God is bringing you into a new present reality.

There are traits of the plowman that will carry over into the prophet. The ability to plow and press and work and toil to break up ground—the very character that the plowman developed in Elisha positioned him to step into his new identity of prophet. These characteristics would continue. They would make the cut. They would endure the transition. Just like who you are—your strengths, your abilities, your knowledge, your skillsets, your wisdom, and your aptitudes. Everything that will keep you moving forward will endure the mantle. Everything from yesterday that will help you step further into today and tomorrow will continue into the your dimension.

At the same time, the stuff that holds you back cannot endure. It cannot go on through. It just can't, as it has no place. You can't let it. Your moment with power exposes you to what can continue—and what cannot. Your glimpse of the next dimension gives you vision for what you can take with you and what you can't take. The only things you can't take are the things that will sabotage your forward momentum.

Just know things aren't going to be like they used to be. Old things might be calling your name, trying to get you to look back. You can't go there. They'll try to convince you that comfortable is better. You just remind them what's on the other side of your unknown and unfamiliar. Elisha stepped into the unknown and unfamiliar and he lived at a new dimension. He walked in a greater anointing. He experienced greater glory. The miracles were greater. He pressed into realms that Elijah never knew.

God has said, *"Behold, the former things have come to pass, and new things I declare; before they spring forth I tell you of them"* (Isa. 42:9). After your meeting with power, you may go back to the same address, but you will not be the same person, because God has done a fresh thing in your life. I repeat, you cannot go back.

After meeting with power, you will not be the same person—God has done a fresh thing in you.

You might try. Elisha did. He tried to go back to his old normal after the meeting, and nothing fit. Nothing made sense. Nothing came close to what he had just received when power passed by. You will go back and look at what you used to call good and say, "What in the world was I thinking?" Whenever God elevates you to the next level, you look at things that you used to call excellent and ask, "What happened to them?" They didn't change. You changed. You received an upgrade. You received a mantle. You were a plower, but now are a prophet. There's nothing wrong with the ox. There's something right with you—you've been exposed to the next level of glory and it's time for you to step on in.

REFLECTIONS

1. Why is it intimidating to leave the ordinary and familiar behind?

2. How is it possible for people to use pain as a source of comfort? How does this prevent you from stepping into the next season?

3. What are the benefits of stepping out into the unknown and unfamiliar?

CHAPTER 12

MAKE FIREWOOD

So Elisha turned back from him, and took a yoke
of oxen and slaughtered them and boiled their
flesh, using the oxen's equipment, and gave it to
the people, and they ate... (1 Kings 19:21).

MAKE FIREWOOD OUT OF THE OLD POSITION

When your potential has awakened it will never rest again. *It will never rest again.* Potential did not orchestrate the meeting with power; it just happened, but since it happened, potential says:

- "I know this is what I've been waiting for all of my life."

- "This is my moment, and I cannot ignore the power to which I have been exposed."

- "I have been plowing on the twelfth yoke of oxen. I cannot go back and assume the family business."

Elisha went back to his home, but did not go back to life on the old level. Even though he physically stood among

127

his family and friends and former living conditions, he was now functioning at the next level. You can live in the next dimension among those who are still in a former level. You are responsible for *you*. You are the one who received the mantle. Trust God's timing and divine orchestration to deal with others who are not living at the level next. You are not God's commissioned constable. You're not His holy law enforcement agent. Your goal is not to make people feel badly about their present level, when you are living in the next. No—you run with what you have. You live at that next level, and the on-looking world will want what you have.

> ***God will make firewood out of your former position!***

When Elisha went home, he made a decision. Look at what he does:

> *So Elisha returned to his oxen and slaughtered them. He used the wood from the plow to build a fire to roast their flesh...* (1 Kings 19:21 NLT).

The man was serious about moving forward. In this moment, the shift is established. He received the mantle, but he could have gone back home...and stayed. He could have decided that the future was too frightening and succumbed to playing it safe as a plowman, living with Momma and Daddy. The opportunity was obviously there. But Elisha was cut from a different cloth. The man was made of more than that. He was not intimidated by what was before him. He made a decision in his heart that next level living was his only option; and as a result, he took what represented his former life and identity—the oxen and the plow—and broke it up and made firewood out of it.

God is going to make firewood out of your former position! There are things you might be laying down, but there are characteristics and qualities you are upgrading. There is stuff inside of you that's changing its very structure and makeup as you embrace transition. His plow fueled the fire in the same way that what Elisha learned as a plowman surely contributed to the fire God used to release upon the earth through him. This was Elisha's past. He was a plowman, and that plow became the fire that destroyed the option of going back to yesterday, but a fire that fueled his forward momentum into tomorrow. Elisha's past was his profession. Even though the ox became dinner and the plow became firewood, the things that Elisha gleaned through being a plowman were set ablaze in the fire of surrender. In the same way that Moses threw down his shepherd's rod before the Lord and it was anointed to accomplish the supernatural (see Exod. 4:1-4), so Elisha throws down what he has—the ox and the plow—and it becomes the fire that launches him into the next glory.

FUEL FOR THE NEXT GLORY

God doesn't want to destroy you; He wants to elevate you. A rod in Moses' hand could only accomplish natural things. He could lead sheep. That was Moses' ordinary. That was what he had known and that was his realm of familiarity. God was not looking to take away his shepherd's staff; He was looking to touch it with power and release potential. Let's look at Moses' story, for it illustrates what is going on with Elisha.

> *So the Lord said to him, "What is that in your hand?"*
> *He said, "A rod." And He said, "Cast it on the ground."*
> *So he cast it on the ground, and it became a serpent...*
> (Exodus 4:2-3).

The same God is asking you, "What is that in your hand?" Are you still clinging to the plow of yesterday while trying to live in a new dimension? God doesn't want to snatch your plow away. He doesn't want to steal your shepherd's rod. He's not on some quest to make your life miserable and take all of your stuff away. No, He wants to make the devil miserable by getting you to hand your stuff over to Him, and let Him infuse it with power. He wants to ignite what you have. The key is yielding it to Him. If He sets the plow on fire while you are holding it, it's going to hurt. It's going to burn. If you don't let go, and the fire consumes it, you will die. You won't be able to sustain the fire. It will kill you, not promote you.

God doesn't set a plow on fire while it is still in the care of the plowman; in the same way, He doesn't turn rods into serpents while they are still being held by the shepherds. Why? Because if we are unwilling to submit these things to God, we are unable to sustain what He wants to release through them.

God wants to take the very things that define your position and profession, and set them on fire.

God wants to take the very things that define your position and profession, and set them on fire. That's living in a new dimension. It can be shocking because it's so different. Moses was shocked when his shepherd's rod turned into a serpent. In Exodus 4:3, Moses watches the supernatural transformation of staff to snake, and we read that *"Moses fled from it."* We've already covered this ground. We cannot become intimidated by the next level of glory. God is taking things we were comfortable with and charging them with supernatural power. Skills we had in the old season are being touched by His power. Potential's coming out that we didn't know was there. It shocks us. We're frightened. At times, we want to run away. The whole thing is too glorious, and a bit too much.

But you can't go back.

The plow's burning. The ox is dead and cooked. People are eating its flesh. You've gone too far and there is no reversing it. Keep going. The same staff that scared Moses saved the nation of Israel. The rod that led sheep was the same rod that led God's chosen people out of bondage. God's taking your old position and setting it on fire. Moses led sheep in the wilderness in one level; but in the next, he led people in the wilderness. Elisha plowed the ground in one dimension; but in the next, he plowed the soil of human hearts to receive the seed of God's prophetic word. I dare you to get excited about God taking what you had in your previous level and empowering it in a new level.

MAKE FIREWOOD OUT OF YOUR PAST

Elisha's plow was not only his position and profession, it also symbolized his past. This is what he had known and had been defined by. He was Elisha the plowman. We've already talked about the need to leave the past behind, move forward, and refuse to look back. I want to take it a step further. I want to take this opportunity to encourage you that the same God who sets fire to your profession and position can also set fire to your past. It's one thing to talk about how God uses our talents and our giftings and our accolades and our triumphs—it's another thing to talk about how He uses our past. And I'm not talking about your past a school teacher, your past as a dentist, your past as a construction worker, your past as a taxi driver, your past as the star quarterback for the high school football team. It's easy to accept that He uses these things because they are noteworthy and safe.

> *The same God who sets fire to your profession and position can also set fire to your past.*

I don't want to play it safe and keep it cute. I don't want to talk about the good stuff; I want us to get into the grit. It's one thing to believe God uses your past successes—it's another level of thinking that emboldens us to believe that He wants to use our past failures, messes, mistakes, shortcomings, train wrecks, disgraces, shame, and sins. When power hits potential, we run—we don't argue. We don't argue with power, giving it every reason why we shouldn't be called. You know how people give God their reasons, "But God, don't You know who I am? Don't You know what I've done?" Power comes; and instead of embracing it, we resist it. We remind power that our past disqualifies us for the present calling. We try to persuade power that we are unworthy of the summons because in our past we feel like we have squandered our potential.

Let me remind you, God is not a man and does not operate according to how we think He should work. Your past does not intimidate Him. We remind God of our past as if He is clueless about what happened. When He summons us, it is absolutely ridiculous to start reminding Him why He should *not* be calling us. He knows what He's doing. He's not blind. He's seen our faults. He sees our struggles. Those things done in the darkness that no one else knows about. God saw them, and still loves you. Those memories that bring you shame every time you invite them back into your mind. God was there. He was there in the darkness, and He was there in the light. He was there when you were with the person you shouldn't have been with, and He was there when you weren't in the place you should have been. He was there in the pit, and He was there in the palace. He was there when you lied. He was there when you cheated. He was there when you prepared your taxes. He was there when you lost your mind. He was there when you crossed the line. He saw every moment, still loves you, and is still summoning you. Don't insult Him by asking, "Why me?"

None of us deserve anything. We didn't go looking for grace; grace came banging down our door. We're not good enough for God. Nothing inside of us cried out for God to come and rescue us; He put the cry inside. That's all true. Paul says it best:

> *And you were dead in the trespasses and sins in which you once walked, following the course of this world, following the prince of the power of the air, the spirit that is now at work in the sons of disobedience—among*

whom we all once lived in the passions of our flesh, carrying out the desires of the body and the mind, and were by nature children of wrath, like the rest of mankind (Ephesians 2:1-3 ESV).

This is our past. If anyone had a problem past, it was the apostle Paul. He persecuted and killed believers. He was a murderer. He was the worst of the worst. He recognized this, writing of himself, *"I am the least of the apostles, who am not worthy to be called an apostle, because I persecuted the church of God"* (1 Cor. 15:9).

Paul had a past. Maybe you had a past. Does this exclude you from the present purpose of God? No. Even after Paul gives us the list in Ephesians 2, reminding us of every bad, wretched, and unspeakable thing we have done, we are invited into a new present and a new future. God is not blind to our former trespasses. He watched as we walked in league with the devil, doing his bidding. He saw as we made passions and lusts our gods and idols. We think the next verse should be a disqualifier, when in fact it simply reads, *"But God..."* (Eph. 2:4). These two words are your invitation to live in a new reality where your past is not counted against you.

Paul continues:

But God, being rich in mercy, because of the great love with which he loved us, even when we were dead in our trespasses, made us alive together with Christ—by grace you have been saved—and raised us up with him and seated us with him in the heavenly places in Christ Jesus" (Ephesians 2:4-6 ESV).

Power brought you into a whole new dimension of living. Your present and your future are not dictated by your past. In fact, God uses your past as a tool of measurement. Your past reminds you how far He's brought you and how deep you've gone. This is how power makes firewood of out the past. When you view your past in light of your present summons, your heart is ignited. You can't shut down the thanksgiving. You know you're not worthy, but He called you worthy. Of course you're not deserving, but God said you are deserving. The King is calling. The courier is handing you the royal invitation. Don't hide your face. Don't run off into the shadows in shame. Stand tall. Remember where you came from, but feel the fire of where He's bringing you.

> *Your present and your future are*
> *not dictated by your past.*

If you don't have a past, you don't have the fire. I believe God wants to take your past and make firewood out of it. It will be the flame that ignites your future, sets off your destiny, creates your passion for your purpose, and releases you into another dimension. The past brings everything into perspective.

Set the ox on fire. Turn that ox into food and feed the neighborhood. Elisha might have said, "This can feed you, but it can't feed me. I cannot continue to follow a dumb thing. I know I've got some more rows to be plowed, but I cannot stay in my position, for the traditions of men will make the Word of God of no affect. If I continue to stay in the sensible circle, making the acceptable motions, trying to live up to the status quo, I am going to miss my moment. So here, you eat it. It's not that it is bad. It was good for me at one time—but a shift has occurred."

REFLECTIONS

1. How can you make firewood out of your position or profession? How does it provide fuel for your next level?

2. What does it mean to make firewood out of your past?

3. How should you respond to your past when God summons you into your future?

CHAPTER 13

LIVE ON A NEW LEVEL

...Then he [Elisha] arose and followed Elijah,
and became his servant (1 Kings 19:21).

DISCOVER WHO YOU BECAME

No longer shall your name be called Abram, but your
name shall be Abraham; for I have made you a father
of many nations (Genesis 17:5).

In the same way that Abram received a divine name change to Abraham, Elisha experienced a similar transformation. Elisha returned from burning the plow and feeding the ox to the townsmen, and stepped right into the flow of his next level. We read that Elisha, *"arose and followed Elijah, and became his servant"* (1 Kings 19:21). Note the word *became*.

Elisha was not dating a new dimension. He wasn't flirting with it. He wasn't testing out the waters. He wasn't satisfied with a touch of power that made him feel good, but didn't transform his life. The result of Elisha's meeting with Elijah? Power awakened potential, and potential was unleashed. Elisha stepped into his new identity. He *became* Elijah's servant. He didn't walk with Elijah for a little while, get tired, and then go back to plow and cook oxen with the folks back home. Home was redefined for Elisha. "Plan B" was removed from his equation. His only option was moving forward with Elijah, because when you become something, it's difficult to un-become it.

When you *do* something, you can stop doing it. Elisha could have *done* the whole serving thing for Elijah, but then turned back when things stopped making sense. When Elijah got too cranky, Elisha could have said, "This is not for me. I don't want to deal with you and your temper and your craziness and your strangeness. I'm out, I'm through. I served for a season, but now I'm going back." There's no going back to something for someone who *became* something.

> *There's no going back to something for someone who became something.*

When the teacher was taken up in the flaming chariots, Elisha could have turned back and run for his life. "I didn't sign up for this. I wasn't planning on this taking place. Nobody warned me. Nobody told me what was coming. I want out." If Elisha chose to simply serve Elijah as an act, it would have been easier for him to turn back. But Elisha's encounter with power didn't just sustain him for a season. His DNA was changed. The plowman started to become a prophet when he *became* Elijah's servant.

THE LOW PERSON IN A NEW LEVEL

And whoever exalts himself will be humbled, and he who humbles himself will be exalted (Matthew 23:12).

Somebody might say, "Well Elisha, you're still following." He says, "Yeah, but I'm following on a whole other level." He wasn't following an ox, he was following a prophet. What he was following before was the family business. He was following the trajectory of his history. Now he was following in the direction of his destiny. The same is true for you. Don't get discouraged if the encounter with power has you still following something or someone. Following is not the problem; it's what or who you are following that determines at what level you choose to live. Was Elisha going to keep following an animal around, or was he going to follow Elijah?

> *I'd rather be the low man in my destiny than the lead man in my history.*

Elisha did not mind following. Why? When you're following at a new level, everything's different. I'd rather be the low man in my destiny than the lead man in my history. You know what I'm talking about. That moment comes when we're invited into a new level, and what happens? We look back at what *was*, because what *was* kept us in a high position. But where was that high position? Elisha's "high position" was following around an ox and plowing. Elisha's position might have been high in his old season; but now, he was invited into a whole new dimension of living. He was exposed to a realm of reality beyond his current living conditions. Yes, he was going to have to start at the bottom, following Elijah, but I'd rather follow Elijah into my purpose any day than stay around in some worn-out season that holds nothing else for me.

The same is true for you.

Don't get discouraged if you keep following into your new season. Think about it. You're not following an ox anymore, you're following Elijah. You're following the person or the thing or the opportunity or the business or the career or the idea or the path that is taking you into the next level. You see, the season of the ox prepared Elisha for living at the next level, but it would never bring him into the next level. Where you were, before your meeting with power, had its purpose—in its season. Your old season made sense *before* power came walking by. But it makes no sense for us to choose to remain in the old season. I don't care if you're the prince in your old season when power pays a visit, because the pauper in the new season is leagues ahead of the prince in an old season.

Now, you're going to come in on the bottom level of a new dimension. Up until this point, everybody in your life has been pulling after you, looking to you for answers, looking for solutions, calling you about this, and calling you about that because you were the plower of the twelfth yoke of oxen. That was your identity in the old season. You were large and in charge. You felt special. You had the answers. You knew the solutions. You had it all figured out.

But don't be afraid. In the new season, you're going to start out knowing nothing, and I'd rather know nothing in the new than keep on knowing everything in the old. You're carrying what you learned in the old season into the new season. God's not erasing your memory. The key is, you're stepping into the unfamiliar and unknown. Celebrate it. Every step you take toward where you don't have a clue where you're going, be confident that you are walking farther toward your purpose. Your potential is being released. You're taking significant strides toward fulfilling destiny.

How to Walk in the Dark

For we walk by faith, not by sight (2 Corinthians 5:7).

We throw around phrases like, "Walk by faith, not by sight." In church, when the preacher talks about this truth, we shout "Amen," and get excited; but when everything changes and we start walking in the dark, we cannot depend on sight. What you've seen has not prepared you for where you're going. What you saw in the old season won't help you as you begin navigating your new dimension. If Elisha tried to see life from a plowman's perspective in his new season, he would have been lost. He didn't know from what perspective he would be seeing. The terrain was alien. All he knew was this guy passed by him, tossed his mantle upon his shoulders, and kept on going. Using what sense he had, Elisha had to assume that this prophet who passed by and kept on walking *knew* where he was going. Elisha didn't know where Elijah was going, but Elijah looked like he knew. In turn, Elisha followed the leader.

Faith is your anchor and sustainer in the new season. Faith that the One who called us is faithful (see 1 Thess. 5:24). Faith that our steps are ordered by the Lord (see Ps. 37:23). Faith helps you see in the dark. And when you feel like you can't see, faith steadies your heart to trust what you know. What is true. What is constant. What is unchanging. What is invisible. Faith is the only way we are able to see in the dark of transition.

Faith is the only way we are able to see in the dark of transition.

Earlier on, we studied how your meeting with power transitions you into a realm of unfamiliarity and un-knowability. You don't know where you're going because it's unfamiliar. It's unfamiliar because you've never been there. Now, I want to help you learn how to walk in the dark. That's what living at a new level is like. You're walking forward. You may not see where you're going, but you know that you're walking. You put one foot in front of the other. Things aren't clear. They don't make sense. You may trip and fall. There's even a good chance you're going to fail and make mistakes. That's okay. It's legal. I'd choose failure in a new dimension over success in an old season that's passed me by. Think about it. Success in an old season actually does not move you forward into your destiny and purpose. If you choose to stay behind in the old and settle for success as a plower, when you're really called to be a prophet, you could be the most successful plower there is, but your purpose as a prophet is still waiting for you to step up.

You're going into a new dimension, living at a new level. With it comes a level of uncertainty, a level of humility, a level where you have to learn and you have to grow and you have to pray and you have to read. This will be unfamiliar territory. For all of your life, up until now, you have been operating in the familiarity of your comfort zone. You do the same things over and over again, following the routine that you always knew. You had the field mapped out and knew every corner and every crevice. You understood it. You knew where the rocks were. You knew where the roots were. You knew where the snakes hid. You knew where the opposition was. You knew where everything was. Your life was defined by the old system and old cycle. But ever since power hit, your potential is coming out and it demands something new. The old wineskin can't contain what's about to break forth in your life.

BREAK THE CYCLE

...but one thing I do, forgetting those things which are behind and reaching forward to those things which are ahead (Philippians 3:13).

I want you to proactively pursue discomfort. You read this right—don't adjust your eyes. This is what Paul was saying in Philippians 3:13. He had a lot to rest on. He had his education. He had his theological pedigree. He had his affluence and influence. All of those things were in his past. They represented his old level. How does he respond? He chooses to forget what was in the past and presses and reaches and pushes into the things which are ahead. This is the key to breaking the old cycles associated with the old season—simply starting new ones.

For so many people, comfort is an idol. It's only when you step out of your comfort zone that you can start learning how to navigate the unfamiliar terrain of your new season. Paul was a Pharisee turned preacher of the Gospel. He was an academic turned traveling evangelist. He was ushered into a dimension of living he had never conceived of, and yet he preferred to press toward the glorious unknown than choose to rest in his pampered past. He knew that what was ahead was greater than what was behind.

> *When you step out of your comfort zone, you will learn how to navigate in your new season.*

I pray that this releases a stirring in your spirit that what's in your future, what's ahead and on the horizon is overwhelmingly superior to what was behind, even if what was behind appeared to be a benchmark. Too many of us get stuck in old cycles because we put limits on God. We limit what He can do with our potential. We think that the old life and all its trimmings was as good as it gets. God wants to bust apart your idea of what "as good as it gets" looks like. You haven't dreamed of what God can do. You can't comprehend what's up ahead. Your mind cannot begin to fathom what the Almighty has on the other side of your new season. I declare to you, according to the Word of God, that *"Eye has not seen, nor ear heard, nor have entered into the heart of man the things which God has prepared for those who love Him"* (1 Cor. 2:9). That statement alone is grounds for a shout, but don't stop there.

We look at verses like this, get a spiritual high, and then go right back to our cycle. Why? Because we isolate ourselves from the incomparable, unimaginable things God wants to bring into our lives. This verse wows us, showing what God wants to do, and yes, even has prepared *"for those who love Him,"* but look at what Paul adds in the following verse—*"But God has revealed them to us through His Spirit"* (v. 10). Right here we discover that even though we're stepping into new dimensions, there is a promise that we will *not* always have to walk in the dark. The Spirit of the living God dwells inside you. The One who searches and knows the mind of God, the deep things of His heart, dwells in you and tells you where to go (see 1 Cor. 2:10-12, 3:16; John 16:13). He directs your footsteps. He gives you wisdom. He releases understanding. He brings clarity. You have not been left alone as an orphan—God Himself has come to live inside you as the Holy Spirit (see John 14:18). Yes, you will walk through the dark, but you will not walk through the dark of a new season alone because God is always with you. God is in you. God is for you. God is in your corner.

I believe the Lord is saying to you, "The cycle has been broken over your life!" It's completely broken. You're never going to be the same. How you used to do things will not define how you do them in your next dimension. You're going to speak differently. You're going to stand differently. You're going to teach differently. You're going to run numbers differently. You're going to sing differently. You're going to practice medicine differently. You're going to raise your kids differently. You're going to love your spouse differently. Everything's different because it's a new dimension!

REFLECTIONS

1. What's the difference between doing and becoming?

2. How is it a good thing to be the "low person at a new level?"

3. Describe what it looks like to walk in the dark. How have you experienced this in your life?

CHAPTER 14

THE FINAL TESTS

*And he [Elijah] said to him, "Go back again, for
what have I done to you?"* (1 Kings 19:20).

In this last chapter, I want to give with some practical tools that
will help you identify whether or not you are living in alignment
with your new level. When you get there, you need to stay there.
Remember, you're changed. You're a new man. A new woman.
Elisha *became* Elijah's servant. One of the worst things that we
can experience is living out of alignment with our new level.
Why? It produces purposelessness. You will always be making
strides toward fulfilling your purpose as you live in alignment
with your level.

Here are some simple tests that will help you recognize
whether or not you are living in the place that power promoted
you into.

THE ROOM TEST

First, we have the *room test*. I always say that if you are the
smartest person in a room, you are in the wrong room. Get out!
You are too big for that room. Think about it for a minute. If

you are going to live at another level, you need to always be learning. You need to always be progressing. There's always something to read. There's always a seminar to watch or listen to. There's always room for development. I'm not saying become a workaholic. What I am inviting you into is a process. Process means there is room to grow.

> *If you are the smartest person in a room,*
> *you are in the wrong room. Get out!*

Elisha might have been the smartest guy in town—or at least the smartest when it came to what he knew. But everything changed when Elijah came by. The master plower was touched by the master prophet, and now the guy's whole identity shifted. The master quickly became the apprentice. This is truly the test of whether or not you are living in alignment with your new level. If you continue to seek out places where you are the smartest person in the room, you need to find some new rooms. Pursue some different influences. Find people who challenge you and draw out your potential.

THE WOMB TEST

Most assuredly, I say to you, unless one is born again,
he cannot see the kingdom of God (John 3:3).

Second, is the *womb test*. If you want to *see* at a new level, you are going to have to be born again. In the same way you needed to experience a birthing process to see the Kingdom of God, you need to be reborn in order to see your new dimension of living. We are going to stay here a little bit longer, as I believe if you truly get this, you will never try to squeeze back into an old season again.

If where you currently are cannot fit you anymore, you need to be born. You need to come out. It is like a mother who is ready to give birth. I believe this is where you were when power passed by. Elisha was ready for transition, and all it took was a push from Elijah to turn the plowman into a prophet in training.

The womb got too small to hold you, and you needed to come out. You needed to make a transition from the womb to the room. You needed to get out of a small place and step into a larger place. You might have been the largest person in that womb, but now, on the outside, you feel like the smallest person in the new world. That means you've graduated to a new level. Now it's time for you to grow. It is time to develop. It's time to learn how to say "Ma-Ma" and "Da-Da."

That womb is too small to hold you. You've outgrown it, and the discomfort that exists is between the womb and the infant. It is painful to the mother and it is painful to the baby when you have outgrown the space you have been in. The only choice you have is to be born. Your only option is to come out. This is what happened when power met potential, and Elijah gave Elisha his mantle. That was the push Elisha's potential needed to come forth.

Can you imagine if, along the way, Elisha turned around and tried to go back to his old way of living? Sometimes that happens. Even though we've been born, and we have become a new person at a new level, we can get distracted by old level stuff. Old level situations. Old level places. Old level people. Old level activities. We try to participate, but they hurt. Why? It's like a two-year-old trying to go back into the mother's womb. It's just painful. It doesn't work. It doesn't look right. It makes no sense. The baby doesn't belong there.

How are you feeling right now?

YOU ARE BREAKING OUT

Are there things in your life that are to squeeze you back into your former level? It won't work. It can't. You're new. Elisha was a prophet, not a plowman. You're a new person on a new course living at a new level. If you feel the strain and the pain of being pushed back into the womb, get out of those situations. That's not where you belong. The same was true for Nicodemus in John 3. The man was not like the Sanhedrin court that he came from. You are not like your background. How do I know you're not one of *them?* Because you see on a whole other level. Nicodemus perceived something about this Man Jesus that none of his colleagues and peers were pressing into. Nicodemus was in transition. He recognized something about Jesus that his cohorts did not understand. He could not convince them because he has been birthed into a new dimension, and they were still operating at the old one.

> *You're a new person on a new course living at a new level.*

It was time for the teacher to become a student again. Nicodemus was *"a ruler of the Jews"* (John 3:1). He was a leader and an authority. He had power and position. His old level was full of prestige among his people. But there was a problem—the water had broken over his life. He met power. Something was happening inside him. He started to see at a new level.

I want to announce to you that the water has broken over your life. You will have to be fed on another level. You're not going to get nourishment through the cord from which you used to receive food. You are going to have to take more responsibility for your food. You cannot just live from sermon to sermon.

In the past, the Lord fed you manna falling down into your tent, but now you're coming into your promised land. Prepare your victuals; for in three days you will cross this Jordan. You are coming into another dimension. You have got to begin to feed on another level. Learn on another level. Read on another level. Interact with people on another level. Parent on another level. Run a household on another level. Build a business on another level. Treat patients on another level. Everything is upgraded.

You have got to get out of that womb. And if you are already out, don't go back there. Don't be drawn back to a place that won't fit you. Don't be enticed by those rooms where you are the know-it-all. Deep down, you know you've got to get out. You've got to get out of this rut. You've got to get rid of that plow. You've got to burn the ox.

POTENTIAL'S FINAL TEST

Potential, here is your final test. Elijah says to Elisha, *"go back home."* We have looked at that process already, where Elisha returns home, deals with the townsmen, prepares them a meal, burns his plow, and moves onward. We have already gone through all of that. Now I want us to look at the test of discouragement. This is the last test Elisha needs to pass before he moves forward.

> *You cannot earn the right to lead until*
> *you pass the test of discouragement.*

You cannot earn the right to lead until you pass the test of discouragement. If I can talk you out of it, you are not the one for the new level. Elijah tried out this test on Elisha to see what the plowman was made of, to see if he really was the one. Yes, he caught the mantle. Yes, he ran up to Elijah. Obviously, he knew he got something within him. He recognized that power touched something. Here is the true test. Will your realized potential survive discouragement? Look at how Elijah responded to the excited Elisha. He looked at him and said, *"Go back again, for what have I done to you?"* (1 Kings 19:20). This wasn't nice. It did not sound affirming at first. The one who brought power that called forth potential was now telling Elisha to go back home.

More than anything, Elijah was looking to see how Elisha would respond. Would he get bent out of shape? Would he go home and not return? Would Elijah's harsh attitude push the plowman away? How much did Elisha really want his new level? The test had been given. How would Elisha respond?

How will you respond?

Will you keep moving forward if things do not unfold the way you think they should? Will you keep following even if you get offended? Upset? If someone talks to you harshly? If someone corrects you? If somebody criticizes you? If others point fingers and laugh at you? Will you keep moving forward if you forget why you were doing this to begin with? *What got into me? Why am I going in this direction? I can't see at this new level. It's all foreign. It's all unfamiliar. At least in the old level I knew where everything was. I knew how everything worked. Everything made sense.* What will you follow? These thoughts are not unusual; they aren't bad. They are entirely normal. They are the common assault upon everyone who is invited into a new dimension.

The test is passed or failed in how you *respond* to the thoughts and feelings and temptations and persecutions and offenses. You don't fail if you feel. You don't fail if you think. You don't fail if you catch yourself asking why. You don't fail if your mind starts trying to make sense of what you're doing and where you're going. These things do not determine your grade. It is what you do that determines where you go. The next level has to be that real to you. That necessary. It has got to become so real to you that you cannot breathe without it.

THE NEXT-BREATH TEST

A young preacher saw an old retired preacher who had a massive, huge, anointed ministry. The old preacher was fishing down by the riverbed. This young preacher approached the old preacher and said to him, "I hate to bother you, but this is my opportunity. I may never get this chance again, and I want to minister under the same kind of glory that you minister under." The old man didn't even look up at him. He kept on fishing. The young preacher started to walk away, and he thought to himself, *I may never have this chance again.* He said, "Mr., I hate to bother you, but I can't walk away. I may never get this chance again, and I want to minister under the anointing that you minister under."

And the old man kept on fishing. And the young man kept bothering him and bothering him and bothering him. Finally the old man put down the fishing rod, got up on his feet and snatched the young guy by his neck. He picked him up and threw him into the water. The young man couldn't swim. He couldn't swim in that dimension, so he started going down in it and coming up again. "Help!" he cried. He went down under the water again, and then popped back up, "Help!" Up and down he went, all the while crying out for help.

Finally the old man reached down into the water, stretched forth his hand, and snatched the young man out of the water. The young preacher was panting. He was gasping for air. He was confused and crying. "But I don't understand. I respected you. I admired you, and you picked me up and threw me into the water. I can't swim." The old man looked at him and said, "You remember that last time when you came up out of the water?" The young man was still catching his breath, "Of course, I remember. I can't forget it." He said, "You remember how badly you wanted that next breath?" He said, "Of course I remember. If I didn't get another breath, I was going to die." The old preacher said, "That's how badly you have to want it. You have to want it like you want your next breath. When you want it like that, then you're ready."

You have got to walk into that next level like you need your next breath of air. You are not playing with it. It's not some game. When you want purpose badly enough to do whatever it takes to get there—to control your passions, your foolishness, and your craziness to get there—that is when you're ready to step into it.

Purpose awaits the ready. God's not playing hide and seek with your purpose. He's looking for those who are actually serious about stepping into what they've been designed to do.

> *God's not playing hide and seek with your purpose. He's looking for those who are serious about stepping into their destiny.*

When you're ready to stay up and study while other people play games to get there, then you're ready. Nobody's going to give you purpose on credit. Nobody's going to give it to you because you look cute. You have to pay the price to operate in the next dimension, and after you've suffered awhile, and after you've been talked about a while, and after you've faced all kinds of discouragement and come through all kinds of hell and say, "I still want it," then God says, "I'm going to release another wave of glory in your life."

If you want it, you have got to run after it. Not walk. Not slug. Not wade. Not shuffle. Not jig. Not dance. You've got to run into it and run with it. Elisha got the mantle and ran toward Elijah. He could have gotten discouraged when Elijah told him to go back. But he didn't. He thought, *Go back...to what? I've got nothing to go back to. I've been ruined and wrecked for anything I could possibly go back to. Forward's the only option. That's the only route I want to travel.* The pace has changed. You almost drowned several times. You nearly died several times. You almost went completely under—but there was something down inside that kept you fighting your way back up again.

Because of your potential, because of the purpose you have been marked for, He did not let the waters drown you. He said, *"When you pass through the waters, I will be with you; and through the rivers, they shall not overflow you. When you walk through the fire, you shall not be burned, nor shall the flame scorch you. For I am the Lord your God"* (Isa. 43:2-3). The Lord your God is with you. He was with you through the past, He is with you in the present, and He will be with you for the future. He is not leaving or changing, for He says, *"For I am the Lord, I do not change"* (Mal. 3:6).

Anybody else would have drowned in the hell you went through. Anybody else would have died in it. Anybody else would have lost their mind. Anybody else would have had a nervous breakdown, but you kept fighting your way back up to the top. And now there is a glory that God is going to release on your life. Don't be mistaken, it has to be released on the extraordinary. Not the perfect. Not the all-cleaned-up. Not the goodie-two-shoes. Extraordinary is the one willing to do whatever it takes to walk in the new dimension.

> *Your purpose fulfilled releases solutions to the world.*

It cannot be released on people who haven't been over their heads, almost went under, nearly collapsed, almost fainted, and almost lost their minds. You are the future. Your purpose fulfilled releases solutions to this world. A double portion is at your disposal. Just when you thought you had it all, God says, "I'm taking you higher. I'm about to blow your mind." If you thought the last level was the best, I've got good news for you—your eye has not seen, nor has your ear heard, nor has your heart even imagined of what God is bringing you into.

REFLECTIONS

1. What is the room test? The womb test?

2. How have you experienced either one of these tests in your life? What did they look like?

3. What does the next-breath test look like to you? How have you experienced this one?

AN IMPARTATION

Then the hand of the Lord came upon Elijah... (1 Kings 18:46).

Now to Him who is able to do exceedingly abundantly above all that we ask or think, according to the power that works in us (Ephesians 3:20).

In our final moments together, I don't want you to simply close this book, put it on a shelf, and go back to living life as usual. I hope you received some good information; but most of all, I want to see you experience impartation. I want these pages to serve as your escort into the next level, your new dimension. I pray the Spirit of God whetted your appetite for new realms of glory, anointing, potential, and power that you didn't even know were inside of you. They were waiting, just locked up inside of you, for a collision with power.

So here is my prayer for you—that the powerful hand of the Lord would come upon you, even now while you read these words. As the hand of the Lord was upon Elijah, and the hand of the Lord was upon Elisha, was upon Moses, and the hand of the Lord was upon Joshua, I pray that you experience this same touch of power that launches you into your new dimension. Into your new season. Into your new level.

I pray that the powerful hand of the Lord would be upon every area of your life. Not one gift or talent remains untouched. Not one ounce of potential misses out. The hand of the Lord is upon your house. The hand of the Lord is upon your business. The hand of the Lord is upon your ministry. The hand of the Lord is on your family. The hand of the Lord is on your schooling. The hand of the Lord is on your finances. The hand of the Lord is on your past. The hand of the Lord is on your future. The hand of the Lord is upon *you*.

So let this be your prayer:

Lord, whatever You are doing in the earth right now, don't do it without me. Touch me with Your power. Orchestrate the divine appointments. Bring me into collision with destiny-defining moments. Give me eyes to see what You are doing. Ears to hear You speaking. And a heart that responds to how You are moving in my life. I run toward everything You have for me, not looking back. Thank You, Father, for bringing me into my purpose.

This is what happens when power meets potential.

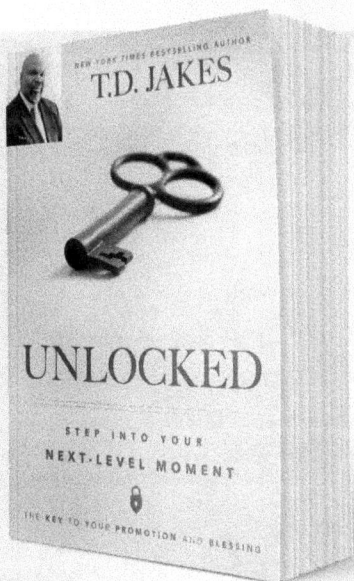

FREE E-BOOKS?
YES, PLEASE!

Get **FREE** and deeply discounted **Christian books** for your **e-reader** delivered to your inbox **every week!**

IT'S SIMPLE!

VISIT lovetoreadclub.com

SUBSCRIBE by entering your email address

RECEIVE free and discounted e-book offers and inspiring articles delivered to your inbox every week!

Unsubscribe at any time.

SUBSCRIBE NOW!

LOVE TO READ CLUB

visit **LOVETOREADCLUB.COM** ▶